EARLY CHILD CARE
IN THE UNITED STATES OF AMERICA

INTERNATIONAL MONOGRAPH SERIES ON EARLY CHILD CARE

A series of monographs, prepared by the International Study Group for Early Child Care, edited by Halbert B. Robinson and Nancy M. Robinson

Monographs on early child care from the following countries are in active preparation:

CUBA	INDIA	THE UNION OF SOVIET SOCIALIST
FRANCE	ISRAEL	REPUBLICS
GREAT BRITAIN	POLAND	YUGOSLAVIA

Developmental Psychology Laboratory, University of Washington

FIGURE 1   Frontispiece

Early Child Care in the
UNITED STATES
OF AMERICA

by

Halbert B. Robinson
Nancy M. Robinson
Martin Wolins
Urie Bronfenbrenner
Julius B. Richmond

GORDON AND BREACH

London   New York   Paris

First Published   July 1974
Reprinted June 1976

This report was made possible in part by funds granted by the Carnegie Corporation of New York. The statements made and views expressed are solely the responsibility of the authors.

This monograph was also published as a complete issue of the journal *Early Child Development and Care*, Volume 2, Number 4 (1973).

Printed in the United States of America

Contents

Introduction to the Monograph Series

IN MOST countries of the world, the decades of the 1960s and 1970s have witnessed intensified efforts to safeguard and enhance the development of infants and young children. Among nations which differ widely in their material and human resources, their industrialization and urbanization, their economic, political, and social systems, the era of early childhood is being viewed with increasing interest. A new worldwide consensus has emerged about the crucial nature of these early years and their role in the future well-being of the individual and, implicitly or explicitly, the nation. Some countries have had extensive programs for infants, young children and their families for many years and have devoted substantial public resources to ensuring the care of the young; others have more recently established programs to serve broad sections of their populations; still others are now beginning to embark upon ambitious programs. Whatever the degree of their previous engagement in this area, however, today there tends to be a heightened enthusiasm for the potentialities of the infant and very young child.

Despite the international concensus regarding early childhood, there has been surprisingly little international communication. There have, of course, been visitors from one country to another, and especially in the fields of health care and early education there has been some interaction among professionals. For the most part, however, when windows have been opened, the viewing eyes have been those of the foreigner making an all-too-brief visit or reading literature aimed at those who already understand the social and cultural "givens." Programs viewed out of context and distorted by a foreign point of view are difficult to comprehend, and significant errors of perception are a hazard often overlooked.

Yet, in all these countries there exists a hunger to learn, a conviction among responsible persons that they could profit from a thorough understanding of the systems which have emerged elsewhere. They realize, too, that knowing "the facts" alone is not sufficient, that many factors outside a program affect its effectiveness.

Recognising this situation, and in the hope that meaningful communication among the world's professionals, citizens, and planners might be enhanced, the International Study Group for Early Child Care was established in 1969. This group of concerned professionals in early child care, each a voluntary participant and none an official representative, is comprised of specialists in education, medicine (pediatrics, psychiatry, and social medicine), psychology (developmental and social), sociology, and social welfare. The twelve countries from which they come are, for the most part, highly urban industrial nations. These diverse countries—Cuba, France, Great Britain, Hungary, India, Israel, Poland, Sweden, Switzerland, the United States, the Union of Soviet Socialist Republics, and Yugoslavia—all take their responsibilities to their young citizens very seriously. Some, however, have had much more extensive experience in this field than others, and their solutions to common problems represent a broad sampling of those to be found throughout the world.

As a first step in promoting international exchange, members of the International Study Group have prepared a series of monographs describing child care in each of their twelve countries. Each author has concentrated in particular upon his own country's arrangements for the partnership between family and state in the care of the young child. Describing specific programs has been considered only a part of this task; rather, the focus has been upon the system of early child care within its total context—past and present, tangible and intangible. Each of the monographs has been written according to a common outline. The reader is not expected to be knowledgeable about the country nor is it expected that he is a professional in any of the disciplines related to children; on the other hand, it is assumed that he is concerned with the welfare of children everywhere and it is hoped that he is open to new ideas and alternatives.

The distinguished group of professionals who constitute the International Study Group for Early Child Care have been exceedingly generous with their time and energies in the pursuit of an exchange of ideas and in their commitment to improving conditions for all children. They have created a hearty and viable coalition, evidenced not only by the work they have accomplished but by their continuing collaboration in writing and in research. It has been our great pleasure to have been associated with them individually and collectively, and to have been a part of the sedulity and cameraderie which have characterized their activities. We should like to take this opportunity to express the gratitude of all the members to the Carnegie Corporation of New York, which has been so generous in its support of this project since its inception, and most particularly to Mrs. Barbara Finberg, Executive Associate of that organization, who has been an active participant in many of our deliberations. We should also like to thank the Rockefeller Foundation, the U.S. National Institute of Mental Health, and the Institute for Social Work of Croatia, Yugoslavia, which have helped to support the annual meetings. Our primary debt, however, is to the participants in this association. They are a very special group of human beings.

Halbert B. Robinson
Nancy M. Robinson

Preface

AMERICA emerged from the depression years of the 1930's and the war years of the 1940's with rather brash self-confidence and optimism. The birth rate soared; economic development was remarkable; few domestic problems seemed impervious to the capacity of the burgeoning technology. It was not until 1958, with the advent of Sputnik, that some penetrating questions began to be asked about the rather easy-going American way of bringing up children, ushering in a wave of reaction, an intensified interest in education, and a frantic awareness that the children who would be the citizens of tomorrow were growing up today.

After berating the schools for a time over their apparent lack of attention to academic excellence, Americans began to be aware that there were other, perhaps more pressing problems. During the early 1960's, the plight of the poor, of various minority groups, and of the handicapped began to receive popular attention. By that time, the weight of scientific opinion had come to be that the most fundamental components of man's nature are learned and that the most important nurturing years are the first four or five.

Much about America can be divined from the crazy quilt of programs and services which sprang up to ensure that young children would be more effectively nurtured. Generosity, good intentions, optimism, impatience, and perhaps most important of all, guilt over past and continuing injustices—all these characterized the groundswell of concern, compassion, and commitment for all the nation's children, but particularly the least privileged.

The International Study Group was established in 1968 and this monograph was begun a year later. During the four years between 1969 and 1973, it has continually been revised, not only because some of the facts were out of date but because the spirit of the times was changing so rapidly. In 1969, the possibilities seemed limitless. If something couldn't be accomplished today, it probably would be tomorrow. Hundreds of thousands of thoroughly committed people, both professionals and laymen, had been mobilized to built a better tomorrow, and the nation as a whole seemed solidly behind the effort.

Times have changed, however, and more than anything else this monograph is a testament to that change. Since 1969, it has become all too clear that the problems of poverty, disease, prejudice, and alienation are formidable indeed and that many of the proposed solutions have been naive and ineffective. We are perhaps beginning now to understand what may be needed, but the new approaches will take time to prove and develop and even then progress will be slow. The dominant mood in America has also changed since 1969, and it is no longer clear that the people will support or even tolerate new social action programs. There has been a reassertion of the doctrine that everyone in America is capable of making a good life for himself if only he will work hard and be prudent. Yet, the generosity, the compassion, the good intentions, and the guilt, have not disappeared. The active partnership described in this monograph between the American society and all its families will surely be modified, but it will not be dissolved.

Individually and together, the five of us have relied on the help of many people—too many to mention here, though they have our sincere gratitude. We are especially indebted to Lois-ellin Datta and Sandra Mitchell for their generosity in providing information about compensatory programs and for critically reading the manuscript, and to Susan Varnum for her energetic and skillful editing.

Halbert B. Robinson
Nancy M. Robinson
Martin Wolins
Urie Bronfenbrenner
Julius B. Richmond

I

Introduction

THE PEOPLE of the United States have long regarded their nation as particularly responsive to the needs of the young, and they have taken great pride in the many accomplishments for children, notably in the fields of health care and education. With their high regard for youth, permissive and accepting child-rearing attitudes, and willingness to tolerate and adapt to young people's demands for social reform, the adults of America have, in fact, been accused of domination by their youth. As a perceptive British playwright once observed, "The youth of America is their oldest tradition," (Wilde, 1893).

Since the first Anglo-Europeans settled on her eastern shores some 350 years ago, the growth of the United States in both population and area has been continuous and at times prodigious. The vigorous pioneer spirit of America's earlier years—the self-confident, persevering, even brash acceptance of life's challenge—has been accompanied by the conviction that everyone has a chance for happiness, that in this "melting pot" everyone has work to do and will reap the fruits of honest labor.

Slowly, however, the realization has evolved that not all have had their chance. Many Americans have begun to reevaluate the nation's progress towards helping children reach their potential as fulfilled, participating adult citizens : the consensus seems to be that success in this area has not been so pronounced as previously thought. It is clear that many parents still lack opportunities for full social, economic, and political participation, and that their children are often unable to escape repeating the cycle of poverty and despair.

The crisis of conscience concerning the poor in America has been coupled with the growing conviction that the man will be whole if the child is adequately nurtured. Those who have waged the "war on poverty" have stressed that even by the age of six, many children from disadvantaged homes are severely handicapped and unable to participate effectively in the educational system. Somewhat belatedly, it has also become apparent that, quite aside from moral responsibilities,

Early Child Development and Care
Vol. 2, 1973, pp. 359–368

society's own self-interests are best served by creating the best possible conditions for all children.

A. A DEMOGRAPHIC VIEW OF THE UNITED STATES

The United States is a richly varied country. Its citizens trace their ancestry to every region of the world. Its political spectrum ranges from far left to far right, although the governing process is dominated by two modern parties which accommodate widely disparate views. Its geography encompasses frozen ice packs of the Arctic Circle, tropical swamplands, sunny Pacific Islands, rugged mountains, fertile plains and arid deserts. Diversity characterizes every aspect of American life, a fact which is often hidden in statistical analyses.

1. Political and administrative subdivisions

Political and administrative structures in the United States are numerous and complex, yet almost all levels of government follow a basic tripartite organization which consists of a legislative branch responsible for enacting legislation; an administrative, or executive, branch to implement and enforce these laws; and a judiciary, which determines whether the actions of individuals, corporations, and the government are in accordance with laws of the land. Each branch functions independently, but tries to act as a check against disproportionate power gains or abuses in the other two branches. This system of "checks and balances" is reinforced by the fact that most leaders of the administrative and legislative branches are elected officials whose tenure must be periodically reconfirmed by the voters.

At the national level, the tripartite organization includes a bicameral congress (legislative), the presidency (administrative), and a hierarchy of courts (judiciary). The 50 states parallel this structure with only minor differences. States are subdivided into counties which in turn may include one or more municipalities (cities, villages, towns, etc.). Finally, one finds innumerable county and municipal districts performing specialized functions (e.g., school districts, water and sewage districts, transportation districts, and so forth); these

[2]

special purpose districts may be smaller or larger than a county, or may combine portions of more than one county.

The governing units described have the advantage of offering wide opportunities for "grassroots" (popular) political participation. On the other hand, the complexity of the system and the large number of people involved constitute formidable barriers to change and require enormous expenditures of manpower. In 1970, for example, 12,639,000 persons or 16.2 percent of all U.S. workers were employed by some level of government. It is in the milieu of this intricate political structure that efforts have been mounted to improve early childhood care, especially for the poor.

2. Population

The population of the United States has increased from 179,323,000 in 1960 to 205,614,000 in 1971. Its land area totals 9,356,889 square kilometers—a density of 22.16 persons per km^2. Different sections vary widely in population densities and degree of urbanization. Alaska, for example, has only about 0.2 persons per km^2, the eight western-central mountain states average 3.7 persons per km^2 while the three populous Middle Atlantic states average 139.6 persons per km_2. About three quarters of the population (73.5 percent) live in urban areas and about one quarter (26.5 percent) in rural areas or settlements of 2,500 or less. The actual farm population is only about 10 million persons (5 percent).

The composition of the United States' population is now predominately native-born, though about 11,000,000 persons were born abroad and an additional 30,000,000 have at least one foreign-born parent. Most persons (87.4 percent) are Caucasian; the rest are predominantly classified as Negro (11.2 percent). American Indians, who constitute a particularly impoverished group, represent only 0.4 percent of the population.

There are 97 males per 100 females, the disparity reflecting higher mortality rates among males at all ages. Married or ever-married women comprise 86.3 percent of all women 18 years of age and older. Divorce rates, however, are approximately one-third the number of marriages each year (e.g., in 1970, there were 10.7

marriages and 3.5 divorces per 1,000 population). About one in ten families is headed by a woman (about half of these widowed and about half divorced or separated). Among poor families with young children, however—a crucial target population for many early child care programs—approximately one-third are headed by a woman.

The United States has recently experienced a significant drop in its birth rate attributable to popular use of birth control methods, easy availability of abortions, and concern with overpopulation. In 1935, the birth rate per 1,000 population was 18.7; in 1950, 24.1; in 1960, 23.7; by 1970, it had declined to 18.2; and during the first half of 1971 to a low of 17.2 (or 82.3 per 1,000 women of child-bearing age). Even so, these figures are rather high compared with many other developed countries.

Families tend to be rather small. Of all families in 1970 with at least one child under the age of 18, 31.7 percent had only one child; 29.6 percent had two; 18.8 percent had three children, and 19.9 percent had four or more. The average number of children per family with at least one child is about 2.3. Birth rates among poverty families are approximately 40 percent higher than the national average. It appears that women in all groups, however, are now spacing their children farther apart and decreasing the eventual size of their families. For example, the number of children under age 5 in families of women ages 15-24, dropped from 433 per 1,000 families in 1960 to 291 in 1969.

3. Economy

The United States is a wealthy and productive country. The gross national product in 1972 was $1,152 billion, or about $5,500 for each person. Hourly pay for an average factory worker in June, 1971, was $3.57 including overtime, or about $143 for a 40-hour week. There was, however, considerable variation in pay from one skilled occupation to another. Construction workers in 1970 received an average of $200 per week, while furniture makers, farmers, and bank employees earned only about half that figure. Unskilled workers earned less, managers and professional workers received substantially more. To earn the money for his family's rent (excluding utilities) in 1969, the average production worker spent the wages for about 3 days of work each month. In 1970, to buy a used car, he spent his wages for 8.5 weeks; to purchase a popular-priced new car, 26.1 weeks. He could earn a dozen eggs by 11 minutes of work; a half-gallon of milk in 10 minutes; a suit by 23.2 hours of work.

Consumer goods are relatively plentiful. In 1971, there were approximately 440 registered passenger cars and 563 telephones per 1,000 persons. In 1969, at least one television set was found in 95 percent of homes (29 percent had two or more and 32 percent of the homes had a color set). Good housing is available to most families: 91.8 percent of families had at least one room per person, and 93.1 percent had both a flush toilet and hot-water bathtub or shower for their exclusive use in 1970. Even so, the 1966 White House Conference on Civil Rights concluded that the United States had to construct two million housing units annually to make headway against deterioration. It was recommended that one-quarter of these be subsidized for the poor, but of a total of 1.5 million units built in 1970, only about 33,000 were constructed with public funds for the poor.

The sad fact is that in the midst of plenty, a significant segment of the population lives in poverty. Although estimates vary from one year or standard to another, it is probably fair to say that about one person in five lives in poverty (but about one child in four, because the poor have more children). About 70 percent are Caucasian, but this should not disguise the fact that a very high proportion of American citizens of ethnic and/or racial minorities are poor. Many poor families exist in an enveloping culture of poverty which they have known since birth and from which they will never escape. About half live in the cities and half in rural areas—but wherever they live, they are only marginal to the greater and more affluent society.

B. HISTORICAL OVERVIEW

Child care traditions were family traditions during colonial times in America, the early years of nationhood, and the great westward migrations which took place in the 19th century. The family was expected to look after its own children, as it was expected to care for its elderly, its ill, and its handicapped. From birth to adulthood, nearly all the child's needs were supplied within the family, and in return he was expected from an early age to be a contributing member of this primary group.

The principal institutions outside the family with an interest in the child were, in those early years, the churches. They also served as social centers for families, and through them was funneled much of the charity support for the poverty-stricken and much of what was available in the way of "book learning."

Industrial development increased opportunities for employment, brought about a need for trained manpower and evoked the opposition of the labor unions to the continued employment of children at low wages. This in turn brought about the establishment of a public school system. As was true in Europe, the middle of the 19th century witnessed the beginnings of some socially supported programs for children including a few public kindergartens, but these tended to be limited and localized. Since that time, the public school system has expanded remarkably; the proportion of children attending and the number of years offered at public expense have steadily increased and are doing so even now. Today, schooling is compulsory for all children, usually from 6 to 16 years of age, and is available at virtually no expense to the student. The upbringing of preschool children has, however, continued to be viewed as the exclusive responsibility of families, which until recently have been given very little aid. Most Americans still believe that a mother of young children should stay at home, and that the "good" family needs little outside support.

Industrial development has changed the American life style as thoroughly and as quickly as any nation in the world. It has led to many beneficial outcomes but it was also responsible for very bad living and working conditions for the millions who emigrated from foreign countries and rural areas to urban factories in the 19th century. Exploitation was widespread. Young children, for example, were often required to work long hours, six days a week. At the turn of the century these conditions crystallized in a heightened interest in the welfare of children, the enactment of protective laws, and the establishment of institutions on their behalf. Child labor legislation was passed; children's courts were set up in a number of states; infant and child health stations were established; and the discipline of child psychiatry and social work were inaugurated. A major manifestation of the interest in children at this time was the first dicentennial White House Conference on Children and Youth in 1909. This conference involved many professional and lay individuals and resulted in the establishment of the Children's Bureau as a federal agency. The first two decades of this century were indeed

Ithaca Journal

FIGURE 2 Independence day parade

vintage years for children's programs and institutions, an era unparalleled in action or commitment until the mid-1960's. For the most part, though, private citizens initiated and financed almost all important social and medical programs, such as the settlement houses,† family social agencies, maternal and child health programs, and child psychiatry clinics.

The growing influence of Freud and his followers became apparent in the 1920's. Psychoanalytic doctrines coalesced with other themes

---

† Neighborhood centers rendering recreational, educational and social services.

in American life leading to new attitudes about the importance of the early years and the role of the family in development. The Horatio Alger theme that a good man could overcome almost any obstacle by hard work was gradually replaced by the theme that the good and the bad in all men is determined by past experiences. In this way, society in general—and parents in particular—came to be viewed as determinants of all that was felt to be wrong with America, and the conviction grew that all could be made right by reforming child rearing practices and important socialization agencies.

A large number of the programs started for young children at the turn of the century continued until the major economic depression of the 1930's. At that point, many worthwhile programs collapsed and economic assistance for large segments of the population came into existence. The most important measure was the Social Security Act of 1935, which among other provisions, made funds available for financial aid to dependent children, maternal and child health, and crippled children's programs. Many important programs today are amended forms of the provisions of that bill. During this same period, the federal Works Progress Administration (W.P.A.) nursery schools and day care centers were established to provide employment for adults. As economic conditions improved, however, these programs were discontinued.

During World War II, another major national program of early child care was initiated. The Lanham Act funded day care centers for children whose mothers were working in war-related industries. When the emergency situation which had necessitated the employment of large numbers of women ended, most of these centers were also discontinued.

Following World War II, there was a heightened interest in the health and welfare of children. Industrial development proceeded very quickly, accompanied by increased migration of the poor from rural to urban areas. The growing visibility of people living in poverty—the contrast between their lives and the growing affluence of the majority —stimulated the interest and concern of many. During the late 1950's and early 1960's, several currents surfaced almost simultaneously on the national scene to force some major changes in American life.

One current was the initiation of an active movement to eradicate laws and customs which had for centuries abrogated Negros' civil rights. Many schools, for example, had remained segregated despite a 1954 Supreme Court decision declaring segregation by race unconstitutional. Some public facilities were not open to Negros; restrictive and employment housing patterns were common. The resulting social and educational handicaps supported segregation, limited job opportunities, and resulted in poverty and discouragement. Efforts of concerned citizens to direct attention to these conditions attracted the participation of political leaders, and during the presidencies of Kennedy and Johnson, several strong civil rights acts were drafted and passed by the Congress.

Another current was the growing conviction that the richest nation in the world could eliminate completely the blight of poverty. President Johnson sought such a "Great Society," and instituted the "War on Poverty" to bring all citizens into the mainstream of the society. The Office of Economic Opportunity was established in 1964, primarily to provide federal funds to communities for the purpose of developing projects which would increase educational and employment opportunities for the poor.

Still another current was the belief that the problems of the poor could be traced to conditions which determined their original life adjustments. In the words of one group of child development experts who followed the development of 250 premature infants from low-income families:

The inadequate incomes, crowded homes, lack of consistent family ties, the mother's depression and helplessness in her own situation, were as important as her child-rearing practices in influencing the child's development and preparing him for an adult role. It was for us a sobering experience to watch a large group of newborn infants, plastic human beings of unknown potential, and observe over a five-year-period their social preparation to enter the class of the least skilled, least educated, and most rejected in our society (Wortis *et al.*, 1962).

By the middle 1960's, then, a preventive approach was clearly indicated to solve the problems of the poor, especially poor Negros. As the new Office of Economic Opportunity joined with existing agencies (Maternal and Child Health Service, Social and Rehabilitation Service, and Children's Bureau) to fight the War on Poverty, funds were made available for early child care programs to supplement the families' care of the children. The most important program was Project Head Start, initiated in the summer of 1965 for approximately half the poor children who were to be enrolled in school that fall. (See Section VI, F.) As Project Head Start continued, it was argued that if its favorable developmental effects on health, personality development, and achievement were to be enduring, a follow-through into the school years would be necessary. Accordingly, some funds were directed toward this goal. Efforts were also made to develop more favorable home environments for infants and young children living in poverty.

The War on Poverty has lasted long enough to make it abundantly clear that the enemies are indeed formidable. New programs have shown no more than mildly encouraging potential, even though careful evaluations point to new directions which show promise. (See Section VI, A, F.) None of the programs has been as effective as its advocates hoped, and some of the proponents of the "war" have already become disillusioned. President Nixon has declared that the efforts initiated in the 1960's to build the "Great Society" were largely misguided, and that many of the programs have been failures.

This position appears to be unwarranted in its extremity, and ignores some of the constructive gains which, however small, have been made. Debates on the fundamental issues are bound to be acrimonious and prolonged during the next few years, and one can only hope that the recently aroused population will not retreat in discouragement. It is clear that this democratic nation must pursue the goal of equal opportunity for all, especially all its children.

II

Conceptions of the child and the upbringing process

A. NATURE, NURTURE, AND RECIPROCITY

IT IS ALMOST impossible to find a genuine consensus among American citizens regarding any common endeavor. "The American Way" is, in fact, a myth : there are many "American Ways." In most aspects of daily living, individuals and families are free to conduct themselves as they see fit, so long as their behavior does not infringe upon the rights of others. Among the areas protected as private, individual matters are most aspects of parents' behavior toward their children. Certainly, there is no agreed-upon way to bring up children in America.

Furthermore, there exist no official doctrines concerning the nature of the young child, and it would be considered highly improper for any government unit to presume to tell parents how to raise children, or to assume the initiative in any matters related to the very private realm of family life. As a service to families who seek advice, a number of government agencies have issued pamphlets dealing with child care. (See Section VIII.) These materials, however, which are made available only on request, are the joint work of a number of specialists, most of whom have little or no official connection with the government. As such, the publications represent combined views of independent professionals rather than governmental or political viewpoints. Even in the more active federal programs recently undertaken to assist disadvantaged families with young children, few official policies are espoused. Local control over programs is encouraged, and parents are very much involved in shaping the nature of the endeavors (e.g., in Parent and Child Centres and Project Head Start, described in Section VI, F).

Nothing seems more obvious about family life in America than the fact of change. Many grandparents shake their heads disapprovingly at permissive child rearing practices, egalitarian parent-child interactions, and the unparalleled affluence of many of today's children. Many parents feel that family life has changed so dramatically in their lifetime that they have no clear conception about either the goals or the methods of child rearing.

Controversies have raged for many years in America as elsewhere about the essential nature of human development. Are the child's temperament and abilities primarily the products of his hereditary endowment? Does his development primarily reveal the working of a sort of universal (but individually paced) inner clock, best not tampered with? Or is he almost totally the product of his environment? This last position, of course, places more responsibility upon the shoulders of parents, who control most of the environment of the young child; the former position relieves some of this burden, placing parents in the role of managers rather than *de novo* creators. The pendulum of what is known popularly as the "nature-nurture" controversy has tended to swing back and forth rather broadly. Slowly, however, a truly interactional position has begun to characterize professional attitudes, and probably the views of most middle-class parents as well. Lower-class mothers still profess, however, to have relatively little control over the development of their children (Hess, 1970).

Whatever the source of their personalities, children's individuality and their unique effects on their parents have recently become a legitimate object of inquiry. Previous accounts of parent-child interactions had assumed—common sense to the contrary—that influence flowed in only one direction: from parent to child. One of the most important recent investigations has highlighted temperamental differences of newborns, their consistency over the early years, and the effects of these differences on the subsequent behavior of their parents (Thomas *et al.,* 1968). One U.S. Children's Bureau manual, *Your Child from One to Six* (1962), tells parents of the one-year-old, "He's been teaching you to manage him." At the same time, the Children's Bureau publication *Infant Care* (1963), says, "It is true that some qualities about the baby are settled before he is born. Nobody can do anything about these. . . But through the pattern of his days, his personality is shaped. Through his experiences with you, the people who are the most important to him, the baby learns the dimensions of the world." It is up to parents, then, to assume responsibility for the young and helpless infant, whatever his constitutional qualities, and to create an environment which enhances optimal growth.

B. STAGES OF CHILDREN'S DEVELOPMENT

By common assent, the period before school is roughly divided into three phases: infancy (birth to walking), toddlerhood (walking to age $2\frac{1}{2}$ or 3), and early childhood (3 to 6). A number of transient "stages" of a different nature also enter the vernacular of professionals, practitioners, and parents. One finds in parents' manuals, for example,

Developmental Psychology Laboratory, University of Washington

FIGURE 3   The backpack stage

discussions of the "age of accidents," the "negativistic stage," or the "chatterbox stage." Parents are encouraged to think of these behaviors as natural phenomena, to be coped with as graciously as possible. The transitional behaviors are often expressed as age norms:

THREE is a kind of coming-of-age . . . You can bargain with THREE and he can wait his turn . . . FOUR (and half-past) tends to go out of bounds . . . FIVE is a SUPER-THREE with a socialized pride in clothes and accomplishments, a lover of praise (Gesell & Ilg, 1943).

Some theories espoused by professionals emphasize stage conceptions and others do not. Theories which focus on learning and the effects of environmental events (e.g., Hullian theory [Dollard and Miller, 1950] or Skinner [1938]) ignore stage sequences, hypothesizing instead several universal laws of development which fit both growing children and adults. On the other hand, some of the most popular theories of development (e.g., Erikson [1950] and Piaget [Flavell, 1963]) portray the child as an essentially different kind of organism as he progresses from one stage to another. All these theories have had an important impact upon scientific research and have slowly filtered through to practitioners and families as well. Some informed mothers are acquainted with the Freudian conceptions of the stages of early development (oral, anal, phallic, Oedipal); a few with Erikson's formulations of the major periods of infancy and early childhood ("trust vs. mistrust," "autonomy vs. shame and doubt"); hardly any with Piaget's formulations ("sensorimotor stage," "pre-operational stage").

There has been considerable debate in the professional literature regarding the existence of "critical periods" in human development, i.e., crucial time-spans during which a given bit of development must take place if it is ever to occur successfully. Although most professional workers now conclude that the evidence is almost nonexistent for such irreversible effects among human beings, they recognize that aspects of early development which have gone awry are often in practice extremely hard to repair; cognitive deficits and personality problems tend to persist and to compound. Even this cautious point of view, however, is increasingly subject to criticism by those who favor a more maturational or nativist position.

[14]

A number of issues in the field of child care are relevant to this notion of continuity in human development. The contention that group care is harmful to infants and toddlers, for example, assumes the earliest stages of development to be critical for personality development. Specifically, it is argued that intensive one-to-one relationships must be set up then if development is ever to proceed normally. "Maternal deprivation"—interpreted as the absence of one's own mother-figure for even part of the day, whether or not substitutes are available— is seen as a danger to be avoided if possible. The theory contends that once a child so deprived has passed this crucial period, he will be forever unable to form intensive, meaningful relationships. The work of Spitz (1945) and Bowlby (1952) was extremely influential in this idea, as were longitudinal studies by Goldfarb (1945) of children adopted after living for their first three years in institutions. The maternal deprivation hypothesis, as broadly and indefensibly stated as it was during the 1940's and 1950's (see Yarrow, 1961), contributed to the prohibitions on group day care of children, and discouraged even family day care if the mother could possibly remain at home. It also led to a substantial reduction in residential institutions for young homeless and/or mentally handicapped children, and it contributed to the emphasis on permanent adoption and foster family care for children needing homes.

C. AIMS OF UPBRINGING AND EDUCATION

American parents in most walks of life tend to share many common goals for their children. Thus, studies looking for major differences have instead usually found major areas of overlap with all parents wanting their children to be healthy, happy, competent, responsive to others, and so forth. Differences do exist, however (Bronfenbrenner, 1958; Hess, 1970). Working-class parents, for example, are more likely to be traditional in outlook, to stress neatness, cleanliness, obedience, respect for authority, and acceptance of adult norms. These values are even stronger in the overcrowded and disorganized homes of the poor, where the ideal child in one who learns to "get along," to stay out of other people's way, to cause as little trouble as possible. The middle-class parent, by contrast, is more likely to value the child who is curious and eager to learn (even if his explorations make more work), cooperative, happy, self-controlled, and open with his parents. The "bright" child is valued as highly—perhaps even more so—than the "good" child. Middle-class parents expect their children to achieve independence within the family context; the poverty family also urges the child toward independence but outside the family—taking care of himself without supervision, and even moving away from home while still an adolescent. Hence, many young people from poor homes establish their own families very early, only to renew the intergenerational cycle of poverty.

Most parents also share a common desire to see their children succeed in school, but there are sharp differences in specific goals and expectations. Hess (1964) asked a group of Negro mothers from four different social classes, "Imagine your child is old enough to go to public school for the first time. How would you prepare him? What would you tell him?" One middle-class mother said:

First of all, I would remind Portia that she was going to school to learn, that her teacher would take my place, and that she would be expected to follow instructions. Also that her time was to be spent mostly in the classroom with other children, and that any questions or any problems that she might have she could consult with her teacher for assistance.

In contrast, a lower-class mother replied:

Well, John, it's time to go to school now. You must know how to behave. The first day at school you should be a good boy and should do just what the teacher tells you to do.

These mothers conceptualize the school situation very differently, yet they both hope fervently that their children will succeed there.

Most nursery school teachers tend to stress nonacademic developmental tasks—learning to get along with other children, creative self-expression, improving fine and gross motor skills, broadening curiosity, and individuality. This fits in well with the expectations of middle-class families about the kind of enrichment they seek for their children, but to many lower-class parents it seems to be "just play." One Head Start father who had taken an hour off from his job to visit his daughter's preschool center asked as he left, "Well, when does it begin?" Yet, here is what his daughter had done during that time:

She . . . completed a 16-piece puzzle, built a delicately balanced block building with three friends, decided to wash the school's doll clothes and hang them up to dry, poured water thoughtfully in and out of a new measuring cup at the small sink, conversed with her teacher about the numbers on the side of the cup, climbed to the top of the indoor jungle gym and jumped off with a group of other children, crayoned and painted on large paper, returned to the block corner to assist in clean-up, before joining the children gathering for a story. (Project Head Start, 1967).

D. ACCELERATION OF LEARNING

Until very recently, the responsibilities of parents during infancy and early childhood were relatively simple: to provide a good physical start in life, build the child's sense of trust in others and himself, gently begin to impose the rules of family living, and set the stage for a few zestful, joyful years before the onset of the "real work" of living. The pace of teaching during this era was regarded as best when it was relaxed and natural, responding to the needs of the children without hurrying them along.

Complicating matters in the past few years, however, has been a recognition of the potential of infants and young children for important cognitive growth, and, at the same time, a strong suspicion that it is "now or never." Some have posed the challenging question: since the child can learn so much, shall we assume that within limits, the faster he can be taught, the better? As a matter of fact, the earlier view—which still has many influential proponents—maintains that purposeful, concentrated encouragement of cognitive development actually competes with and hampers the child's most important task during this period, the accomplishment of basic social and emotional growth. Milton Senn, Gesell's successor at Yale, has said, "Too frequently today the emphasis is on speed, on hastening learning. Children are denied time to reflect, to cogitate, to dream. I believe this denial hinders the development of the intellect as distinguished from the development of intelligence" (Senn, 1969). Others have observed, though, that the more cognitively competent children also tend to be those who are best adjusted socially (White et al., 1969).

Most, but admittedly not all, professionals agree about the

[17]

desirability of enhancing the cognitive development of "culturally deprived" children, whose development is typically slow. The major controversy revolves instead around whether or not the usual development of children from normally favorable (e.g., middle-class) homes can or should be hurried. The consensus among practitioners can probably be characterized as encouraging gentle efforts toward acceleration, reserving the more heroic efforts for "deprived" children. Young middle-class mothers have heard this message. They may be spending more time "teaching" their babies, and certainly they are buying more "educational" toys. It is clear that middle-class mothers, however, were already more effective and dedicated teachers of their children than were lower-class and poverty-level mothers (Hess, 1970).

E. THEORY AND METHODS OF UPBRINGING

1. Relevant theory and research trends

No single theoretical position about children's development is pre-eminent today. There are, rather, several "camps." One major group gives primary allegiance to Sigmund Freud and other contemporary psychoanalytic theorists such as Erik Erikson, although the dominance of this group has steadily declined over the last decade. Another important group champions behavior theory as presented by psychologists such as Pavlov, John Watson, Clark Hull, and more recently B. F. Skinner. A group of increasing strength during the past few years subscribes to the cognitive theories of Jean Piaget and his followers. There is still a small group which identifies with the maturational theory of such men as Arnold Gesell. By far the largest group of professional workers, however, identifies itself as eclectic and subscribes to various components of these theories and still others.

Major areas of research activity regarding the practical problems of raising children have focused on systems and timing and reinforcement (rewards and punishments) which determine and regulate performance; the consequences of varying degrees of limit-setting on children's development; and the nature and importance of possible models for the child to emulate. Practical problems surrounding the management of learning environments by parents and teachers, especi-

[18]

ally for children from poverty families, have received a great deal of attention recently.

The focus on reinforcement is a natural product of the preoccupation of American psychologists with learning theories. While such theories have differed in their details, they have all shared a common emphasis on the events surrounding behavior—whether they be natural outgrowths of the behavior itself (a burned finger that touched the stove), or the parentally- or societally-engineered consequences (a loving pat on the head or a grade received on an examination). Most theories have emphasized the greater power of positive reinforcements to cement and shape effective behavior patterns. Research has also consistently revealed the greater potency of reinforcers occurring in the context of an important, and especially a loving, relationship with the child. Recent investigations have been concerned with the power of inattention to extinguish undesirable behaviors. It appears that misbehavior is actually strengthened when it earns the attention of parent, teacher, or peer—although this is quite the opposite of the intended effect. Extensive research has shown the efficacy of withholding attention in these situations, at the same time seeking an opportunity to reinforce a desired behavior. So far as punishment enters this picture, professional advice based on psychological research maintains that the punishment should be contingent and prompt, should inform the child precisely what he has done wrong, and should be designed to suppress the undesirable behavior so that approved patterns can be substituted and reinforced. "Love-oriented" disciplines (temporary withdrawal of affection, disapproval, shame, guilt) are preferable to physical punishment; natural consequences ("Go to your room until you are fit to live with,") are preferred to arbitrary inflictions ("No dessert tonight because you hit your sister,").

One of the most strenuous debates regarding American childrearing practice has had to do with the handling of freedom and restrictions. During the 1940's and 1950's, a popular understanding of psychoanalytic and other theoretical positions led many parents to remove all but the most necessary restrictions on the behavior of children, fearing that adult-imposed rules would harmfully inhibit and repress natural instincts. Casual observation seemed to reveal that children brought up in this manner were difficult to live with and tended to lack the very self-confidence that "permissiveness" was said to encourage. Negative reactions grew, and such parents were eventually said to be neglecting their responsibility as socializers in the name of a misguided permissiveness. Fortunately, the pendulum did not swing to extremes of restrictiveness; rather, the idea gained strength that effective child-rearing must involve "freedom within limits."

Until recently, the major theoretical position emphasizing the power of models for children was psychoanalytic theory. By little-understood means, the young child was expected to adopt not only the overt behaviors but also many of the internal attitudes of his parents and others important to him. While some theorists (e.g., Dollard and Miller, 1950) discussed the role of imitation in this process, its nature has been viewed as a mystery and for the most part outside the conscious influence of parents. It should be noted that much of the concern about the effects of the father-absent family and the absence of men in child care and early education programs rests on the assumption that both the young girl and the young boy, but particularly the latter, need male as well as female figures with whom to identify.

Modern social learning theories (e.g., Bandura and Walters, 1963) continue to emphasize the power of models in socialization of children. A number of laboratory studies have demonstrated that which has always been obvious to mothers: children learn by watching and imitating others. Very little of the research on modelling has been directly concerned with the parent-child relationship, though, or on the relationship of children to their peers and siblings. Most of it has been conducted in laboratories where interaction patterns can be rigorously controlled. Even so, the results point unequivocally to the importance of within-family interpersonal interactions. It is clear that potency increases to the extent that the model is seen as competent, nurturing, rewarding, of high status, and controlling potential resources (who more than the parent?), and to the extent that the model is viewed as similar to the viewer (who more than siblings and peers?).

2. Advice to parents

Recommendations concerning the manner in which children should be reared come from many sources in the United States. The recognized experts tend to be scientists and practitioners from the various disciplines related to child development—pediatricians; members of university faculties; staffs of research institutes or agencies serving children and their parents, such as child guidance clinics, preschools, etc.

There is evidence showing some correspondence between recommended values and practices, and those subsequently espoused by parents, with a somewhat greater time differential in the case of working and poverty classes as opposed to middle-class families (Bronfenbrenner, 1958). One may question whether professional recommendations do in fact influence the public, or whether the views of both reflect economic and social changes in the culture as a whole (Kohn, 1969). It is clear, though, that the recommendations provide a reasonably valid basis for inferring the beliefs of a large segment of parents and professionals.

To provide a first approximation of trends in the ideology and methods of childrearing in the United States, more than a dozen manuals published in the quarter-century since World War II have been systematically examined (Bronfenbrenner, 1971, unpublished). Materials included were the most popular publications prepared for use by parents, nursery school teachers, day care personnel, and others engaged directly in the care of children under seven years. The resulting analysis revealed both continuity and change, the most enduring and salient theme emphasizing the importance of the child as *an individual.* The potential for development has been viewed as lying within the child and the central aim of childrearing—whether in family or group settings— as assisting him in the self-realization of his potential. Inhibiting this potential through the imposition of unwarranted or inappropriate external constraints has been seen as the greatest danger. Consistent with this theme has been the stress on the development of independence. In the middle 1940's, both parents and professionals were advised to "let the child do things for himself" and to "let him make his own decisions as much as you can." Similarly, in the 1960's, Ginott told parents, "Deliberately present the child with situations where he has to make choices," and Nimnicht instructed the staffs of nursery schools to "Let the child make a choice in every possible situation."

[21]

Within the continuity, however, there has also been change. The most pronounced shift occurred in the potentialities of children which were brought into focus. Especially in the 1940's—but throughout the 1950's as well—the overriding emphasis was on the emotional life of the child. Parents were repeatedly enjoined to allow children to express their feelings: "Let a tantrum take its course," "Never try to break the thumb-sucking habit," "Allow masturbation as long as it doesn't become compulsive." By the late 1950's, however, the emphasis began to shift. There were fewer references to emotional experience and a growing concern with cognitive development. By the turn of the decade, the latter theme began to predominate, and the "self-actualization" of the 1950's was transformed into the "self-discovery" of the 1960's. Parents and other caretakers were urged to leave the child free to explore and to make a series of interrelated discoveries about his physical, cultural, and social world.

A second, though less pronounced trend, occurred in the sphere of method rather than content. It is perhaps most clearly reflected in the writings of Dr. Benjamin Spock, who has often been described as having had the most important influence of American child rearing methods during the past quarter-century. For almost ten years, from the middle 1950's to the middle 1960's, Spock wrote a monthly column for *Ladies' Home Journal,* a leading women's magazine. The first 18 and the last 18 articles published during this period have been analyzed, and his specific recommendations classified into 18 categories under four general headings: Expression of affects, Nurturance, Discipline, and Activities. The analysis revealed virtually no change over time in the first area, but a number of noteworthy changes in the other three. Admonitions to engage in nurturant behavior dropped from 22 percent of all recommendations to 2 percent, whereas calls for discipline increased. Entries classified under "permisiveness," for example, dropped from 29 percent to 10 percent, while "setting rules and limits" doubled from 6 percent to 12 percent, and "re-directing child's behavior" rose from 1 percent to 10 percent. Finally, in keeping with earlier observations, recommendations for cognitive experiences increased from 1 percent to 9 percent. The significance of these shifts is underscored by the fact that the advice emanated from a single source over the period of a decade.

Probably the most important change in the past twenty-five years concerns the audience to whom the publications have been directed. In the 1940's and 1950's, the manuals were written almost exclusively for parents, with only occasional books discussing the care of children in settings outside the family. In the middle 1960's there was a radical change : a series of booklets published as training materials for Project Head Start ushered in a stream of publications on child care in group settings. There was, accordingly, a distinct shift from the predominantly middle class orientation of the earlier works to concern with children from disadvantaged families. Most of the recent publications have been highly cognitive in their emphasis, the only notable exceptions being Project Head Start manuals, and a later series of child care manuals published by Arlie House, which have given balanced coverage to areas such as health, nutrition, social services, and parent involvement.

The most stable and salient feature of the American approach to childrearing does not become fully apparent until one compares American manuals with those from other countries. The American trademark that then becomes so clearly recognizable can be summarized in a single word : "individualism." The rights of the individual and the emphasis of independence are of course central themes in the history of American society. It should perhaps be pointed out, however, that the manner in which these themes are reflected is not altogether reassuring. Throughout, the focus is on the individual child, his "self-realization" through "self-discovery" and "self-motivated behavior." While other people are to assist him in this process, they are not to get in his way. As for the question of the child's obligations to others—especially to those not his own age—the training manuals are strangely silent. Perhaps in a deeper sense than Americans intended, their ideology of upbringing is indeed "child-centered."

[23]

III

The compact between the family and society†

A. ORIGIN OF ATTITUDES ABOUT THE COMPACT

There are several major belief systems which in large measure determine the nature of the compact between families and society in the United States. Parents are held to be unequivocally responsible for the care of their young children; it is assumed that for the most part, they will have the knowledge, the desire, and the means to carry out this responsibility effectively. The free-enterprise market economy and cooperative exchanges of goods and services are viewed as capable of adequately supplying all but a few families with everything they need. It is felt, therefore, that government need not—indeed, should not—interfere with the freedom of parents to raise their children as they see fit.

The origins of these positions are rooted deeply in the American past and are intermingled with a strong adherence to fundamentalist religion traditions, the need for personal and familial self-sufficiency, and a continuing desire for maximum freedom of thought and action limited only when there might result severe encroachments on the rights of others or on the common good.

A major determinant of American attitudes about families has been the Protestant ethic which, although increasingly modified and detached from religious conceptions, is still a strong force in American life. This ethic is fundamentally concerned with the relationships between productivity and social rewards, and assumes that success is a reward for virtue while failure is a consequence of sin—especially the sin of laziness. Given such an orientation, it is not surprising that formulations of governments' relationships with individuals and families have often been couched in social Darwinist "survival of the fittest" terms. Life has been pictured as a fierce and competitive struggle in which the capable, strong, and virtuous survive and prosper, while those who are weak, indolent, and sinful suffer and perish. The proper role of the

† Suggested for further reading: Wilensky and Lebeaux (1958); Wolins (1967).

state has been viewed as helping to promote this process, or at least refraining from weakening it by rewarding those who do not produce.

The Protestant ethic and social Darwinism have never, though, been the sole philosophical or value determinants of society's relationship to families and children. From the earliest times of the nation, and with increasing force in the nineteenth century, these harsh doctrines have been modified by a fundamental humanitarianism which has stressed the dignity and equality of all people. Many national leaders from diverse backgrounds have, over the years, advocated a variety of programs to relieve the problems of children and families in need. Although each era has had its prophets, posed its particular view of man and society, and offered its own paradigm for a better life, one enduring theme emerged long ago: the belief that education is an effective means of opening to all the doors to a better life. Hence, the strong emphasis on development of an egalitarian school system.

As the failings of man and the family system have been studied from various perspectives, another consensus has emerged in America: there are a variety of human tragedies, such as severe mental retardation, substantial emotional disturbance, and prolonged physical disability, with which few families can successfully cope. Such severe instances are now viewed as burdens which must be shared by all. For many decades, then, concern for the least fortunate has grown, thus generating increased number of hospitals for the chronically incapacitated, social measures for destitute families, institutional and foster family care for children in need, and so forth. There has, of course, been the stigma of being labelled "incompetent" to balance the ledger for recipients of aid.

Throughout the 20th century, but particularly after World War II, social policies have undergone a considerable broadening. Government organizations have become increasingly involved in helping children and families, although there are strong indications of at least a temporary reduction in governmental aid (1973). Even so, a popular stance has slowly emerged that to begrudgingly "help the hindermost" is not good enough. Almost all would now agree that the goal should be to enhance the quality of life for all. The most telling examples of this new creed have been in the areas of health and education, but the impact has been felt in the area of welfare as well. The statements of two presidents, separated by only seven decades, illustrate the degree of change that has occurred :

The lesson should be constantly enforced that though the people support the government, the government should not support the people (Grover Cleveland, 1887).

The human problems of individual citizens are a proper and important concern of our government (Dwight Eisenhower, 1954).

Values may, of course, change more rapidly than the social instruments which give them meaning. Although President Eisenhower may well have reflected the general desire of the people to participate positively and actively in helping needy children and families, it is clear that the devices for doing so are still painfully evolving. Even more, it is clear that the quest for social justice does not always run a straight path to its goal. Witness this succinct statement of the Protestant ethic :

Ask not what your country can do for you; ask what you can do for yourself (Richard Nixon, 1973).

B. THE DICHOTOMOUS COMPACT

There have evolved two relatively different systems for meeting the needs of young children and families in the United States. Those families with economically adequate means tend to operate within one system, while those who are poor are generally forced to function within another. Most parents, perhaps 75 or 80 percent of them, can afford to draw on market economic facilities to meet their children's needs : not only for food, clothing, shelter and medical care, but also for recreation, education, etc.

Most of these families also have some protection against the vagaries of life in a market economy. The majority are insured against major medical expenses; most carry some insurance on the father's life which, together with social security payments (for almost all who have worked) protect for at least a year or two against loss of income due to illness. None of these families is completely secure, since there are always potential financial catastrophies against which one cannot adequately insure. Essentially, though, insurance mechanisms place a

[26]

stable floor beneath the financial status of the families who use them by spreading among many people the effects of disasters which would overwhelm an unlucky few.

Ithaca Journal

FIGURE 4   Private swimming lessons

While the importance of government in directly promoting the well-being of the majority of children is relatively small, the activities of government do affect all families in several important ways. The only legal requirement for families is that they send their children to school at age six or seven; no specific requirements impinge on them during the preschool years. Nevertheless, government action influences all children by various preventive measures. Eradication of poliomyelitis and other dread diseases has lead to a healthier environment for the rich as well as the poor. Governmental controls over the quality and safety of foodstuffs, medications, appliances and toys, while perhaps less critical for the middle-class child than for the poor one are nevertheless important. The available public services (e.g., institutions for the retarded, programs for the physically handicapped, etc.) constitute a backup to the need-meeting capabilities of all families. While they are rarely used, the sense of security is probably of some psychological consequence. Finally, and most significantly, the penetration of government is very circumscribed and discreet.

The compact between poor families and society is markedly different. The importance of market mechanisms is reduced and government mechanisms are correspondingly more important. Failing to meet the needs of their children through acceptable market means, poor parents must turn to public sources for assistance which may be grudgingly given and may entail a high level of intrusion. A mother with young children who receives financial aid under the Aid to Families with Dependent Children (AFDC) program (see Section VI, C), for example, is given minimal support in return for which she will probably have to submit to an investigation which may review many aspects of her personal life, including her relationship with the children's father(s), her employment status, spending habits, childrearing techniques and philosophies, and other similar familial issues which more affluent families consider extremely private.

In contrast, the ability of poor families to influence the social welfare bureaucracy is quite limited. AFDC parents do participate in planning a budget which determines the size of their grant, and they have some control over their contacts with social workers who run the program, but their impact on the total organization is limited. In recent years, through more unified action (see the description of the Welfare Rights Organization, Section IV), greater resort to the judicial process, and the subversion of some arbitrary AFDC rules, the recipients of welfare have had a greater impact on the programs. Compared with options open to more affluent families, however, the influence of indigent families upon the social instrumentalities designed to serve them is small indeed. In short, recipients of welfare exchange a considerable amount of freedom for a limited amount of help with their problems.

Cooperative exchange arrangements which could in many instances substitute for the market economy, governmental action, or privately sponsored welfare arrangements, have not been particularly popular in the United States. There are church groups, cooperative baby-sitting arrangements, cooperative nursery schools and play-groups, social and recreational clubs, and community associations which essentially fit this model, but they provide for only a small fraction of the needs and activities of a family with small children. Similarly, American cities, whose taxes may be considered a form of citizen cooperation, tend to have relatively few locally supported parks, community recreation facilities, meeting places, etc. The implicit ideal is evidently for every family to have its own home, complete with recreation facilities and/or to belong to a club restricted to paying members who share the facilities.

Poorer families have tended to involve themselves in cooperative arrangements even less than the more affluent. They have limited capacity to exchange material goods, and there have been few opportunities to engage in meaningful exchange activities. One exciting exception to this general situation has been Project Head Start (see Section VI, E), which has provided government support for cooperative activities and thus has brought to light the hidden reserve for cooperative behavior among poor people.

As we have already noted, the compact in America between families and society, for the rich and poor alike, is based on an assumption of high family capability in all areas. Parents must, in fact, markedly neglect or abuse their children before the supervisory or coercive powers of society are brought to bear, and even in such cases, the burden of proof is on the state. The reluctance of governments to invade the privacy of the family extends even to providing information about child-rearing (see Section II). Similarly, publicly supported services in the form of counselling centers, family service agencies, and maternal and child health departments exist in many communities, but are used only by families which seek them out. Supplements of food, income, housing assistance, and medical services may also be available, but again the family must take the initiative.

Some analysts view the existing relationship between families and society in the United States as callous. Others see it as the proper relationship between a free people and their government. Most probably regard the relationship as a mixture of freedom and irresponsibility, in which the lack of societal responsibility makes the guarantee of freedom quite meaningless for those who are economically deprived. To be sure, most American parents know how and have the means to make good use of available public and market services, and they exercise the options provided by this very loose compact. For the poor, though, "freedom of choice" is a meaningless and mocking abstraction, and the paucity of effective social welfare programming leaves some of their fundamental needs unmet.

A final major difficulty in the compact between family and society stems from the essentially dichotomous nature of the model. It tends to assert that families are either "competent" (i.e., need no help they cannot buy) or "incompetent" (i.e., need the intervention of society). The overwhelming majority of families fall between these two extremes, however, needing help in meeting some needs of children and not others, and perhaps at one time and not another. The outcome of this melange is a maladjustment between societal helpfulness and familial needs for most families much of the time.

IV

Planning for children

EVERYONE and no one plans for children in the United States. Countless individual citizens, technical specialists, administrators, and elected officials, are concerned with the problems of children and families. Often the interests of separate groups are in concert (as in the united effort to combat rubella); at times they are in conflict (as concerns racial integration in the schools). The interests of children in the United States are never the province of a single central planning or policy-making organization, though, regardless of the issues involved.

It is perhaps useful to distinguish between planning (i.e., the development of alternative goals, strategies, and timetables) and co-ordination (i.e., the process of integrating the actions of various individuals and organizations). Although the two are related, dominant American values are much less favorable to the former than to the latter. Government plans tend to be construed as con-stricting or limiting the freedom of action of citizens, special interest groups, and future administrations—which, of course, they do—and as such are more or less suspect. A prominent American economist has commented fairly :

To suggest that we canvass our public wants to see where happiness can be improv-ed by more and better services has a sharply radical tone. Even public service to avoid disorder must be defended (Galbraith, 1958).

Coordination, by contrast, fits well into the American ethos of efficiency and productivity. As previously indicated, there is a general tendency in the United States to consider that government best which governs least intrusively, however many or difficult the problems it must handle. Yet once a consensus has been reached on particular goals which require sustained public efforts (e.g., the exploration of outer space, the establishment of a school system, the development of public health and environmental protection measures), everyone agrees that the efforts should be efficient. The usual re-sponse is to appoint a committee to coordinate the many related activities which are progressing independently of one another. Unfortunately, such committees often have little power and the coordination achieved is illusory. Programming for day care constitutes a blatant example of such a situation. There is practically no coordination of effort despite interagency committees at the federal level and coordinating committees at regional, state, and local levels. (See Section VI, D.)

Planning and coordination generally occur during or in response to periods of difficulty. The great depression of the 1930's, for example, led to legislation protecting the economic well-being of families. World War II led to the development of child care schemes enabling young mothers to work in war-related industries. The severe problems of inner cities and minority groups have led to a broad-range attack on poverty which has been greatly concerned with improving conditions for children. All of these measures constitute components of what could become an overall plan in behalf of children, but no such plan currently exists, nor is there any institution empowered to develop or implement one.

There are, of course, various government groups at the federal, state, and local levels which are responsible for planning and implementing specific children's programs. The U.S. Department of Health, Education, and Welfare, a gigantic federal conglomerate with expenditures of some $80 billion in 1972, has broad authority to develop programs for young children. Within this department is the Office of Child Development, which carries a direct mandate to develop forward-looking programs for the nation's children, especially for those below school age. There are many other groups in federal departments such as Agriculture, Commerce, and Labor, which plan and run programs vitally affecting children. In addition, countless state and local bodies interpret and carry out federal programs or provide their own. Add to all of these the privately sponsored groups —national and local, religious and secular, formal and informal, permanent and *ad hoc*—which exist to plan and implement programs for young children and their families, and it becomes clear why it is that everyone and no one plans for children in the United States.

[32]

A. THE MARKET ECONOMY

Most families in the United States satisfy the needs of their young children for food, education, health care, recreation, day care, etc. by purchasing goods and services in the free market economy. (See Section III.) It is assumed that, if there is a demand for a service, a supplier will appear to provide it; it is also assumed that parents will refrain from purchasing "shoddy" goods and services, or any not in their children's best interests. This free enterprise approach has

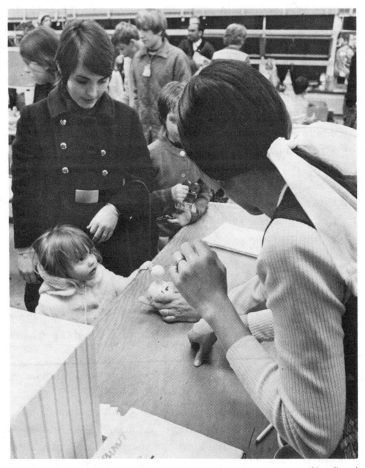

Ithaca Journal

FIGURE 5   A mini-consumer

produced a relatively complete array of goods and services (e.g., baby foods, children's clothing, children's books) which are, for the most part, of good quality, convenient, and inexpensive. In this system, no one has planned for children but there has evolved a give-and-take which has been astonishingly successful in meeting most needs of most American children.

The problem is, of course, that some needs are inadequately provided for in most families because the expense is too great (e.g., day care and early childhood education programs) and that some families have insufficient resources to meet even the minimum needs of their children. It is to overcome such difficulties that, one by one, programs to meet specific needs have been added. These programs constitute the patches on the frayed fabric of the free enterprise system.

Another problem is that parents cannot always judge the safety, durability, and other properties of the goods and services they are considering. They cannot know the sanitary conditions under which infant foods are prepared, the flammability of fabrics, the qualifications of a physician, dentist, or day care giver. To protect the consumer, there have evolved a variety of regulations concerning standards of production, labelling, professional training, etc. In addition, during the past few years there has been substantial activity to protect the public health, the total environment, and individual consumers.

B. PUBLIC AND VOLUNTARY AGENCIES

Following an extended visit to the young United States of the nineteenth century, Alexis de Tocqueville wrote in *Democracy in America* that :

In no country of the world has the principle of association been more successfully used or applied to a greater multitude of objects than in America.

The principle of association is, of course, the tendency of Americans to form voluntary organizations to accomplish limited goals. There are literally thousands of private groups which plan and run programs to help others. Most of them are constituted of groups of citizens who themselves are relatively homogeneous with respect to social class, religion, age, and/or ethnic characteristics but who may extend help to others quite different from themselves. In 1968, over $11 billion was donated for such philanthropic activities, a substantial part being directed to programs for young children. There is still a strong consensus that private programs are more innovative, are more efficiently run, and serve the needs of their clients better than public programs. The difficulties associated with problems such as poverty, though, are of such magnitude that most people tend to agree that a combined private and public effort is required.

Arguments in favor of voluntary efforts on behalf of children are numerous and persuasive. In addition to variety, efficiency, innovation, and program flexibility, there are other positive points which are possibly more telling. First, voluntary action increases the number of individuals who are knowledgeable and concerned about the problems of children, and who will give financial and personal support to the programs. In 1968, at least 32 million individuals or married couples made some contribution to philanthropy. The average contribution during the year was $281, or 3 percent of personal income. An unknown but significant portion of these contributions was used to help young children.

Second, distinctive characteristics (cultural, religious, political, etc.) of helpers and of those helped can be maintained. Catholic schools, Jewish adoption and foster home agencies, Chinese or Mexican day care centers all exist, some in substantial numbers. Many parent, community, religious, and other special groups are formed for specific purposes : to organize a nursery school for retarded, palsied, or very bright children; to develop an after-school recreation program; to provide safe access to a playground; to lobby in a state legislature for free kindergartens, etc.

Third, given the likelihood that public services will not meet all the needs, voluntary efforts supplement even when they do not substitute. Volunteer activities in schools, hospitals, and many public welfare agencies clearly belong to this category. Of the more than two million children under the age of 21 who were receiving child welfare services from agencies and institutions in 1970, for example, 7 percent were attended to primarily by voluntary agencies (National Center for Social Statistics, 1972a).

Critics of voluntary efforts can, of course, point to substantial problems. First, individual and special interest groups tend to focus on very selected problem areas and population groups, often at the expense of others. A disease affecting a small number of victims, such as muscular dystrophy, for example, is emphasized because the association concerned with it is aggressive and powerful, while the major problem of malnutrition receives inadequate attention. Foster home care for Jewish children in New York City is excellent, but less good for most Catholic and Protestant children.

Second, tax exemptions given to nonprofit service organizations and their supporters effectively shift part of the burden of support to the general public without at the same time permitting any public control over services offered or populations served.

Third, centralized planning is very complex, perhaps impossible, in the face of so many independent special-interest voluntary agencies which are both politically active and powerful. While some of these groups would favor a central planning authority, others would surely resist.

C. CENTRALIZED AND DECENTRALIZED PLANNING AND ADMINISTRATION

Until recently there has been a continuing tendency of the federal government to assume responsibility for centralized planning and program development. Most of the noteworthy programs for children in the last several decades were started by Congress and/or by various agencies of the Presidency. Income maintenance schemes, maternal and child health services, day care programs, special education projects, and most other programs affecting the young child have emanated from the nation's capital. Furthermore, the legislation which established and funded such programs as Project Head Start and Aid to Families with Dependent Children, invested federal agencies with the authority to set standards, to supervise and review, and to withhold funds if standards were not maintained.

It would be a mistake, however, to assume that federal agencies can usually exercise more than a general surveillance over programs.

The Aid to Families with Dependent Children (AFDC) program provides a telling example. Somewhat more than one-half of the funds are provided by the federal government with the remainder coming in about equal shares from state and local sources. The program is optional, however, and a state may elect to participate in all, some, or no components. (In actual fact, all states do participate in most components.) The federal program lays down certain criteria defining a "suitable home" in which a child receiving help may remain. This requirement, intended to protect the well-being of the children, was for a time used by some states to reduce the number of recipients. Such states declared some homes unsuitable but made no alternative provisions for the children who were affected. It is possible, then, to move counter to federal intent and to deprive some children of needed service; it is also possible to move independently in a more constructive direction. California, Illinois, and New York, for example, provide at their own expense far more liberal benefits and lenient interpretations of the AFDC plan than federal rules require.

In an effort to achieve more effective federal control and to encourage local innovation and initiative, some programs have by-passed state and local government agencies. Project Head Start provides for programs run by local groups without any state or local government participation. Community Action Programs designed to aid poor families were set up in the same manner. Many favor such procedures because they make it possible to avoid local prejudices and to allow the recipients of aid a larger voice in programs. State and local government officials often dislike such procedures, which reduce their power and make it difficult to plan and to implement comprehensive, coordinated programs. Since 1973 there has been a drastic reduction of such programs—e.g., the dismantling of the Office of Economic Opportunity may be attributed in part to the fact that many of its programs circumvented the conventional power structures.

Although the past 40 years have seen a continuing trend toward centralization of programs and a strengthening of presidential powers, the pendulum seems about to swing in the other direction. Historically, the proper relationship between national and state governments has been the subject of countless debates. The Constitution provides that powers not specifically granted to the federal government should remain with the states, but the exact balance of power has shifted broadly from one time to another. At present, there may be a swing of national opinion away from federal power and in favor of state responsibility. One prime reason for federal assumption of programs has been the fact that the tax structure provides the federal government with most of the tax revenues. President Nixon is now proposing that many federal programs in the areas of health, education, and social welfare be eliminated and the funds be granted instead to the state in lump sums, to be disbursed as they see fit. This solution to an old question has never been tried in the United States on a large scale, nor it is certain at this point that it will have a trial now. It would appear, however, that many states are anxious to reclaim planning and coordination responsibilities: according to the Education Commission of the States (February, 1973), 12 states have already created offices of child development, or the equivalent, and 3 others have initiated action to "bring orderly planning to programs and services from young children."

D. THE SPORADIC NATURE OF PLANNING

Planning for children takes place in private as well as public agencies, at all levels of government, and is highly susceptible to the general political milieu. It is clear, too, that interests sometimes conflict and communication is often lacking. There have been, however, some sporadic efforts which have managed to cut across various interest groups and which have yielded considerable planning on behalf of children.

The White House Conference on Children and Youth has already been mentioned as a tradition in which representatives of voluntary and public agencies, interested citizens, and government officials meet once every ten years to discuss the problems of children and to draw general policy positions. These conferences, endowed with the prestige of the White House and attended by several thousand laymen and numerous experts, are concerned with all aspects of child development. They have been effective in establishing policy guidelines and in exerting pressure for specific programs. A review of the 1960 Conference indicated that in six years, 14 percent of the stated goals had been actually or nearly achieved, and that 52 percent of the other goals were being followed (Wright, 1968).

The 1970 White House Conference on Children (a separate conference on youth took place in early 1971) was composed of 25 working forums which considered six cluster areas: individuality; learning; health; parents and families; communities and environments; and laws, rights, and responsibilities. The most important recommendations were that the nation should:

- establish comprehensive family-oriented child development programs, which will include health services, day care, and early childhood education;

- develop programs to eliminate racial prejudice;

- establish a guaranteed basic family income adequate to meet the needs of children;

- improve the nation's system of child justice so that the law responds in a more timely and positive way to meet the needs of children;

- establish a federally financed national child health care program which will assure comprehensive care for all children;

- develop a system of early identification of children with special needs, together with a system which will deliver prompt and appropriate treatment.

Conference members also called for the reduction of injuries to children caused by perinatal events, traffic, poisoning, burns, malnutrition and rats; for greater federal support of independent research and dissemination of information relating to education; for education which achieves individualized, humanized, child-centered learning; for establishment of a National Institute for the Family to encompass action, advocacy, implementation, legislation, and research; for establishment of a Department of Education with Cabinet status and backed by a National Institute of Education; and for establishment of a high level, independent Office of Child Advocacy with a network of local advocacy programs. At this point (1973), none of these recommendations has yet been acted upon. The report has not, in fact, been publicly acknowledged by President Nixon, for whom it was prepared.

A second planning mechanism which has sometimes proved effective is the task force or commission, such as the Joint Commission on Mental Health of Children. Brought into existence by an Act of Congress, the Commission investigated mental health problems of children with the assistance of numerous voluntary and government agencies. A general resport issued by the Commission in 1970 lists recommendations for a child advocacy system, community services in several areas, research, and manpower training.

A third planning procedure involves special interest efforts. The mechanism may be a governmental task force such as the President's Panel on Mental Retardation, or more likely a voluntary fund raising drive with a massive publicity campaign and research and service investments. While some of these efforts are duplicative, divisive, and unnecessarily costly, they often involve many citizens, effectively focus on an important problem, and contribute significantly to its solution. A measure of the potential magnitude of such campaigns is illustrated by the millions of contributors who in 1945 alone gave nearly $19 million to finance the National Foundation for Infantile Paralysis which was a major factor in developing the Salk and Sabin vaccines.

Finally, on the tide of public concern, there have arisen new policy studies, advocacy, and action groups whose broadly conceived goals are the protection and enhancement of children's rights and the conditions of their lives. These privately funded groups include the Carnegie Council for Children, the Washington Research Project/ Children's Defense Fund, and other established institutes now turning attention to children (e.g., the American Academy of Science, the Brookings Institution and the Center for the Study of Public Policy).

E. CONSUMER INTERESTS IN PLANNING

There is increasing sentiment in the United States that recipients of services should be involved in planning them. Consumer participation has been a strong tradition for some time among the middle and upper classes. The Parent-Teachers Associations (PTA) have long been a force in educational planning, for example, as has more recently the National Association for Retarded Children. Many now feel that the poor, particularly those from minority groups, must be given the same opportunities. The planning bodies of some federal programs are legally required to assure "maximum feasible participation" of the poor. This newly-heard voice of the poor in planning has become increasingly strong during the past few years. A voluntary organization of public welfare recipients (mainly AFDC mothers) has introduced new techniques and new wants. The Welfare Rights Organization is now heard by community welfare councils, state legislatures, and Congressional Committees and was a major factor in the 1970 White House Conference. More than ever before, everyone plans for children in the United States.

F. PLANNING AND RESEARCH

It seems reasonable to suppose that in a modern, technologically advanced society, there would exist a close relationship between planning and research in all aspects of development. In the United States, however, planning for children is seldom firmly based on empirical evidence. There are, of course, some notable instances in which plans were dictated by research findings. The appearance of retrolental fibroplasia in the 1940's, for example, led to a research effort and successful plan of action. Poliomyelitis has been combatted with similar planned vigor.

The relationship between planning and research efforts has been markedly different in programs seeking to solve more complex problems. The various programs directed against poverty, for example, have primarily reflected the strong desire for a more egalitarian society and an overriding belief in the power of education rather than any solid research evidence. Similarly, attempts to combat crime, the decay of the cities, and the growing alienation of young people have been inspired by weak research evidence coupled with strong convictions.

On the other hand, once such programs are launched, they tend to be scrutinized meticulously and often prematurely by stringent evaluations. When they fail—as so often they must—to achieve desired goals at the level promised, they may be summarily dismissed as failures long before they have reached a mature level of operation. Project Head Start is a case in point. (See Section VI, F.)

It is paradoxical that a nation which can carry through a highly complex, well-orchestrated, and successful space research program costing billions of dollars, has not initiated a similar long-range research program to discover how to cure the social ills of the nation. There are, however, a number of reasons for this falure.

First, the American people tend toward "fads" of interest and are extremely impatient. Once a topic becomes the object of concern, immediate action is demanded; if scientists, like other citizens, have followed the mainstream, the research base simply is not there yet. The lead time in terms of basic and applied research is a luxury not afforded social scientists, although other scientists have been able to demonstrate the absolute necessity of preliminary research for their programs.

Second, social science research and social scientists are viewed with suspicion by a broad spectrum of American society. In some respects this suspicion is justified, for social scientists have tended to be more liberal politically than average American citizens and have not been averse to using insufficiently developed "science" to bolster ideological or political convictions. Some years ago, for example, most liberal thinkers tended to favor family care over group care arrangements for young children. In defending this view against proponents of institutional and day-care programs alike, many social scientists cited the research work of Bowlby (1952), Goldfarb (1945), Spitz (1945) and others. These projects had all been challenged on methodological and other grounds (e.g., Pinneau, 1955), and none of them dealt with children in part-day arrangements. In short, they had little relevance to important questions concerning day care for young children.

Many of the "generals" in the war on poverty have defended their battle strategies, including those involving the day care of young children, on similarly ambiguous and irrelevant research grounds. The overwhelming fact is that we do not yet know the consequences of many existing and proposed programs for young children and their families. At the same time, *ex post facto,* some extremely interesting and valuable data are being gathered now which suggest that building on existing strategies and modifying others may lead to more positive outcomes. Yet, many promising programs about which we are just beginning to acquire good research data, are currently in danger of being discontinued. In some measure, this crisis reflects the disillusionment of many, whose unrealistic expectations—inflated by overoptimistic predictions by social scientists—have been shattered, despite the fact that much has been accomplished against overwhelming odds for poor children and their families.

V

The family

BY TRADITION and practice, it is up to American parents to provide everything that their young children need. No one else will intrude; no outside services will be forthcoming unless they are sought; it is altogether possible that until the child is four or five years old, the family will constitute his entire social environment. How do the parents carry out their responsibilities? The answer to this important question is, unfortunately, for the most part unknown.

The study of human development is nowhere more highly developed than in the United States, where hundreds of investigators monthly fill the pages of numerous journals and books devoted to scientific inquiry concerning children's development. (See Section IX.) But most of this research has little to do with the process of development as is occurs in daily life, especially within the family. A striking reflection of this "ivory tower" bias is the scarcity of basic information on how children are cared for during the early years of life, where, how, and by whom they are fed, fondled, played with, talked to, taught, or disciplined. The human interactions which constitute the family *in vivo* remain in large part a mystery to scientists, for many reasons having to do not only with the kinds of questions which researchers prefer to ask, but also with the seductive ease of conducting research in group settings such as nursery schools.

The only comprehensive study of child rearing practices over time and social space (Bronfenbrenner, 1958), covering the period 1932-1957, has never been up-dated, and subsequently there have been only sporadic publications concerning circumscribed aspects of parent-child interactions. Our scattered research knowledge by no means permits a complete picture of child rearing in the United States, but some specific findings are rather interesting. For example, as of the early 1960's, about 40 percent of American infants were breast fed but the great majority of these were weaned during the first six months of life; by 1969, only about 30 percent were breast fed during the first week after birth, only 17 percent at age two months (Kram and Owen, 1972). Formerly, the higher the social class and the larger the community, the more likely was the mother to employ bottle feeding; by 1969, the social class distinction, at least, had disappeared. The modal age for beginning bowel training in the early 1960's was the second half of the first year; for over 80 percent of children, training was completed by the age of two and one half. Mothers with college education tended to start training later and to use milder methods of control.

Children under two years of age are seldom disciplined, but the disciplinary measures used are often of a physical nature. In a California survey, over a third of mothers reported that their 18-month old infant never did anything wrong that required correction; 41 percent of the boy babies and 33 percent of the girl babies were disciplined at least once a week; about 20 percent of these mothers reported that they punished their infants daily. Corporal punishment was far more frequent than other forms of negative sanction (isolation, censure, "talking to") and accounted for about half of all disciplinary acts. Interestingly enough, fathers emerged as more lenient than mothers, especially in their treatment of boys, although this finding may have been due in part to bias in the mother's report, which was the only source of data. As the child grows older, the frequency of misdeeds and punishments increases. Only about 5 percent of mothers of children between three and six years of age reported that the child never does anything wrong. The most frequent ground for discipline was "misconduct towards others." Again, fathers appeared more lenient than mothers, boys were punished more often than girls, and the use of physical force was the method of choice for both sexes (Heinstein, 1965).

The widespread resort to corporal punishment, even for infants under two years of age, may have broader psychological and social significance.

. . . the context of child-rearing does not exclude the use of physical force toward children by parents and others responsible for their socialization. Rather, American culture encourages in subtle, and at times not so subtle, ways the use of "a certain measure" of physical force in rearing children in order to modify their inherently nonsocial inclinations. This cultural tendency can be noted in child-rearing practices of most segments of American society. It is supported in various ways by communications disseminated by the press, radio, and television, and by popular and professional publications.

[45]

Approval of a certain measure of physical force as a legitimate and appropriate educational and socializing agent seems thus endemic to American culture (Gil, 1970).

A. THE CHANGING AMERICAN FAMILY

Even if little is known about the process of child rearing in the United States today, an objective observer of the American scene can say a good deal more about other aspects of family life. Two salient facts stand out. First, there is extreme variability from one group of families to another, with an especially wide gap between poverty groups—perhaps the bottom 20-25 percent of families ranked on income—and the much larger and dominant middle class. In almost all aspects of family living, the "have-not" families function at a considerable disadvantage, and their children suffer accordingly.

The second, and perhaps the most compelling fact about American families is not the *status quo,* but the rapid and fundamental changes which are taking place. The evidence is everywhere, and the fact of change itself probably constitutes the most important force affecting the development of children today.

Some changes can be objectively quantified. Over the years, for example, the average family has become better able to provide for the material needs of its children, and indeed most children of the middle classes are well supplied with those advantages which money can ensure. There is ample space in most of these homes; there is plenty of food, clothing, access to health care, etc. Virtually all children sleep in a bed alone and a great many have a bedroom to themselves, private space for their own belongings, and a bountiful supply of toys, books, records, etc. Some city dwellers, especially the poor who live in the central areas, live in apartments, some of them very massive and impersonal; but children in other city neighborhoods, suburbs, smaller towns, and rural areas live in single-family houses which often have protected yards outfitted with sand boxes, swings, and other play facilities. (At the same time, however, we must remember that rises in the cost of living have put poor families at an even greater relative disadvantage in many of these respects.)

Increased general prosperity has brought shorter working hours and also many labor-saving devices and services. The standard work week is 40 hours, but many—especially supervisors, managers, etc.—work overtime. Most employees are paid for about 10 holidays plus a minimum vacation of two weeks; and there is an increasing trend to one-month vacation periods. The amount of necessary housekeeping labor has been reduced by the availability of prepared foods and a surfeit of home appliances, from automatic washers and dryers for the laundry to electric can openers and self-cleaning ovens. There is, unfortunately, little indication that parents are spending this extra time with their children (see below).

During the 20th century, the American family has also undergone a process of equalization which—especially now, under the influence of widespread concern about the rights and roles of women—is continuing and perhaps even accelerating. Sharing of authority is more typical of middle-class than lower-class families but the trends are apparently similar in both (Hess, 1970). Like the adults, the child tends to be viewed and to view himself as an individual in his own right, not simply as an appendage of the family.

Studies in the 1960's have reported some shift in parental roles, with fathers becoming relatively more affectionate and less authoritarian. There can be little doubt that traditional distinctions between the sexes—mother as the "soft," "tender," "emotional" caretaker and father as the "final authority" and "disciplinarian"—have been diffusing for a number of years. The softening of the father's authoritarian role and the increasing "equality" of the mother's role have often, though, resulted in an actual weakening of the family structure as a sort of uneasy adaptation to the new ambiguities in the parents' relationships with one another and with their children.

One of the clearest of Bronfenbrenner's findings in 1958 was a turn toward permissiveness, in line with professional recommendations of that day. This was particularly characteristic of middle class families, in which he found "a shift away from emotional control toward freer expression of affection and greater tolerance of the child's impulses and desires." It is unfortunately impossible to say whether this trend toward increased permissiveness has continued. To the extent that the trend was a product of parental uncertainties about their own roles and values, and their involvement with other activities, any reversal seems unlikely.

Even more pronounced changes are occurring in other aspects of family life. Witness the following facts :

Ithaca Journal

FIGURE 6   "Seven, Eight, Lay Them Straight."

In 1971, 42 percent of the nation's mothers worked outside the home; in 1940 the figure was only about 10 percent. One in every three mothers with children under six is working today.

As more mothers have gone to work, the number of other adults in the family who could care for the child has decreased. Fifty years ago, about half of all households included at least one adult besides the parents; today that figure is below 5 percent.

The divorce rate among families with children has been rising substantially during the last 20 years. The percentage of children from divorced families is almost double what it was a decade ago. If present rates remain stable, one child in six will lose a parent through divorce by the time he is 18.

In 1970, almost a quarter of all children were living in single-parent families, nearly double the rate for a decade before. Over the same period, the number of families headed by never-married women had tripled. Almost half the mothers who are single parents with children under six were in the labor force; a third were working full time.

B. ABDICATING AMERICAN PARENTS

Perhaps the most disturbing trend is a decrease in all spheres of interaction in families. Distance has increased between parents and children and there has been an unplanned and only partly successful substitution of outside relationships for those that previously were found in the home. A comparative study of socialization practices by German and American parents found the former to be significantly more active. A second study, several years later, showed changes over time in both cultures reflecting "a trend toward the dissolution of the family as a social system," with Germany moving closer to the American pattern of "centrifugal forces pulling the members into relationships outside the family," (Rodgers, 1971).

Although the nature and operation of these centrifugal forces have not been studied systematically, they seem readily apparent. The following excerpt from the report of the President's White House Conference on Children summarizes the situation as seen by a group of experts including both scientists and practitioners.

For families who can get along, the rats are gone, but the rat race remains. The demands of a job, or often two jobs, which claim mealtimes, evenings, and weekends as well as days, the trips and moves one must make to get ahead or simply hold one's own, the ever increasing time spent in commuting, the parties, evenings out, social and community obligations—all the things one has to do if he is to meet his primary responsibilities—produce a situation in which a child often spends more time with a passive babysitter than a participating parent (Report to the President, 1970, p. 242).

The forces undermining the parental role are particularly strong in the case of fathers. This fact, coupled with the traditional emphasis upon the mother as the primary agent of upbringing in the early years, brings about a situation in which fathers take relatively little responsibility for child rearing. For example, although in one interview study of middle class families fathers reported spending an average of 15 to 20 minutes a day playing with their one year old infants (Ban and Lewis, 1971), an observational research revealed a rather different story, a mean of only 2.7 interactions per day averaging a total of 38 seconds (Rebelsky and Hanks, 1971).

The greatest share of the child's upbringing falls, then, to the mother. Although the current philosophy of child care tends to put

Ithaca Journal

FIGURE 7   "Trick or Treat" on Hallowe'en (All Saints' Eve)

more stress on the role of fathers and the sharing of responsibilities, in actual fact, mothers and young children are living in a growing isolation. Studies of parent-child interactions at all age levels continue to identify the mother as the principal agent not only of emotional support, but also of discipline. An investigation of parent practices in a large sample of American urban and suburban families found, for example, that there was not a single category in which the father surpassed the mother; the mother significantly exceeded the father, however, in 9 of the 14 variables, including Nurturance, Companionship, Achievement Demands, and Physical Punishment (Devereux et al., 1969).

Another factor reducing interaction between parents and children is the changing physical layout and equipment in the home. The cherished affluence of middle-class families has led increasingly to home situations in which children's activities are relegated to separate "rumpus" and game rooms in the basement, while the "master bedroom" is located as far as possible from the children's areas in order to give the parents privacy and quiet. A similar effect is achieved by modern "child-centered" equipment. A brochure recently received in the mail describes a "cognition crib" equipped with a tape recorder that can be activated by the sound of the infant's voice. Frames are built into the sides of the crib for "programmed play modules for sensory and physical practice." The modules come in sets of six, which the parent is encouraged to change every three months so as to keep pace with the child's development. They include soft plastic faces, mobiles (among them a "changing faces mobile"), a crib aquarium, and "ego building mirrors." Parents are barely mentioned in the brochure except as purchasers.

Another major change concerns a now-ubiquitous feature of the American home. The average American family consists of a mother, a father, 2.4 children, and 1.3 television sets. At least one of the sets is on six hours a day and the typical child in the first 16 years of his life may spend as much time in front of the television screen as in school. The influence of television violence in evoking aggressive behavior under fairly common circumstances has now been clearly demonstrated (Television and Growing Up, 1972) and recently has been a topic of heated controversy in America (See Section VI, H).

But another perhaps more important impact of this medium on the child's socialization has remained unexamined. The principal danger of the television screen may lie not so much in the behavior it produces as the behavior it prevents—the talks, the games, the family festivities, discussions, and emotional scenes through which much of the child's learning takes place and his character is formed. The most relevant investigations about the effects of television on family life were published in the early 1950's before the nation had become irrevocably committed to the "television culture" (see Garbarino, 1972). In one study of more than 300 families, for example, 78 percent of the respondents indicated no conversation during a TV program. The author described the viewing situation in the following terms :

The television atmosphere in most households is one of quiet absorption on the part of the family members who are present. The nature of the family social life during a program could be described as "parallel" rather than interactive, and the set does seem quite clearly to dominate family life when it is on (Maccoby, 1951).

There are indications that a withdrawal of adults from the lives of children is also occurring outside the home. To quote again from the report of the White House Conference :

In our modern way of life, it is not only parents of whom children are deprived, it is people in general. A host of factors conspire to isolate children from the rest of society. The fragmentation of the extended family, the separation of residential and business areas, the disappearance of neighborhoods, zoning ordinances, occupational mobility, child labor laws, the abolishment of the apprentice system, consolidated schools, television, separate patterns of social life for different age groups, the working mother, the delegation of child care to specialists—all these manifestations of progress operate to decrease opportunity and incentive for meaningful contact between children and persons older, or younger, than themselves. (Report of Forum 15, 1970 page 2).

The centrifugal forces generated within the family by its increasingly isolated position have propelled its members in different directions. As parents, especially mothers, spend more time in work and community activities, children are placed in or gravitate to group settings, both organized and informal. For example, between 1964 and 1970 the number of children enrolled in day care centers nearly tripled, and the demand far exceeds the supply. From the preschool years onward, children spend increasing amounts of time solely in the company of age mates. The vacuum created by the withdrawal of parents and other adults has been filled in by the informal peer group. A recent study of school-age children found that at every age and grade level, children today show a greater dependency on their peers than they did a decade ago (Condry and Siman, 1968 b). A parallel investigation indicates that such susceptibility to group influence is higher among children from homes in which one or both parents are frequently absent (Condry and Siman, 1968 b). In addition, "peer oriented" youngsters describe their parents as less affectionate and less firm in discipline. Attachment to age mates appears, in fact, to be influenced more by a lack of attention and concern at home than by any positive attraction of the peer group itself. The children have a rather negative view of their friends and of themselves as well. Compared with other children, they are more pessimistic, lower in responsibility and leadership, and more likely to engage in anti-social behavior such as lying, teasing other children, truancy, or "doing something illegal," (Siman, 1973). Although these children are, of course, older than the preschool group under consideration in this monograph, the beginnings of these patterns are detectible in the preschool years. Informal observation suggests that American preschool children are often not so closely supervised as young children in other countries; playing with friends around the block or in one anothers' backyards, even quite young children may have no contact with any adult for an hour or more at a time.

It might seem reasonable to suppose that as relationships are diluted among family members, there would be a decrease of tension within the family. In fact, the opposite seems to be happening. The breakdown of neighborhoods, the increasing trend toward nuclear families, and the growing number of father-absent homes, have all augmented the responsibility which falls on the young mother. A growing number of divorces are accompanied by the unwillingness of either parent to take custody of the child; married women are for the first time being reported to police departments as missing (a phenomenon until now exclusively male); even more shocking, an increase in infant homicides has occurred together with a probable increase in child abuse. With respect to the latter, it is of special interest to note that severe injuries of children are more likely to be inflicted by parents and other adults under 25 years of age than by older persons, and abusers are more often women than men, especially mothers rearing children alone (Gil, 1970). All this is not to say that America is a nation of parents who desert, beat, and murder their children—but these figures, as indices of stress, give pause to the concerned observer.

C. SOCIAL CLASS DIFFERENCES

A wealth of research has recently been directed at the ways in which poverty-level parents interact with their children. Much of this effort has stemmed, of course, from the concern over the development of young children in environments of poverty, and the hope that early experiences of a more positive nature can halt the erosion in cognitive development which is found so often among poor children. To judge from the growing literature comparing poverty-level and middle-class parents, the latter group tend in almost every respect to conduct themselves in ways more closely resembling those being advocated by professionals. (See review by Streissguth and Bee, 1972.)

Recent research has confirmed the evidence for class differences in parent behavior toward children and has extended the available data into the earliest years of life. In one observational study of interaction between mothers and their 10-month old babies for example, the investigators found no class differences in physical care and affection but noted marked variation in the quantity and quality of verbal expression particularly as related to the infant's cognitive development (Tulkin and Kagan, 1972). Compared to their working class counterparts, middle-class mothers not only talked more to their babies but were more likely to respond verbally to the infant's vocalizations and to engage the young child in stimulating activities.

By the time children are four to five years old, class differences become more pronounced. The following summary from an observational study is representative of findings from a number of similar investigations.

The middle-class mother tended to allow her child to work at his own pace, offered many general structuring suggestions on how to search for a solution to the problem, and told the child what he was doing that was correct . . . In contrast, the lower-class mother as a rule did not behave in ways that would encourage the child to attend to the basic features of the problem. Her suggestions were highly specific, did not emphasize basic problem-solving strategies, and seldom required reply from the child. Indeed, she often deprived the child of the opportunity to solve the problem on his own by her nonverbal intrusions into the problem-solving activity (Bee *et al.*, 1969, pp. 374–375).

It is important to note that such observations may be colored by the differing responses of lower and middle-class mothers in the research setting—a situation usually more familiar, comfortable, and comprehensible for the middle-class mothers.

Low-income parents, especially the father, are more likely to demand unquestioning obedience from the children and less likely to listen to the children's wishes than are middle-class parents (Hess, 1970). Bronfenbrenner (1958), for example, noted that "parent-child relationships in the middle class are consistently reported as more acceptant and egalitarian, while those in the working class are oriented toward maintaining order and obedience." A more recent review indicates a strong tendency among lower-class families to prefer the familiar, conventional, simple interpersonal interaction which is structured (especially with children) in terms of status and power rather than reason and the rational consideration of alternatives (Hess, 1970), but again, this may be the reaction of lower-class families under middle-class eyes.

It is also apparent from recent studies that, in the lowest socio-economic strata, the breakdown of the family and its supporting structures is so severe as to be associated with impairment of the child's cognitive functions. The extent of this impairment in contemporary American society, and its roots in social disorganization, are reflected in surveys conducted at national and state levels. Two reports from the National Health Survey describe intellectual development and school achievement in a sample of over 7,000 children, 6-11 years of age. Differences were assessed across region, race, size of place of residence, degree of educational mobility, income, and parents' education. Although substantial variation was found across each of these domains, the most powerful predictors of school achievement were parental education and income; racial and regional factors were of only slight importance (National Center for Health Statistics, 1971).

Confirmatory and more refined results are available from a New York State survey. In a study of over 300 schools,

58 percent of the variation in student achievement was predicted by three socio-economic factors—broken homes, overcrowded housing, and education of the head of the household. . . . When the racial and ethnic variables were introduced into the analysis, they accounted for less than an additional 2 percent of the variation. . . . One of the most stiking phenomena in the achievement score data is that over time more and more children throughout the state are falling below minimum competence (New York State Commission on the Quality of Education, 1971, Vol. I, p. 33).

With respect to conditions of life, the low-income family is at an overwhelming disadvantage. The poverty-level mother often has little choice but to work outside the home and to work full time. As noted previously, many low-income families are headed by a woman alone; even when the father is present, the mother often plays a dominant role. (There are, of course, exceptions; among the rural poor in the Appalachian Mountains, for example, it is the mother who is often more disorganized and the strong father, his role rooted in proud tradition, who keeps the family together.) Poverty-level parents are much more likely to be overworked, exhausted, distracted and unable to give the child the kind of attention he needs. Further, lower-income fathers spend even less time with their children and more time with their own friends than do middle-class fathers (Chilman, 1966).

The physical aspects of the home are likewise poorly suited to active exploration. The crowded and unordered home may be full of danger for the young child, who for reasons of safety must often be confined. He may, indeed, have to learn to "tune out" much of what goes on around him in order to maintain a reasonable degree of stimulation.

On the other hand, it has been argued that in a few respects, at least, the poverty family may provide a better setting for child rearing than the middle-class home (Riessman, 1962). Low-income children are often more cooperative and less competitive, more like to share what they have, more oriented to loyalty, to sticking together, and to the concepts of brotherhood and sisterhood, all qualities which can soften the impact of the alienation and discouragement which so understandably emanate from a difficult life situation.

D. A DAY IN THE LIFE OF AN AMERICAN FAMILY

To appreciate the nature and impact of typical American child rearing practices, they must be seen in their concrete context. Toward this end, we offer an account of a day in the life of a middle-class family with young children. The data are fictional in the sense that they are not based on observations of a particular family, but they are realistic in being drawn from observed and reported experience in a substantial number of American families of middle income. It must be emphasized, of course, that there is no typical American family. As we have repeatedly pointed out, diversity is the one unremitting characteristic of family life in the United States.

Our mythical family consists of a father, who works full time (8 hours a day, 5 days a week), a mother who works four hours a day, and three children : John 10, Jane 4, and Jimmy, nearly $1\frac{1}{2}$ years old. They reside in a suburb of the city in which both parents are employed. The split-level dwelling consists of a living room, kitchen, laundry, dining-family-room complex on one level, comprising one wing of the house; and in the other wing, the parents' bedroom and a bath on one floor and three small children's bedrooms and a bath on the second floor. The family owns one automobile.

The day in our family begins early, at six in the morning, when Jimmy awakes. He climbs out of his crib and wakes up his siblings. Jane gets up, climbs over the protective folding baby-gate on the stairs (which also blocks the way to the parents' bedroom) and wakens the parents. Mother goes with Jane to the kitchen. There she prepares a bottle for Jimmy and gives Jane some fruit juice. Mother sleepily changes Jimmy's diapers and puts him back to bed with the bottle and some toys. She tucks Jane back in bed and gives her a book to "read." She awakens John and tells him to dress quietly, so as not to rouse the younger children. But in 15 minutes they are both out of bed again and have joined their older brother, who is making his bed. Father has finished breakfast, and it is time to take him to the bus stop. Mother helps the two younger children put on their jackets and boots over their sleepers. She carries Jimmy to the car and straps him in the car seat. Jane sits down beside him. Mother drives father to the bus stop. He kisses all three and waves goodbye as they drive off. On the way home mother stops to pick up milk. The children remain in the car.

When they return home John has already finished his breakfast and is in the family room, watching television. The younger ones join him, while mother prepares their breakfast of eggs and toast. John leaves to take the school bus. Mother scolds the younger children for not taking off their jackets and boots, but she readily assists them with this task, and helps them wash up and brush their teeth. The children sit down to breakfast in the kitchen. Jane serves and feeds herself.

Mother gives Jimmy small portions, which he attempts to eat by himself. Mother cleans up the kitchen while she keeps an eye on the childen and listens to the morning news on the radio. Then she gets herself a cup of coffee and sits down with them. With another spoon, she feeds Jimmy between his own spoonfuls. They talk together over the din of the radio. Mother washes Jimmy's face, lifts him out of his chair, and gives him a hug. He plays with pots and pans in one corner of the kitchen. Mother helps Jane finish her food, praises her, and starts to eat her own breakfast, but is interrupted by a telephone call.

Finally, the children are sent to their rooms to get dressed. Jane begins to put on clothes, but gets distracted by some toys in her room. Jimmy plays in his room. It is now almost nine o'clock. Finding Jane still dawdling, mother dresses her hurriedly and combs her hair. Jane puts on her wraps and takes her lunch box and her favorite rag doll. Mother brings her to the curb, where the carpool car, loaded with four other children, is waiting. Mother kisses Jane goodbye, and greets the driving mother and the other children in the car.

As the car drives off to the day care center, mother turns around and finds Jimmy outside in his sleepers walking in the mud. She picks him up, dismayed, scolds him, takes him to his room and removes his muddy sleepers. She put him on the potty . . . unsuccessfully. Cheerfully, she puts on his diapers again and then puts him on the floor, encouraging him to put on his own clothes. After a few attempts Jimmy gives up and mother helps him, playing "peek-a-boo," both of them laughing while she puts undershirt and shirt over his head. She sits on the floor with him, helps him build a tower with his blocks, and then goes off to answer the telephone. After a few minutes, Jimmy crawls down the stairs, having gone through the now-open gate, and follows mother around while she cleans up the kitchen. Then she puts on his jacket and hat, and puts some diapers, his blanket, and a few toys in a bag. She drives him to the house of the babysitter, brings him in, and then drives off to the city to work. Jimmy cries briefly but the sitter comforts him and distracts him with a candy.

There are four other young children in this day care home. They play in the dining room, which is blocked from the kitchen and living room with wooden gates. There are a few colorful toys on the floor and in a large doll bed. The sitter watches the children from either the kitchen or the living room while she does her housework. The children spend quite a bit of time sitting by themselves and they frequently grab toys from one another. Sitter interferes in their play only if they are hurting each other. At 11:30 she puts lunch on the low table in the play area. The children sit down quietly and eat sandwiches, dry cereal, and jello. The sitter gently urges them to eat, but does not help them. Jimmy eats very little. After lunch, each child is washed, diapered, and put down to nap on a pallet on the floor. The sitter watches television in the living room. One by one, the children slide to the gate to watch. At one o'clock she gives each child a cookie and some Kool-Aid and sends him out to play in a large sandbox in the backyard with plastic containers, old spoons, and some plastic cars. Two neighbor ladies come over to talk to the sitter and the children. At 2:30, mother picks up Jimmy.

Jane too has been cared for while mother worked. Jane attends a cooperative day care center, where each mother assists three hours a week. The center is housed in Sunday school space borrowed from a nearby church. There is one qualified teacher and one untrained aide, both paid from parent fees. About 25 children are enrolled.

The carpool mother drops Jane and the other children off at the center. They are greeted warmly by head teacher, who talks to each one briefly about the adventures of the last 24 hours. She also checks for any signs of contagious illness. Jane shows the head teacher her rag doll's torn dress and says her grandmother is going to make her a new one. Each child puts his lunch box and toys into his own locker and then goes out to play on the well-equipped playground. Some of the children play on the swings and slide; others are "building" a house with the help of the young teacher's aide. Jane joins a group that is busily planting a garden. The aide shows the children how to dig up the soil and prepare it for planting, then she encourages them to do it. At ten, the children go indoors, remove their own wraps, and sit around low tables to have juice and crackers.

The aide brings a can of clay to Jane's table. One child eagerly fetches a pan of water and another a box of sponges, rolling pins, and cookie cutters. Each child puts on its own smock. The children work with the clay. They pound and roll energetically and joyfully. The aide shows them how to shape the clay, but not what to shape. She praises each child's creation. At lunch time, each one puts his clay object on a tray to dry and helps to clean up the table; Jane washes it with the sponge. The aide helps her with the stubborn spots and then tells her what a good job she has done. The children remove their smocks and wash up for lunch. They bring their lunch boxes to the table. The teachers serve hot soup and milk to the children. Jane has brought carrot sticks to share with her friends. She trades them for celery, raisins, and crackers. From her best friend, she gets a cookie. Everyone seems content.

After lunch, each child lies down to nap on a low cot. They nap with their own cuddly toys. Teacher reads a story to the group, and then plays quiet music. Many children fall asleep. After nap, the teacher plays singing games with the children. Jane's best friend falls and hurts her ankle. Jane is allowed to go to the office to comfort her until the assisting mother takes the friend home. Jane is worried and upset, so the teacher asks Jane to "help" her. She dusts the teacher's books. Then the teacher takes Jane on her lap and reads her one of the books. When Jane hears that some of the children are going outside to plant the seeds, she hurries outside to join them.

Meanwhile mother has gone home with Jimmy. He is tired and hungry. She holds him on her lap and feeds him some leftover pudding, then puts him to bed and he goes to sleep. A telephone call comes from Jane's day care center. They need someone to fill in for the mother who took the injured child home. Mother wraps Jimmy in a blanket and puts him in the car. By the time they arrive at the day care center, Jimmy is awake and crying. Mother has to hold him and talk to him to quiet him down as they enter. Jane asks mother to go out onto the playground. She and Jimmy go to the playground with Jane and enthusiastically admire the garden the children have planted. Mother secures Jimmy in one of the infant swings and supervises the other children playing on the rings and slide.

At four o'clock, mother takes Jane, Jimmy, and the four car pool children to their respective homes. When they arrive at their own home, John is already there. He has a dentist appointment, so he climbs into the car with the others and is dropped off at the dentist's. In the meantime, mother takes the younger children to see her parents. Mother helps the grandfather with his physiotherapy exercises, while the grandmother talks to Jane and Jimmy. She has made a new dress for Jane's doll. Jimmy, sad-faced, feels left out, so the grandmother starts to make a bunny for him from some yarn. The bunny is not finished when it is time to pick up John. Grandmother suggests that the children stay and that father can pick them up on the way home from work. Jane is happy to stay, but Jimmy refuses, despite the pleadings of both grandparents, who seem to feel a little hurt. After mother and Jimmy leave, grandmother invites Jane to have "tea." She sits at the table with her grandparents and has milk and cookies; then she sits on grand-father's lap to watch Sesame Street on television. At 5:30, father picks her up and they walk together to the bus stop. The bus is very crowded, and both have to stand up. In the pushing and shoving, Jane loses the yarn bunny for Jimmy.

After mother and Jimmy left the grandparents' house, they picked up John at the dentist's and drove home. Both boys now watch television while mother starts dinner and cleans house. John's friends call him out to play and Jimmy wants attention. Wishing he had stayed with his grandparents, Mother reads him a short story, interrupted by two telephone calls. Finally, she puts him in the car to go to the bus stop. It has started to rain, so they wait in the car, mother singing nursery rhymes, Jimmy clapping, and both watching for Jane, father, and bunny. By the time the bus comes, Jimmy has begun to fuss, and when he discovers that the bunny has been lost, he breaks into tears. Father drives and mother holds the now-screaming toddler in her arms. Everyone arrives home damp from the rain and cranky. Father brusquely puts Jimmy in his bed and then goes off by himself to the toolshed to sharpen the blades on the lawnmower.

By the time dinner is ready, Jimmy has fallen asleep. Jane serves herself and tries to participate in the conversation with her parents and John. John teases her and she cries. Both children are asked to be quiet while father and mother talk with one another. After dinner, father plays a game with Jane, tickling and rough-housing with her. He has to stop to drive John to a youth group meeting. Jane asks her mother to read her a story, but mother is now feeding Jimmy. Jane turns on the television, finally selecting a police thriller from the four programs available.

After Jimmy finishes his supper, he has his bath. He plays in the tub, crowing and splashing, with boats and floating toys, Mother keeping an eye on him and chatting with him as she puts away the laundry in the children's rooms. After-ward, Jimmy is wide awake and does not want to go to bed. Father plays ball with him on the family room floor while Jane takes her bath. Each parent puts one child to bed and sings a good night song, then goes in to kiss the other one good night. Jane falls asleep quickly, but Jimmy gets out of his crib after 15 minutes. He shakes the stair gate and calls for his mother. Father comes, gives him a firm pat on the bottom, and puts him to bed. Jimmy fusses, sings to himself for a while, and finally falls asleep. John, who was brought home by a neighbor, briefly joins his parents who are watching television and then goes to bed. Father leaves for a nine o'clock meeting and mother brings out the ironing board to touch up her husband's "drip-dry" shirts as she continues to watch the television comedy.

In the foregoing account, we have sought to bring to life in concrete form some of the patterns of family life that are reflected in contemporary research studies. The general picture is one of well-intentioned parents attempting to do their best for their children under increasingly hectic conditions of life and with decreasing assistance from other family members or the community at large. The consequences of such patterns of living, both for the child himself and the family as a whole, are not yet fully understood, but some Americans are now beginning to question whether the "good things in life," as they have been defined, do not require some redefinition and reordering of priorities.

VI

Programs

A. HEALTH SERVICES

There is growing dissatisfaction with the system of health care in the United States. Three successive presidents have described comprehensive health care as a right, and public opinion increasingly endorses this position but it is still very far from a reality for many citizens. Although the system provides a broad spectrum of high-quality services, costs are rising rapidly and services are increasingly fragmented and complex. These concerns have precipitated what has come to be known as "the health care crisis," and substantial public debate envelops the health care system.

1. The health status of infants and young children

Americans have been accustomed to think of their health care system as the best in the world. In view of the many recent medical advances which have occurred in the United States, it has been reasonable perhaps to assume that the nation would rank high in health status. Yet, according to several standard indices, this is not the case. At least 15 countries have reduced infant death rates to lower levels; many have done a better job of preventing handicapping conditions and accidents. U.S. statistics uniformly reflect the fact that the uneducated, the poor, and the non-white minorities tend to have poorer health records and to receive less adequate care.

a) *Infant mortality* There has been a gradual decrease in infant deaths for several decades, but from 1950 to 1965, progress in this respect was disappointingly slow. In those 15 years, deaths dropped from 29.2 to 24.7 per 1000 births. With the introduction of new health services as part of the broad-scale attack on poverty, infant mortality then began to fall much more rapidly, to 19.6 in 1970 and 18.5 in 1972.

Even though since 1965 deaths among non-white infants dropped faster than deaths among white infants, a tragic contrast remains. In

Table 1 are the 1971 statistics for neonatal and post-neonatal deaths, white and non-white. The differential between the groups is especially striking and disheartening with respect to deaths between one month and one year of age, because such a large proportion of these are potentially preventable.

TABLE 1

Infant mortality rates by age for white and non-white populations, 1971[a]

	Under 1 year	Under 28 days	28 days to 11 mo.
White	16.8	12.9	3.9
Non-white	30.2	20.8	9.4
Total	19.2	14.3	4.9

[a] From Wegman (1972)

b) *Maternal deaths*   Maternal deaths are now very infrequent for the population as a whole—only 2.47 in 1970 for every 10,000 births —yet the rate for non-white mothers was about four times as great as for white mothers.

c) *Childhood mortality*   In 1970, there were approximately 7.90 deaths for every 10,000 children ages 1–4 in the United States. The figure for children ages 5–14 was 4.14. Accidents, poisonings, and other forms of violent death were by far the greatest killers, in 1967 accounting for 38 percent of deaths in children 1–4 and 48 percent of deaths in the 5–14 age span. Other causes of death in the younger group were congenital anomalies (11 percent), influenza and pneumonia (11 percent), and malignant neoplasms (9.5 percent).

d) *Therapeutic and preventive health care*   Good health care has not been, nor is it now, the birth-right of every American child. In such indices as general level of nutrition, number of untreated health problems, and prevalence of chronic illnesses and disabilities, low-income persons are much less well off than persons with higher incomes (e.g., Bauer, 1972; Birch and Gussow, 1970).

[63]

Children from poor families receive less attention in the early stages of illness, a delay resulting in longer and more serious illness. In 1967, for example, three-quarters of children under age 17 with family incomes over $7,000 saw a physician at least once during the year, but only about half the non-white children and those from families with incomes below $3,000 did so. The overall average of visits per child was 3.6, but it was only 2.0 for non-whites and nearly double that (3.9) for whites (National Center for Health Statistics, 1970).

Innoculation rates constitute one index of the preventive health care children are receiving. The 1970 Immunization Survey revealed that the percentage of immunized children was only 57 nationally for measles, 41 percent in central city poverty areas; for polio the figures were only 66 percent and 51 percent. This situation represents a deterioration from earlier coverages, probably because the special federal funds which formerly supported immunization programs had recently been blended with general health funds granted to the states for such health programs as each deemed fit.

The most striking evidence of inequality in the health care system is in dental care. Examination of children in Head Start programs in 1966 revealed, for example, that 40–70 percent had untreated caries (depending on whether the water supply was fluoridated). When poor children receive dental treatment, their carious teeth are likely to be in such bad condition that they are extracted. Black children tend to have teeth extracted almost three times as frequently as white children (45 percent vs. 17 percent) and to have fillings for caries about half as frequently (23 percent vs. 43 percent) (National Center for Health Statistics, 1966 b). Little wonder, for in 1968 the average number of dental visits for children from families with less than $3,000 income was only 0.4, compared with 2.3 visits for children from families with more than $15,000 income.

e) *Birth rates* One area in which many Americans take some pride is the recent success in reducing the birth rate. In 1972, for the first time in U.S. history, fertility declined to replacement level, 73.1 births per 1,000 women aged 15–44. Should this rate continue, the result would be a stable population about the year 2040.

Many groups now discourage young couples from having more than two children. Birth control information and materials are widely available, and abortion laws have gradually been liberalized. In 1973, the Supreme Court decreed that laws regulating abortions during the first trimester of pregnancy are unconstitutional, so there is now a situation in which it can be assumed that almost every child who is born is wanted by his parents, or at least by his mother. The profound changes concerning attitudes about conception and birth are related to equally profound changes in the roles of women, to a fear that human beings may have already exceeded the population supportable by this planet, and an awareness that the United States uses much more than its share of the world's irreplaceable resources.

Here again, the picture is different among poor families than among the middle class. Although there is some controversy about this topic, it appears that poor families want about the same number of children as do more affluent families. Yet, until recently, their birth rates have been about 40 percent higher than the average for the nation. Other figures underline this problem. Illegitimacy rates are also much higher among the poor, and first children in poor families are generally born much sooner after the marriage than children in more well-to-do families. More than 90 percent of first births in families with less than $3,000 annual income occurred within the first two years of marriage in 1964–66 (37.5 percent within the first 8 months), whereas only 48 percent of first babies born into homes with $10,000 income or more were born in the first two years (8.2 percent within the first 8 months).

2. The system

The American system for the delivery of health services is very much a product of its national context (Yerby, 1969). It is highly pluralistic and combines a number of different ways to organize personnel and deliver services. It is a multicentric system centered largely in the domain of private enterprise, but with substantial voluntary components and with growing state and federal government involvements. It is also a very fragmented system.

Changes have been slow, largely because they have been so strongly resisted by physicians' groups jealously guarding the fee-for-service

[65]

system. The American Medical Association (AMA), the largest organization of physicians, has wielded great influence to maintain the *status quo*. Since the 1930's, it has lobbied relentlessly to delay the development of health insurance programs, to restrict new forms of medical practice, and above all, to limit government participation in medical education, in research, and in the payment for and direct delivery of health care services. In recent years the AMA has relented to some extent and in fact no longer occupies quite the position of dominance which it formerly held among physicians' groups. Another reason for the slow pace of change has been that most people who could pay for medical services have been relatively satisfied. There are, though, strong forces including some physicians' groups which find the present situation inadequate and seek new forms of delivering services for better and more economical results.

a) *Components of the system* The basic ingredient of the American health care system is private practice. A physician who has been licensed by his state may elect to provide health care by establishing a practice alone or with one or more partners. He may be a specialist and receive both self-referrals and referrals from other physicians, or he may be a generalist rendering primary health care. He determines his own fees within the bounds of the market economy, and he may augment his income by high fees, by working long hours, and/or by seeing many patients as rapidly as possible. The average income of physicians is, in fact, among the highest of any occupational group in the country.

There are some variants in the private practice system. Some physicians have banded together into groups or larger clinics with a variety of arrangements for financing. These clinics provide a convenient means for sharing specialized services and onerous duties (e.g., night calls) and reducing office expenses, but they retain the essential private practice characteristics.

Since World War II, a growing pattern of service has been the prepaid health plan or health maintenance organization. Although these still cover only a small minority of the population, they are important because of their rapid growth. Under such plans the individual or family pays a stipulated amount each month, sick or well, and receives comprehensive care, sometimes including all medications. There may or may not be a token fee for each visit. Such non-profit corporations hire their own physicians and other staff and pay them a salary. In some the physicians control the corporation; in others control is invested in a board chosen from the users. They build their own clinics and often their own hospitals. In so doing, they offer a number of advantages. They tend to be less expensive, particularly because of the inherent incentive to reduce hospital stays and to render regular preventive care and prompt curative care. They are able to avoid many hospitalizations and to shorten others by preparing for them in advance on an outpatient basis. Generally, as in private care, patients choose their own physicians from among the group, and all the work of specialists and technicians is coordinated by this physician. In such a group, it is relatively easy to utilize health technicians trained for specifis tasks and to make use of technologically advanced methods such as computer aids in preventive care. Recently, the Department of Health, Education, and Welfare has developed a plan to encourage communities and groups of physicians to develop health maintenance organizations with characteristics of prepayment plans.

Special services are also provided by voluntary organizations. Much birth control information, for example, is dispensed through the voluntary organization, Planned Parenthood and World Population. The free clinic movement provides a substantial amount of care to poverty groups, young alienated individuals, users of drugs, etc. They operate with a combination of people ranging from the untrained to the highly specialized professional. In addition, there are a number of voluntary, nationwide organizations which try to stimulate services and research in their special areas of interest. The largest of these are the American Heart Association, the American Cancer Society, and the National Association for Mental Health.

The emergency rooms of local hospitals have become the largest single source of medical care for the poor, together with the outpatient clinics of public hospitals and medical centers. Originally intended to give only prompt treatment for unexpected events such as accidents and acute illnesses, the emergency room has become a catch-all for the health problems of the poor. Here one finds the father who has not been able to afford a day off to see about his sore throat and therefore arrives in the evening or on Sunday, a baby whose fever has persisted for days but whose mother has not been able to obtain transportation to bring him in, a five-year-old with a painful abscessed tooth who has never seen a dentist, etc. Under such circumstances, treatment is likely to be impersonal and superficial. There is no room in the emergency service for preventive care, no time for delving into underlying health problems. Despite the fact that some emergency rooms are now manned by full-time, well-trained staffs, continuity of care simply cannot occur here. Patients will be admonished to use other facilities, but many find this difficult and furthermore, many poor families also believe that care of this type is better than that they obtain in the regular clinics.

Some outpatient clinics have been designed to serve poor families, but in practice they often do a rather poor job of it. Most such clinics are located in schools of medicine, city or county hospitals, and are seldom close to the neighborhoods they serve. Too often the personnel show insufficient respect for the person's privacy, time, or dignity. Rarely is there provision for the comfort of other children who must be brought along. If the clinic is part of a teaching or research program, as is often the case, it tends to be organized to meet those needs rather than the needs of the patient. Recently, there has been an effort to provide comprehensive, family-centered primary care for poor families through the organization or neighborhood health centers. Financing these programs has been difficult, and as a consequence, maintaining professional staffs has become a serious problem.

Variations on the practice of public medicine have tended to improve the health care of the poor, but they remain only an addendum to the regular system.

b) *Distribution of personnel* There are, in all, about 3 million health care workers in the United States. In 1970, there were approximately 300,000 active physicians, one for every 666 persons, and approximately 725,000 registered nurses. In 1940, there were 345 general physicians for every 100,000 people; the corresponding figure in 1970 was 100. During this 30-year period, the number of specialists increased dramatically to 70 percent of the total; the number of pediatricians more than doubled, from 7 to 18 per 100,000 persons.

Medical care of children has correspondingly shifted from general practitioners (who now supply about 25 percent of health services for children) to pediatricians (who supply about 50 percent).

Pediatricians are usually very busy and often overworked. Despite concerns about a substantial manpower shortage, however, recent analyses have led to the conclusion that soon there may be close to an adequate supply of pediatricians, especially if the low birth rate persists (Haggerty, 1972).

The greater problem concerning personnel and services has to do with their distribution. Low income and rural areas have had fewer resources and have had difficulty in maintaining adequate services. The solution to the problem of distribution will depend in part on the provision of adequate financing so that ability to pay will cease to be an important factor in determining access to services. A new incentive or regulatory system will also have to be devised to ensure the availability of services in rural areas and others which commonly fail to attract personnel.

c) *Insurance* Over the past few decades, private insurance companies have developed schemes to cushion the shock of major medical expenses. Some pay most of the expenses, while others come into play only when expenses mount very high. Fees vary accordingly. A family may join a private plan on its own initiative, may belong to a group (e.g., a union) which has arranged insurance for its members at a favorable rate, or may be given the insurance as a benefit of the mother's or father's employment. None of these plans changes the basic fee-for-service relationship between physician and patient. In fiscal 1971, the private health insurance companies paid $16.6 billion in benefits, or approximately 40 percent of the non-governmental health costs that year.

A federal plan (Medicare) for all those over 65 years old was introduced in the mid-1960's. This is essentially a form of government insurance which came into being because of the financial crises caused by the repeated and prolonged illnesses and the nursing needs of the elderly. It does not directly affect the care of many preschool children, but plans like this, which make the elderly financially independent of

[69]

their children, effect subtle and important changes in family situations and thus do have their influence on the young.

d) *Health care, American style*   To see how the free-enterprise system operates in practice, let us take a look at a typical pattern of health care for a relatively healthy child born into a middle-class family.

Soon after she suspects that she is pregnant, the mother sees her family physician or an obstetrician for confirmation of the pregnancy, blood tests, etc. If all is well, she will be given advice on caring for herself and a prescription for nutritional supplements, and told to report back monthly. On each subsequent visit, a urinalysis will be done, weight and blood pressure will be measured by the nurse, and the baby's heart will be listened to by the physician; toward the end of pregnancy, she will see her doctor weekly. If he is in group practice, she will see each of the other obstetricians at least once, because one of them may deliver her baby if her own physician is unavailable. For pregnancy and delivery, she will pay her Doctor a standard fee agreed upon beforehand (averaging $300 or more); should complications occur, she may have to pay more. Once labor is established, she will go to the maternity section of the hospital for delivery, after which she will usually remain three or four days before going home with the baby. For her hospital stay, she will pay an average of $80 a day or more. Six weeks later, she will be seen for a postpartum checkup by her physician and will receive a prescription for birth control pills or a diaphragm, if she desires. Her health insurance may or may not cover maternity and newborn care; this is a special problem with prematures and other babies needing costly, protracted care.

The baby will be checked by the hospital staff at delivery, and will be seen within the next several hours by the pediatrician or family doctor designated by the mother. He will see the baby daily during its hospital stay. Neither he nor the mother's own physician will encourage her very strongly to breast feed the baby.

The mother may, if she desires, ask the County Visiting Nurse to visit her at home, but very few take advantage of this free service. During the first month, she will probably speak to her baby's physician several times over the telephone, especially if the infant is a first child. Beginning at about one month of age, the baby will be seen monthly or bimonthly during the first year of life, unless there is reason to supervise him more closely. During his first year he will receive combination injections for diphtheria, pertussis and tetanus, innoculations for rubella and rubeola, and polio vaccine by mouth. Neither a BCG vaccination nor a routine smallpox vaccination will be recommended. Depending upon the physician, the baby may be seen every two or three months until he is two or two and a half, and then at intervals of six months to a year. His posture and coordination will be observed, and beginning at age four or five, his hearing and vision will usually be checked. There will be no formal developmental testing unless there is reason to suspect a problem.

The types of upbringing problems discussed during the visits are greatly influenced by the particular mother-doctor relationship. The doctor is, in any event, unlikely to discuss the child's diet after he is well into his second year of life, or to bring up other matters relating to general health such as exercise or outdoor play. He is likely to assume that the mother, being reasonably well educated and of the same social class as he is, will see to it that the child's diet is balanced and that she will know "how to bring up children" in other ways as well.

During the ordinary intermittent episodes of illness, the mother will often telephone and discuss matters with the physician or his nurse before deciding whether to bring the child into the office. Very rarely will a physician visit the child at home; in case of crisis, the child will be taken to the hospital emergency room and the physician will be alerted to meet him there.

The above is, of course, the pattern for the relatively well-to-do and concerned family. Even for such a family, continuous, integrated health care may be interrupted when the family moves, the mother forgets to make some appointments, the family grows dissatisfied with one physician and tries another, etc. It is important to notice that at no time has anyone outside the family contacted them to remind them to see their physician, to offer help or health information—nor may anyone in the community in fact know that the baby exists.† The infant's birth will, of course, have been registered by hospital authorities, and when the birth certificate is mailed it may be accompanied by a printed reminder to make sure the baby is immunized. Not even immunizations are compulsory, however. This state of affairs surely respects the authority of the family, but at what cost to the children?

e) *Programmatic attempts to meet the needs of special groups* The contemporary role of the federal government in personal health care began in 1935, with the landmark Social Security legislation which has been progressively expanded to include many important programs for the young. The double-pronged public concern for the mentally retarded and the poor which characterized the mid-1960's resulted in a further spurt of health legislation which has had both direct and indirect effects upon the health of children. An analysis of significant American health legislation lists only ten federal laws between 1935 and 1964, but 19 important pieces of legislation in 1965–66 alone (Lee and Silver, 1972). Since then, there has been much less legislative activity.

---

† In some communities, the public health nurse will attempt to visit families to ensure continuous health care, but in fact these services are almost entirely now limited to the poor.

The largest public program of health care for children is the *Medical Assistance Program* (Medicaid), established in 1965. The primary target population consists of families eligible for public assistance payments, but children whose families are "medically indigent" (unable to handle the health costs even if they are not legally poor) may also be included. This federal program provides grants to states, ranging from approximately half to over 80 percent of the total cost, depending upon per capita income in the state and the amount which the state is willing to invest. The program does not affect the patient-physician relationship; it merely pays for it. Most care financed is for acute or chronic illness rather than for comprehensive or preventive services. Since 1972, however, the states have been required to undertake health screening and follow-up treatment in children of families eligible for Medicaid; unfortunately, this part of the program has been slow to come into operation. The total federal appropriation for the program in 1972 was approximately $4 billion.

A variety of programs designed to improve the health status of disadvantaged mothers and children are run by the states under the supervision of the *Maternal and Child Health Services* of the Department of Health, Education, and Welfare, under authorization of the original Social Security Act of 1935. These include maternity and well-child clinics (the medical profession having opposed the inclusion of sick-child services), public health nursing services, immunizations, and screening and referral programs in schools. Some projects provide full maternity care and comprehensive infant care during the first year of life. Others provide comprehensive care to poor children living in areas with concentrations of low-income families. Still others offer family planning services, and a special project begun in 1971 provides dental screening and treatment to children in low-income families. The combined federal appropriation for all these projects, some of which are also funded in part by other sources, was approximately $200 million for 1972. The target populations for most of these programs were originally rural, but with the migration of the rural poor to the cities, the emphasis has shifted to include the city poor as well.

Two programs, both part of the Maternal and Child Health Services, deserve special mention because they are specifically designed for mothers, infants, and very young children. The *Maternal and*

Infant Care Projects (M & I) came into being in 1964 following the report of President Kennedy's Panel on Mental Retardation, which pointed out the apparent relationship between inadequate obstetric care and the number of defective or retarded children. As the inner cities became the residential areas for the poor, and the more well-to-do (and their physicians) fled to the suburbs, prematurity and infant mortality rates in the cities actually reversed direction and began to rise. The M & I programs for poor families provide full maternity care and care of the infant during his first year. They have a limited geographic scope such as a city, a convenient subdivision of an urban area, or a whole rural county. Although there has been no overall evaluation of these projects, some specific results—such as the drop in infant mortality already mentioned—suggest that the M & I programs have been worthwhile. The total federal expenditure for 1972 was approximately $43 million.

The other direct-service project of special import, the *Children and Youth Project* (C & Y) was authorized in 1965 in response to the observation that too many children were being taken to overcrowded emergency rooms rather than to a pediatrician. The C & Y projects were intended to promote the health of both preschool and school-age children in areas inhabited by low-income families; many are operated by medical schools and teaching hospitals and provide comprehensive medical care to all children under 21 living in prescribed geographic areas. Children registered in the C & Y projects have experienced a 50 percent decrease in hospital admissions since the program was initiated, and the diagnosis of "well child" on recall examination has increased over 50 percent. The cost of care per child in the program decreased from $201 in 1968 to $150 in 1970. The total federal appropriation for C & Y projects was approximately $47 million for 1972.

Another set of health oriented programs was established by the *Community Action Programs* of the Office of Economic Opportunity. High on the lists of priorities drawn by citizens in most communities have been health services, not only in greater numbers but closer to the homes of these families and operated by socially sensitive professionals (including minority group members) who are able to understand and to respect the living patterns of poor people. Some programs aim at comprehensive care for families; others are more specifically concerned with family planning, the provision of emergency food, and emergency medical services. The combined federal appropriation for these programs was approximately $135 million for 1972.

An important program with the goal of extending comprehensive health care to all segments of the population is the *Comprehensive Health Planning and Public Health Services Program* (Partnership for Health). This program provides funds for planning, for health services development, and for the actual provision of health services. A major component has been the establishment of Community Health Centers to provide comprehensive health services to families in disadvantaged communities. A number of similar programs started by the Community Action Programs (above) have been transferred to this program after becoming well established. The total federal appropriation was approximately $125 million in 1972.

A few major programs offer medical components as part of other services for children of disadvantaged families, e.g. *Head Start, Health Start,* and *Follow Through* (see VI, F). Services consisting of screening and referral services including dentistry, health education for children and parents, and a nutritional component are required. The budget for the health component of Head Start was approximately $22.6 million in 1972; Follow Through's total budget was approximately $58 million in 1972 for such social, medical, nutritional and other services supplementing the ordinary public school budget. *Title I of the Elementary and Secondary Education Act* of 1965 (see VI, F) provides, on local initiative, special assistance for groups of children whose level of achievement is below normal. The health component of this program amounted to $28 million, 1.8 percent of the 1972 budget of $1,565 million.

Finally, there are some children for whom the federal government assumes total responsibility for health care services. Comprehensive medical services for Indians on or near reservations and natives of Alaska are now provided by the Public Health Service. Since it assumed responsibility in 1955, the infant mortality rate among Indians has declined 51 percent. The federal appropriation in 1972 was $153 million. Actually, the largest program is the comprehensive health care rendered to the approximately 2.2 million dependent children of military personnel, partially through direct services and partially through reimbursement for the use of non-military health services. The total cost in 1971 was approximately $600 million.

In addition to these major programs, the federal government sponsors a bewildering array of programs for specific target populations, such as the mentally retarded, those with physical handicaps, the children of migrant workers, etc. Federal appropriations for these miscellaneous health programs have approximated $150 million per year. An equal amount is spent for various programs having to do with the care of the mentally ill. Some attention has been given recently to health problems arising from the damage to the environment, but funds for programs in this area come from many different federal sources and it is impossible to say now how much has been made available in all.

It must be stressed that only a portion of funds for health care comes from the federal government. A total of approximately $9.3 billion was spent in 1970 for the health care of children below the age of 19; private funds provided 73 percent and public funds only 27 percent. Of the public funds, $1.47 billion (59 percent) came from the federal government and $1.01 billion (41 percent) from state and local governments (Lowe and Alexander, 1972).

3. What is right and what is wrong with American health care?

a) *The assets* In present practice, perhaps two-thirds of American children receive adequate health care. The free-market structure leads the children into contact with reasonably skilled practitioners whose understanding of the subtleties of childhood illness and behavior leads to prompt amelioration of early disease states. Their immunizations are complete and their nutritional status adequate. Their families are able to provide a supportive environment and are reasonably wise in the ways of upbringing. When their illness requires special technologies, these are generally available and of high quality.

1) Standard of living. Many factors in the life of the American child which support good health do not resemble health measures at all. For the nation as a whole, food is abundant and of good

[75]

quality. Housing is good, centrally heated, plentifully supplied with refrigeration, hot water, and often sanitary dishwashers. Furthermore, the availability of the physician by private telephone and the accessibility of his office or the hospital by use of the family car also bring the health care system close to home.

2) Research. Biomedical research is conducted on a broad scale and for the most part is technically excellent. The federal government supports a broad variety of research efforts, ranging from the attack on specific disease entities to basic, theoretical research. Since its beginning in 1937, federal expenditure for health research has grown to more than $2 billion annually (Lee and Silver, 1972).

3) Public health measures. Americans have recently become deeply alarmed at the state of their ecology. In addition to improving water and sewerage treatment, there is presently a broad attack (fragmented, however, as usual) on pollution of the rivers, seas, and air. New automobiles must, for example, meet stricter standards for control of harmful emissions and for safety than those of any other nation.

4) Qualified personnel. Despite shortages and maldistribution of health workers, the qualifications of health professionals tend to be quite satisfactory. The key person in the system is the physician, and for the most part the field of medicine enlists bright and capable people. Nurses, too, are highly trained in the U.S. and in many instances can assume considerable autonomy.

5) Physician-patient relationships. For the middle-class patient, the relationship with his doctor offers a maximum of flexibility and personalization. The patient and his family can choose someone they like and respect, important ingredients especially in the subtle and private areas of child rearing. They may have access to a specialist on their own volition, and there is reasonably good give-and-take between the physician and the intelligent patient.

6) Insurance. With the advent of insurance supports, the major danger of a modified fee-for-service system—disastrously costly episodes of illness—has been made remote. The patient feels that he gets what he pays for and he usually need not worry that the cost will significantly exceed his means. The lack of a centralized delivery

system also minimizes the paper work and the bureaucratic super-structure which would otherwise be called for, although the new public programs and insurance repayment plans are beginning to erode this benefit.

7) Integration of preventive and curative care. The field of public health, which treats the group rather than the individual, is fairly isolated from the personal health care system and suffers from a traditional lack of status. Yet, when one looks at personal health services, the preventive and curative aspects are thoroughly inte-grated—when the system works as intended. The child is usually cared for by the same physician whether he is sick or well, whether he is seen in the hospital, the office, or (very rarely) at home. Even if a specialist is needed, the primary physician is typically expected to supervise the carry-through.

b) *The liabilities* Within this rosy picture, there are many loop-holes and failures. Improvements are overdue, but some are on the horizon.

1) Rising costs. In 1972, the cost of all components of the health care enterprise was approximately $80 billion, or nearly $400 for every man, woman, and child. The total represents approximately 7.5 percent of the gross national product, up from 5.3 percent in 1950, a much more rapid rise than the general cost of living index. This can be traced to a number of features inherent in the overall system which is, as we have seen, rather chaotic and out of the control of any single responsible group. The costs of using specialized personnel are high; there are few incentives for economy; there are costly duplications of facilities; and hospital costs are spiralling.

2) Health care as a privilege, not a right. The amount and quality of health care given to a child is a direct product of the knowledge, commitment, and resources of his family. This is an undue burden to put upon parents, and unfair to children denied, by the chaos of the system, services ostensibly "available to all."

3) The narrow perspective of medical practice. The social and behavioral problems of children tend now to be viewed as legiti-mate health concerns, but there is not really adequate provisions for

helping parents who are having ordinary problems of upbringing. Furthermore, personnel are far too often exclusively oriented to the individual patient. The family must be looked on as a unit existing in and providing for itself a particular environment which deeply affects its health status. Children's development often hinges on the functioning of the adults on whom they depend, and in turn on parental needs (e.g. better housing, a better job, reliable high quality day care, adequate public transportation, etc.). It is often the children's doctor who is in a position to see this most clearly.

4) Lack of planning. Many people are, in fact, aware of the serious problems in our health care system, but no one is empowered to do very much about them. Even with the increasing role of the federal government in this field, authority is divided among so many agencies and departments that integrative efforts are incredibly complex. Planning is almost impossible. This state of affairs is by no means limited to the field of health, but the shortcomings in this field are perhaps exaggerated by the excessive proliferation and the vested interests of specific programs, the strength and special interests of professional groups, the private control of the system, the rising costs of health care, and political differences over the powers of the states relative to the federal government in such matters.

Federal leadership in goal setting and in planning seems reasonable, but efforts in this direction have been consistently sidetracked. There is an Assistant Secretary in the Department of Health, Education, and Welfare, whose job is defined as planning, but so far the holders of this position have been able to make little headway (Lee and Silver, 1972). Congress and the President often fail to agree on plans to reorganize agencies and services, and little action is taken. Inaction also has been the fate of a suggestion supported by a broad segment of the population including the 1970 White House Conference on Children, for the creation of a Council of Advisors for Children (or, alternatively, for Health) similar to the President's Council of Economic Advisors, a continuing group which monitors economic indicators and recommends action. Under the auspices of the National Academy of Sciences, an Institute of Medicine was established in 1971, to survey the current scene and to suggest plans, but highly respected though the Academy may be, this group has no direct power to bring about any sort of change.

5) Hardening of the categories. The health care system in the United States consists in large part of a series of restricted services which have arisen in response to passing, highly specific, public concerns. The result is a system which contains sets of divisions based on (i) the type of disease (e.g., tuberculosis, cerebral palsy, birth defects, cystic fibrosis, cancer); (ii) age (e.g., M and I programs, C and Y programs, Medicare); (iii) institutions (e.g., school health services, Head Start); (iv) geographic or political boundaries (e.g., community action programs, state and local health departments, Model Cities); (v) income (e.g., Medicaid); (vi) occupation (military services, union-based programs); and combinations of all these. Many people fall into the gaps or fail to comprehend the system, and furthermore, the health care of a family is too often segmented to the point that an overall family illness pattern is perceived by no one.

Record keeping is also chaotic, but thus far the establishment of a comprehensive record system has been hampered by justifiable concern with preserving confidentiality of information, traditionally held to be inviolable between physician and patient. Approximately 20 percent of Americans move in any year from one residence to another, usually without any sort of cumulative record and with minimal communication between the old and the new primary care givers.

6) Unmet manpower needs and the underuse of technical personnel. Not only is current medical training of 5–10 years in the rarefied atmosphere of a teaching hospital an expensive way to train a primary-care physician (the estimated cost is $100,000 each), it is also an inappropriate way. The use of auxiliary personnel—nurses trained to give physical examinations, aides to test hearing and sight, surgical assistants who can stitch a minor wound or clean out an eye, midwives who can handle normal deliveries—is only beginning to enter the American scene to any significant degree. Most physicians have steadfastly resisted using paramedical assistants. Although this has produced considerable frustrations (e.g., pediatricians trained to treat exotic diseases seeing an endless succession of

[79]

healthy babies and those with common illnesses), it is difficult to remedy. Technical assistants are uneconomical for small offices and few in private practice would desire such aides, given the economic benefits of doing the work themselves even if they must work long hours to do so.

7) Lack of social supports. There exist in this country few social supports for the health of the child. A mother may take sick leave or vacation time when she has a baby or her child is ill, but there is no systematic provision for granting either parent such leave. There is, in fact, a prejudice against hiring the mother of young children or even a young married woman who may eventually become pregnant. Homemaker services to lighten this load are not at all well developed.

8) Restricted outreach. A self-defeating "hands off" attitude prevails in health care. Respecting the autonomy of the parents is too often used as a rationalization for not offering services which are sorely needed in this day of rapid social change and the prevalence of the nuclear family headed by inexperienced parents. Except for the child whom the welfare authorities have taken under supervision, no one reaches out to the family with reminders or offers of help, nor are there concrete incentives to encourage a parent to seek care for his child; quite the opposite, in fact.

In summary, broad changes are needed to ensure the optimal health status of American infants and children—changes not only in the health care system itself, but in the very fibers of the society. Broad-scale attacks on poverty and injustice will be needed to make significant inroads on many health problems of children, as will a willingness in others to share with parents responsibility for the health care of the young.

B. NUTRITION PROGRAMS

For decades, Americans comfortably assumed that every child had enough to eat. It was unthinkable that hunger and malnutrition could exist in a nation which every year must cope with a grain surplus and pay farmers to let their land lie fallow! In 1967, however, a Senate investigation of the poor, and a report by a team of doctors, brought to light the tragic presence of hunger. As many as 256 out of a total 3200 counties, concentrated in the poorer regions of the country but with some in highly urbanized areas as well, were identified as hunger areas (Citizen's Board of Inquiry, 1968). A series of studies revealed further evidence: 35 percent of poor children five and under showed growth retardation; 4 percent of poverty children below the age of six had rickets; 38 percent below the age of nine showed some evidence of scurvy (U.S. Public Health Service, 1968). Among some subgroups, the situation was even more desperate: 25 percent of the two-year-old children of migrant workers, for example, were found to be at the 3rd percentile or less in height (Bergstrom, cited by Richmond and Weinberger, 1970). Iron deficiency characterized preschool children at all income levels, but especially the poor, for whom intake of ascorbic acid is also low (U.S. Dept. of Agriculture, 1971).

A White House Conference on Food, Nutrition and Health in 1969 urged immediate action, presented guidelines for ending hunger caused by poverty, and outlined a broad national effort to improve the nutritional health of all. Infants, preschool children, adolescent girls, and mothers were identified as special targets, and hundreds of detailed recommendations were contained in the conference report (Simms, 1970). Responding to all these cumulative findings and to strong public concern, White House and Congressional action promptly began to strengthen existing nutrition programs and to initiate new ones.

The most important measure to combat hunger is the Food Stamp program which allows the poor to purchase stamps redeemable for food at neighborhood grocery stores. A poor family of four may, for example, purchase stamps worth $146 in food of their choosing by paying as little as $2 and never more than 25 percent of the family income. There are also programs which distribute foodstuffs directly to the poor, but they are unwieldy and require considerable state and local participation.

Several feeding programmes are aimed specifically at poverty children. The federal school lunch program grants funds ($330 million in 1970) which must be matched by participating states to provide lunches for 6.6 million children in schools and day care centers, and additional funds for food programs in schools serving areas with concentrations of low-income families or migrant workers. Regulations in effect since 1971 standardize the criteria of eligibility, previously up to each state, but do little to compel the states actively to seek out eligible children. Nutrition and nutritional education are also essential ingredients of Project Head Start (Section VI, F). Maternal and child health programs emphasize nutritional education; this is especially true of the Maternity and Infant Care Projects (Section VI, A) and the Parent and Child Centers (Section VI, F), which may in addition participate in a commodity distribution program for expectant and nursing mothers and children under six years.

Twenty-five to 30 million persons are estimated to live in families with incomes low enough to be eligible for food assistance, yet only about 15 million participate in any of the federal programs. Even though a Senate Select Committee on Nutrition and Human Needs found a steady drop in the number of malnourished Americans between 1969 and 1973, the battle against poor diet in this food-rich nation is far from won.

C. SOCIAL WELFARE SYSTEMS FOR CHILDREN

Home life is the highest and finest product of civilization. It is the great molding force of mind and character. Children should not be deprived of it except for urgent and compelling reasons.

This statement from the first White House Conference on Children in 1909 expresses the still-dominant theme of social welfare services for children: first priority should be given to maintaining children within their own families. If this is impossible or for compelling reasons undesirable, the children should be placed with a substitute family. Only if neither of these alternatives is feasible may the children be placed in a non-familial setting, hopefully on a temporary basis.

Welfare services in the United States are of three major types and are delivered by three major systems. The types of services are

[82]

support, supplementation, and *substitution.* Support is usually concerned with giving advice, counseling and psychotherapeutic aid. Supplementation consists of giving financial or other kinds of direct help. Substitution involves replacing a family with another family or some type of group care. The systems for the delivery of services are the *child welfare services* programs, the *family service agencies,* and the *child guidance clinics.* Child welfare services programs, located in city and county welfare departments and private welfare agencies, provide all three types of service to children and their families. Family service agencies provide support and sometimes limited supplementation in the form of auxiliary services (e.g., homemaker services). Child guidance clinics provide support, usually in the form of psychotherapy, to disturbed children and their parents. Some other organizations (e.g., juvenile courts, health departments, probation departments, and some units of the public school system) enter the picture of welfare services for children, but they are of lesser importance to young children.

The social welfare system in the United States does not directly affect most children. A reasonable estimate is that welfare aid including purely financial assistance reaches the families of some 15 to 20 percent of children between the ages of birth and 18. There are, however, some children who desperately do need help and cannot obtain it. Between seven and eight percent of children live in areas with no organized services for children, most of them in poorer rural areas where other programs are also likely to be deficient. Even in those areas which have child welfare services, there is wide disparity in the amount and quality of available help. For example, the average number of full-time professional public child welfare employees per 10,000 children under 21 years of age was 1.5 for all states in 1969, ranging from 4.2 in New York to .1 in Arizona and .2 in Alabama and South Dakota. Similar disparities exist with respect to financial and other forms of aid given.

One outstanding feature of the social welfare system for children has been the considerable involvement of private agencies (see Section IV). Although the proportion of children served has steadily declined to less than 10 percent in 1970 (National Center for Social

Statistics, 1972a), the importance of voluntary agencies is still considerable. Less hampered by political problems and legal strictures, they have greater flexibility and are able to establish more innovative programs which often cross city, county, and state boundaries. They are almost completely free of financial supplementation functions, and have tended to concentrate instead on support and substitution activities. They constitute, for example, a dominant factor in adoptions. They are generally older, better established, and more middle-class in outlook than the public agencies. Until recently, there was a tendency for their services to be simply doled out to the unfortunate. In the last few decades, however, this situation has undergone substantial change, and they now tend to argue for welfare services which enhance the quality of life for rich and poor alike.

In short, social welfare services are potentially available to most children in the United States, though they are actually used by few. There is great diversity, with a tendency to better financing and more availability in urbanized, wealthy, politically liberal states. Privately financed agencies lend assistance, and add variety and a note of competition to government sponsored services. (Selected references: Jeter, 1963; Kadushin, 1967; President's Commission on Income Maintenance Programs, 1970).

1. Social welfare support systems

One source of help for the troubled child and his family consists only of advice or other forms of psychological and social assistance. A professional worker—usually a social worker but at times a nurse, psychiatrist, psychologist, or some other trained person—attempts to help solve the child's and the family's problems by direct therapeutic intervention or by bringing to bear the influence of other persons or social units. Occasionally the child alone will be treated, but with a very young child in particular, at least one other member of the family is likely also to be treated. Sometimes the entire family will be treated individually or as a group. The child may, at times, be treated in a day care setting or as a part of some other extra-familial group. The object of such therapeutic intervention is to improve the condition of the child within the family context.

All three types of delivery units mentioned above supply such services. County welfare departments and family service agencies generally focus on intervention through the parents while child guidance clinics are more often inclined toward therapy directly involving the child. Because the theoretical orientations of these service units tend to be very similar— largely tied to psychoanalytic doctrines—and because their staffs are practically interchangeable, the distinctions among them have become blurred. They differ, however, in that the county welfare departments deal primarily with lower socioeconomic segments of the nation whereas family service agencies and child guidance clinics serve a predominantly middle-class population. These latter agencies have, in fact, been accused of abandoning the poor.

The problems encountered by a typical agency range considerably, including all kinds and degrees of familial conflict, childhood neuroses and occasionally even psychoses. Most often, however, the family needs insights into its own dynamics, the processes of child development, the demands and supports of the society surrounding them. Most support services are of brief duration involving but a few interviews; some, though, are protracted over many months and even years.

The question of whether or not supportive services are effective has been long and hotly debated. Many argue that meaningful psychotherapeutic intervention is usually impossible. The average number of visits is about five per case, slightly higher for families with children. Premature withdrawal from the therapy program—against professional advice—happens in nearly half the cases, indicating perhaps that the staff members are ambitious for more thoroughgoing changes than are the families. The most commonly stated reasons for withdrawing, however, have to do with the clients' feeling that they are not given the services they need and seek. Clients from lower-class families, in particular, tend to find the circumspect, exploratory-theapeutic, highly intellectual approach frustrating. "We come for help and get talk," is a common complaint.

The research evidence concerning specific outcomes of supportive services is rather uniformly negative (Eyesenck, 1965; Levitt, 1963). It should be stressed, however, that research in this area is very difficult and that there are not many good studies. It is somewhat ironic that some 50 years after the establishment of the child guidance clinics, intended by their founders to "demonstrate . . . the value of such psychiatric study and treatment applied to children . . ." (Harper *et al.*, 1940), their efforts have yet to be more precisely described and seriously evaluated. On a rather different level, though, it is clear that these services meet an important need. The public demands them and waiting lists are almost always very long. (Selected references: Beck, 1962; Cloward and Epstein, 1965; Coleman *et al.*, 1957; Levitt, 1963; Maas and Kahn, 1955; Meyer et al., 1965.)

a) *Help for unwed mothers and unwanted children* The American social welfare system has long been concerned with unwed mothers and their children. Until very recently, the number and percentage of illegitimate births were climbing steadily. The estimated number of babies born during the later depression years to unmarried mothers wa sabout 7 per 1,000 unmarried females of child-bearing age; by 1968, however, the 7 had become a disconcerting 19.8. In the same period of time, the proportion of illegitimate births among all live births rose from 3.8 to 9.7 per cent (White House Conference on Children, 1970). The problem has been further compounded by age and socioeconomic factors: about 75 percent of children born to mothers under the age of 15, and half of all those born to nonwhite mothers, have been illegitimate (National Center for Health Statistics, 1966).

The situation appears to be changing rapidly, though, with increased availability of contraceptives and liberalized abortion laws. New York, for example, where out-of-wedlock births had been increasing five to six percent each year, has experienced its first decline ever—nearly 25 percent from 1970, when its abortion-on-request law was first implemented, to 1972. Twenty-nine percent of these abortions were performed on teenagers (Guttmacher, personal communication, February 26, 1973). The most significant result will almost certainly be reduction of unwanted children. According to one study (Ryder and Westoff, quoted by Guttmacher, 1973), the percentage of babies unwanted at time of conception dropped from 19 percent during the period 1960–65, to 15 percent in the years 1965–70.

[86]

In spite of what appears to be a clear trend toward declining numbers of illegitimate and/or unwanted babies, provision must be made for existing unwed mothers and their offspring. Unwed mothers may be found in a variety of residential and familial arrangements. About half of those receiving child welfare services continue to live with their families and/or other relatives; the remaining half live independently or are served by the various types of foster care programs and maternity homes (Jeter, 1963). Maternity homes have an annual service potential of about 10 to 15 percent of girls giving birth out of wedlock. Greater attempts, though, are being made to serve girls in their usual home settings. This has meant substantial expansion of services to school girls and residents of deprived neighborhoods, particularly in urban areas. A number of these programs are being sponsored by the U.S. Children's Bureau, which has focused particularly on the multiple medical and social problems so often attending the birth and living situation of an infant born to a young, unwed mother (Birch and Gussow, 1970). Programs combining schooling and/or vocàtional preparation of the mother with day care for the child are becoming more numerous (see Section VIII, C).

Only one-third of illegitimate children born during 1960–1968 were adopted. The situation differs markedly, however, according to race. The number of illegitimate children born to white mothers was somewhat lower than for nonwhite mothers (155,000 white to 184,000 nonwhite); the number of white children adopted was, conversely, nearly five times higher (87,000 white to 18,000 nonwhite) (White House Conference on Children, 1970). Adoption has long been considered the solution of choice for most children of unwed mothers, but there has been a strong movement in recent years to make it easier and more rewarding for the natural mother to keep her baby (Bernstein, 1971; Sauber and Corrigan, 1970). There is no doubt, though, that it is a difficult task for a single parent to raise a child. The problem of single-parent families is particularly acute among nonwhite groups. In 1969, for example, only 0.3 percent of white children under the age of six were living in a household where the head was a never-married person, while 1.3 percent were living in a foster family or with relatives other than their parents. Of nonwhite children under six, however, the comparable figures were 4.3 percent with never-married head of household, and 12.1 per cent in the presence of neither parent (Bureau of Census, 1970).

b) *Help for the neglected or abused child*   The number of children in the United Satates who are passively neglected or actively exploited or abused is unknown. Estimates vary widely, depending upon the methods and definitions used. Projections based on suspicion of physical abuse alone lead to an estimate of four million children annually. Incidents of abuse admitted by a parent lead to a projection of 400,000 to 600,000 cases (Gil and Noble, 1969). Of the cases which actually come to the attention of authorities, more than half are children under six years of age (White House Conference on Children, 1970). In short, neglect, abuse, and exploitation are phenomena of considerable magnitude in early childhood.

Professional workers tend to agree that except in extreme situations these children should not be removed from their families. The approach usually recommended is a "specialized casework service . . . (which is) preventive and non-punitive and is geared toward rehabilitation" of the parent (De Francis, 1955). Generally, the service agency enters the situation because of a complaint by a neighbor, relative, or professional that a child is being neglected or abused. The tendency is to assume that abuse or neglect is not deliberate or perverse but rather caused by social or psychological factors which the parents themselves wish to see changed. The agency intent is usually quite limited—prevention of further abuse and, if necessary, restoration of the child to normal functioning.

The resistance to infringing upon parental rights is very strong in American society. Social agencies bring fewer than 10 percent of protective service cases into court, and even in these extreme cases the courts remove only a small percentage of children from their parents' custody. Three-fourths of all children in protective care remain with their parents, and two-thirds of the small percentage outside the familial home were placed voluntarily. This situation is ordinarily judged as positive; parents retain their children, supervision is maintained, community involvement and responsibility are minimized—all outcomes consonant with the American tradition of social welfare. An analysis of the available data, though, leaves cause for concern.

[88]

Parents who abuse their children do not typically show visible behavior changes as a result of intervention (Young, 1964). In some agencies about half of the requests for service to abused and neglected children involve cases previously known (Rein, 1963). Abused children show a very high incidence (50.8 percent) of prior abuse (Gil, 1967). There are also indications of generational continuity; one study showed that 14 percent of the mothers and 7 percent of the fathers of abused children had themselves been victims (Gil, 1967). As one practitioner has described the situation:

Most cases which eventually land with a protective agency have been "around the Horn" of community services. They display amazing consistency in their "inability to use help," but the protective agency must do something with them! Thus it finds itself with a large and concentrated load of seriously pathological case situations (Philbrick, 1960).

Neglected, abused, and exploited children appear to be the victims of archaic legal conceptions, public apathy, inadequate alternatives, and, also, of a confused professional conception regarding their problems and effective solutions. Society's reluctance to separate is exceeded only by its inability to help these children and their families. There is a beginning recognition that the present approach does not work and many protective service agencies are attempting new intervention schemes, particularly on the neighborhood level and with young families. Recently some multi-service neighborhood facilities have been established, offering casework and other social service assistance in addition to day care, homemaker services, emergency shelter and foster care. It is hoped that such an array of supportive, supplemental, and even substitute services will reduce parental helplessness, particularly maternal depletion, and will result in better care for these most unfortunate victims of non-interventionist social welfare and legal systems. (Selected readings: Gil, 1967, 1970; Gil and Noble, 1969; Kahn, 1963; Rein, 1963; Young, 1964.)

2. Social welfare supplementation systems

A major correlate of most social problems in the United States—unwed parenthood, malnutrition, child abuse, etc.—is low family

TABLE 2

Major programs for income maintenance[a]

Reason for loss of income	Program				
	Federal	Federal-state	State, or state-local	Private	Miscellaneous
Old age	OASDHI[b-c]	Old-age assistance	General assistance	Insurance	Railroad retirement
	Medicare	Medical assistance to the aged		Pensions	Public retirement
	Veterans[b]				
Unemployment	Unemployment insurance[b-c]	Unemployment insurance[b]	General assistance	Miscellaneous	Special industry provisions
Death	OASDHI[b-c]	Aid to families with dependent children[b-c]	General assistance	Insurance	
Permanent Disability	OASDHI[b-c]	Aid to families with dependent children	General assistance	Insurance	
	Veterans[b]	Aid to the blind	Workmen's compensation[b-c]		
		Aid to the permanently and totally disabled			
Temporary disability	Medicare[b]	Old-age assistance	General assistance	Insurance	
		Medical assistance to the aged	Workmen's compensation	Employee benefit plans	
		Aid to families with dependent children[b-c]	Disability programs (4 states)		
		Medical assistance to the needy[b]			

[a] From Weinberger, 1969, Table 1
[b] Of major importance to children.
[c] Described in this chapter.

income. In order to improve opportunities for children, financial help is often necessary. Such assistance is available either because of parents' rights to insurance benefits acquired during active employment or because of the current impoverished state of the family. Both types of programs are intended to assist families and individuals in periods of financial distress, but they differ significantly in the socio-economic status of recipients, ease and certainty of obtaining benefits, availability of accompanying social services, and public acceptance. Insurance benefits and programs for the indigent provide billions of dollars annually, much of it to families with children; the former, though, are considered a success, the latter a decided failure.

a) *Insurance programs—eligibility by status* Eligibility for social insurance benefits is a function of such circumstances as unemployment, industrial accident, death or retirement of the insured. The benefits are not dependent upon the economic conditions of the recipient. In some instances, the recipients are quite poor, but this is irrelevant to eligibility.

Old-age, survivor's and dependents' and health insurance (OASDHI) covers more than 90 percent of the U.S. labor force, and many of those excluded are in other parallel programs for railroad workers, government employees, and other smaller groups. About 3.4 million children† receive regular assistance under this program, usually because of the death or retirement of the father. The average monthly payment for a mother and two children was, in 1971, about $279 a month. Maximum benefits at that time were $120/month each for three dependents, $145.30/month each for two, and $164.09/month for a widow electing benefits at age 62. Participation of workers is compulsory, the program being financed by contributions from employees and employers who are both assessed about five percent of wages up to $9,000 per year. The coverage, then, is very broad but sizable numbers are still excluded and, since eligibility and the size of payments are tied to prior earnings, OASDHI of necessity fails to protect adequately the most needy, i.e., those irregularly or unprofitably employed. Another problem with the program is that it fails to

---

† Including mentally retarded adults who continue to beregarded as dependent children.

provide social services, which, given the circumstances under which benefits are paid, may often be needed. About half of the OASDHI children known to social service agencies are, for example, living out of the parental home; many others (25 percent) live only with their mothers.

Private pension plan payments also affect the economic standing of many children. In 1970, the President's Commission on Income Maintenance Programs reported the existence of 135,000 private pension plans covering 26.4 million workers. Benefits from these plans vary widely from about $900 per year to $12,000 or more. These benefits are additive, so that most retired workers with private pensions and OASDHI coverage have incomes considerably above the poverty level.

The workmen's compensation program began in 1911, but it was not until 1948 that all states adopted the program. Coverage is based on "liability without fault," i.e., any work accident, regardless of reason, entitles a worker to assistance. Employers pay the cost of the program, with premiums adjusted to their previous accident rate. About 80–90 percent of all workers are covered. Among those excluded are self-employed, domestic, and agricultural workers. The exclusion of the latter two categories again deprives those with lowest incomes and least extensive financial backlog. Even for those covered, the program may not be fully adequate, since both the amount and duration of compensation vary widely among the states. Usually, the amount is 60–67 percent of earnings, but most state laws limit the maximum payment, thus reducing the average to around 50 percent of earnings. Nevertheless, the program is of considerable importance, having provided in 1971, for example, $3.5 billion in compensation for some two million work injuries.

Unemployment insurance was established on a national basis by the Social Security Act of 1935. This is a state-administered program financed by a payroll tax of 3.1 percent (on the first $3,000 per person per annum) collected by the federal government but given to states when their program meets certain requirements of universality and fairness. Only about 80 percent of employed persons are covered (some agricultural, domestic and small firm workers are again excluded). It is, nevertheless, an important supplementary program. There is substantial fluctuation from one year to another because of changes in the labor market and eligibility requirements. In 1968, for example, 4.2 million persons collected $2.03 billion in benefits; in 1970, 6.4 million persons collected $3.85 billion. Both payments and duration of eligibility vary by state. In 1968, the level of payments ranged from 31 percent of income in Alaska to 60 percent in Hawaii. (Selected references: Burns, 1949; President's Commission on Income Maintenance, 1970.)

b) *Assistance programs—eligibility by need* The major program of financial assistance to needy families who do not qualify for or who receive insufficient support under insurance and pension programs is *Aid to Families with Dependent Children (AFDC)*. A parent must take the initiative in seeking out the welfare office and proving a need for assistance. Divorce or desertion by the father is the cause for assistance in about one-third of the families; his death or incapacity account for about one-fourth, and illegitimacy for somewhat more than one-fifth of the cases; with other causes, including low wages and prolonged unemployment, accounting for the rest.

In May, 1972, AFDC affected directly nearly 11 million individuals living in 3 million households with some 8 million children (National Center for Social Statistics, 1972 c). Of these children, 33 percent were under the age of six, and a little over half under the age of nine. Despite a large number of cases and very high costs amounting to $6.5 billion in 1972, some investigators are convinced that not all of those potentially eligible are receiving assistance. There are some 10 to 12 million children in poor families, either in households headed by men who are marginally and irregularly employed or in female-headed households where the mother is rarely employed. All are potentially eligible for AFDC payments, even by the strict standards now generally enforced. Although the AFDC coverage is obviously inadequate, its growth has been quite regular. About 1.6 million children were assisted in 1950; the number had risen to three million in 1964, to over four million in 1969, and as we have just seen, to about eight million in 1972 (White House Conference on Children, 1970; National Center for Social Statistics, 1972 c).

The size of AFDC payments is computed on the basis of need, as defined by the state and as reported by the applicant. In operation

[93]

this means that the family and social worker compute a budget which includes food, clothing, shelter, fuel, and some incidentals. If the family income is below this budget, eligibility is established. There is, however, considerable variability among states in budgeting practices. In 1968, monthly needs for a family of four were determined by three states to be in the range of $123 to $174, by 18 states to be in the range of $175 to $224, and by 29 states to be more than $224.

After having calculated a budget, many states do not meet their obligations because of restrictive administration and/or fiscal difficulties.

At the beginning of 1965, thirty-four states made AFDC payments that were less than 100 percent of need as determined by the state's own minimum standards. In seven states, the highest amount payable was less than 50 percent of need (Burns, 1968).

As a result of varying budgeting criteria and differences in meeting needs, there is a very high degree of variations among the states. In May, 1972, average monthly payments ranged from $8.97 per person ($46.20 per family) in Puerto Rico and $14.72 per person in Mississippi ($54.57 per family) to $71.21 per person ($259.19 per family) in New York and $78.91 per person ($281.69 per family) in Hawaii (National Center for Social Statistics, 1972).

The AFDC program has three major components: it provides money, authorizes payments for medical care, and renders social services. Until recently, social service workers had to conduct a periodic review of eligibility as well as assist the family to become self-sufficient; regulations now separate these tasks so that professional social workers can concentrate on serving the family. The caseload in most states averages about 60 families per worker. Each family can be expected to present five or six major problems, including difficulties in clothing and feeding children, interpersonal strife among family members, various health problems, school difficulties, and problems of employment. It is generally agreed that in order to help, the social worker must visit the families quite regularly. A recent report on AFDC social services in Wisconsin, however, showed that about 60 percent of the families were visited five times a year or less. Although the service component has been increased and eligibility work reduced, the typical caseload of an AFDC social worker in 1965 as charted in Table 3 is still of interest. The problems of the 63 "typical" families are painfully obvious.

TABLE 3
Profile of an AFDC caseload[a]

The caseload of 63 families includes:
  31 families with three or more children
   9 mothers who are less than 25 years old
  27 mothers who have had eight or fewer years of education
  18 mothers with no work experience
  19 mothers who are either unskilled or are domestic workers or farm laborers.
These 63 families have a total of 190 children including:
  63 who are below school age
   1 of school age but too incapacitated mentally or physically to attend school
   3 of school age who are not attending for other reasons
 132 who have no father living at home
  20 who have no mother living at home
  41 who have an incapacitated father
  46 who were born out of wedlock
These 190 children, in terms of their health, include at a minimum:
  11 who have a visual defect
   3 who have a hearing impairment
   4 with a speech defect
   3 with heart abnormalities
   4 with an orthopedic impairment
  17 with a dental impairment
   5 who are mentally retarded
   6 who have emotional or other nervous disorders.

[a] Adapted from: Welfare Administration (1966).

The charity characteristics of the AFDC program, the wide range of payments, the lack of clear purpose, and public suspicion of "welfare chiselers" together with uncertainty (in some cases, hostility) of professionals in the welfare system have resulted in a program which is generally disliked. Perhaps the most important problem is the lack of clearly stated goals. Policy directives have at times, for example, emphasized that recipients of aid should constantly seek employment; at other times they have stressed that mothers should remain at home to care for their children. Such policies usually stem from labor market needs rather than the needs of the families or their children.

Another problem involves the inadequate child rearing settings in families which, by virtue of their own problems and poor social environment, are unlikely to produce healthy growth in the young.

[95]

One national study indicated that 26 percent of the families suffered from severe marital conflict, 14 percent contained alcoholics, 9 percent had members with criminal records, etc. (Burgess and Price, 1963).

Another problem area has been in the conception of an adequate family or suitable home—a requirement for AFDC assistance. In some states, "suitable" has been interpreted so as to preclude assistance for those children most in need. Unsuitable conditions are assumed to prevail, for example, when an out-of-wedlock pregnancy occurs in an AFDC family. The denial of assistance was intended to reduce the number of cases in which an unmarried mother had another baby, but in at least one follow-up study the results appear to have been just the opposite of those desired (Bell, 1965). Recent federal regulations require local authorities to find an adequate substitute setting whenever assistance is denied on grounds of unsuitability.

The AFDC program has been bedeviled by charges of fraud almost from the very beginning. The "upright employed" have traditionally been hostile to the "loose living unemployed." Recipients of this unpopular welfare program are thus widely suspected of cheating. Interestingly, all the studies on this issue show a very small proportion of deliberate deception by recipients. Of those who are receiving assistance, only about one to five percent are ineligible, and some of those are due to professional ineptness rather than clients' deceit.

Finally, there is the "charity versus right" controversy. AFDC recipients recently organized the Welfare Rights Organization and stipulated demands including increased federal (as opposed to state or local) program control and support, bigger allowances tied more closely to need, and less intervention by case workers. Needless to say, these demands have met with considerable hostility in many sectors.

Expensive, hard to administer, painful for recipients, meager in results—AFDC has pleased practically no one. Many insist on its complete abolition, but few can agree on an acceptable replacement. The United States is probably moving toward new arrangements for child support, but the eventual format is obscured by political maneuvering, fiscal constraints, and a firmly based skepticism concerning the long-term usefulness of heavy federal expenditures on social improvement programs, given the current state of our knowledge about how to engineer such programs effectively (Schultze et al., 1972). Some analysts note regressive tendencies in current administrative regulations and legislative proposals. They point, for example, to an increasing emphasis on work requirements for recipients, including those with young children. Other analysts express hope and optimism, citing the fact that the number of children declared eligible is growing and that more and more money is being spent.

Despite many disappointments with the current program and with proposed substitutes, some major features of any new arrangement seem clearly indicated. One thoughtful writer has suggested that a new program must efficiently supplement income to an acceptable level, maintain human dignity, preserve work incentives, and carry benefits for the almost poor. Using these criteria, a number of suggestions have been advanced. President Nixon proposed in 1970, for example, legislation which would have provided for :

1) a $1600 minimum annual income for a family of four (and up to $2400 for a family of seven) with modified payments to a ceiling of $3920 combined earned and public income;

2) Continuation of welfare payments in states where they exceed the federal minimum;

3) Work training for an estimated 150,000 mothers of families headed by women;

4) Day care facilities and after-school care for 450,000 children.

This new approach to welfare has been shelved, as have all other innovative proposals, until ambiguities in the current political, social and economic situation are sorted out. What will eventually emerge is anybody's guess. (Selected references : Bell, 1965; Briar, 1969; Burgess and Price, 1963; Burns, 1968; Handler and Hollingsworth, 1969; President's Commission, 1970; Schorr, 1966; Schultze et al., 1972; Vadakin, 1968; Wiltse, 1960.)

Homemaker service programs, when available, are generally geared to families with young children in which the mother is temporarily absent because of illness or some other reason, or is present but not able to cope with maternal chores. In 1968, 17,600 families with 64,200 children were provided with this service by public welfare agencies. An additional small number of families were served by voluntary agencies (National Center for Social Statistics, 1969). In some instances homemakers are used to instruct incompetent mothers, in others to reduce the impact of demands leading to a "depleted mother syndrome," etc. Because of the complex relationships which may ensue among the mother, father, children, and the homemaker, it is recommended that the service be arranged through a social welfare agency and accompanied by casework. As a rule, homemakers are employed by an agency, although some families assume full costs.

This program provides a relatively simple, direct, and inexpensive service with profound effects in certain situations. On both logical and empirical grounds, it is abundantly clear that prompt, timely intervention can prevent unnecessary removal of children from the home, spare a family considerable grief, and save the community substantial costs. One New York City study of 40 families with 184 children demonstrated a saving of $65,000, as well as a reduced number of short-term separations and the grief these might have entailed (Children's Aid Society of New York, 1962). Success has been tempered, however, by several difficulties, including a general shortage of homemakers and geographic maldistribution of available programs. It is, again, the large urban centers which are best provided for. Other problems relate to fees to be paid by families and to difficulties experienced by homemakers, families, and even social workers in precisely defining the homemaker's functions. Is she primarily responsible for child care or for household maintenance and simple housekeeping chores—or for both? As roles and status are clarified, however, these services will probably see expansion and increased usefulness.

3. Social welfare substitution systems

Alternative care of children in a substitute family or institution may occur for a variety of reasons. In the nineteenth century the major cause of familial disruption was death of one or both parents, usually leading to permanent alternatives in the form of adoption or long-term foster care. During the twentieth century, divorce, desertion, out-of-wedlock births and mental and physical illnesses have increasingly yielded a different type of orphan—those of the living. Because the problems of today are usually not very clearcut, their solutions are often neither as obvious nor as permanent. As indicated, the tendency is to keep the child with his natural family if this is feasible, to attempt to arrange for a foster or adoptive family if it is not, and only as a last resort to use an institution. There are, though, a great variety of familial and institutional arrangements possible.

a) *Foster care* Foster care occurs when a family is disrupted and incapable of caring adequately for its dependent children. The annual rate of such disruptions in the United States has remained nearly constant over the last 100 years at about 30–35 per thousand families. Most of the children remain with relatives and friends. In 1970, some 325,000 dependent, neglected, and/or emotionally disturbed children under the age of 18 were in foster care, constituting a rate of 4.5 per thousand children. Most of these were in the almost 160,000 agency-approved foster homes; the remaining were in institutions for dependent, neglected, delinquent, retarded, or emotionally disturbed children. How many more were placed privately by their own families is unknown, but the number is substantial.

An increasingly large percentage of children in foster care has been judged to be pathological and in need of treatment. In most countries, special institutions care for a large proportion of such children. Institutional care in the United States, on the other hand, has declined continuously, though very unevenly, since the turn of the century. Thus, the proportion of foster children in family homes as opposed to institutions has risen from 35 percent in 1910 to 78 percent in 1970.

The simple dichotomy of family-institution has, it should be pointed out, been used in rather simplistic fashion. A variety of innovative approaches have been tried. They have been described under seven headings connoting a progression from familial to institutional environment :

1) *The traditional foster home* usually cares for one or two children, sometimes three or four. Children range in age. The foster parents provide a close adult-child . . . relationship in a family setting. (They) are reimbursed for part of their cost of caring for children. . . .

2) *The specialized or professional foster home* has foster parents who are selected because of their professional background or special capacity for working with agencies in care and treatment of handicapped children. . . . These families may be paid a monthly service fee, a board rate, or salary. Most . . . care for one or two children.

3) *Foster family group homes* care for more children than regular foster homes—

usually about four to six children. . . . These foster parents usually have a knack for constructive handling of a group of children. They receive board payments, subsidy, service fees, or combinations of these.

4) *The agency-owned foster home* is an apartment or house rented or owned by an agency or institution. A married couple is invited to live at the facility on a free-rent-and-board basis, plus a board rate for each child or a monthly salary. . . . If the foster parents leave, the children remain in the home. Usually about four to eight children are cared for in these agency-owned foster homes.

5) *The agency-operated group home* is usually a single dwelling or apartment owned or rented by an agency. . . . It cares for one group of about four to 12 children. Child care staff are employed and viewed as counselors or houseparents rather than as foster parents. . . . The group home reaches out to the community for many of its activities and resources. Its housing and architecture is usually indistinguishable from nearby homes or apartments.

6) *The group residence* is a . . . small institution serving about 13 to 25 children or youths. In contrast to the group home, it has *two* or more groups of children each with its own child care staff. More agency rather than community services are introduced. . . . The group residence usually differs from nearby homes and apartments by its large size and different architecture.

7) *The institution* serves from 25 to 100 or more children. It has several buildings located on the same campus which is partially or fully separated from residential neighborhoods. The institution may offer a variety of relationships and activities with adults and other children. . . . Some institutions still have a custodial atmosphere. Others have added social services, improved their group living program, and are reaching out for other clinical and remedial education services. A smaller number of institutions have become residential treatment centers with therapeutically designed group living environments within which various individual and group therapies are integrated (Gula, 1964).

The choice of facility for a child is determined by a variety of clinical and other criteria, but the inclination is always to place very young children in smaller, more intimate, family-type settings. The cost and availability of alternatives are also of considerable significance. The costs of the more professionally run foster homes (categories 2 through 5) are about twice those for the traditional foster home, and the costs of institutional care (categories 6 and 7) are about three times as high. (Selected references : Child Welfare League of America, 1959; Gula, 1964; Jenkins and Sauber, 1966; Low, 1966.)

Institutional foster care of a young child is a rare phenomenon in the U.S., although in recent years several experiments concerned with such alternate care have yielded successful results (Gardner, Burchinal and Hawkes, 1961; Gavrin and Sacks, 1963; Witmer, 1967). During the

1960's, no more than five percent of institutionalized children were less than five years old. At any given time, approximately 1200 infants and young children were in 31 infant units in the United States; another 1500 or so in temporary shelters for the abandoned and neglected; and perhaps 1500–2000 others in various children's institutions.

Nearly all young children in institutions are placed there temporarily with reluctance. There is little incentive, therefore, to build and run good institutions for children. Indeed, there is what amounts to a prohibition on the development of such facilities, stemming from the belief that they cannot adequately meet the needs of the young child. When other alternatives fail, however, young children are in fact placed in institutions, usually a hospital or a facility designed for much older children. The prophecy that institutional care is deleterious for young children thus becomes self-fulfilling, and perhaps, a major reason for the "institutionalism" which Bowlby (1952) and others found to be so prevalent. (Selected references: Hylton, 1964; Pappenfort *et al.*, 1968; Witmer, 1967.)

Familial foster care is by far the most important source of alternate care for children from disrupted families. There are probably some 160,000 foster homes in the United States at this time with a large majority caring for one child only. Social welfare agency workers search the community for appropriate foster families, interview applicants, visit them in their homes, often contact references provided by the applicants, and license the families they are satisfied will provide a healthy environment for a child. The license may limit the number, ages, and other conditions of children to be accepted for foster care. It is usually issued for a limited period, often one year, and renewed on a periodic basis. Although licensed foster family homes may accept children directly from parents seeking such care, the great majority continue to work with a licensing agency.

Following placement of a child, it is assumed that the foster care relationships will be a quadripartite arrangement involving the foster family, the child in placement, the child's own parents, and a professional worker from the agency. Usually the agency has administrative control; the natural parents retain legal control; and the foster parents make the day-to-day decisions. With this distribution of responsibilities and authority, foster family care has proven an effective arrangement only when there is reasonably good collaboration among the four parties. The function of the professional in this situation is to enhance the collaboration by appropriately matching the child to the foster family, giving them both the necessary support, working with the natural parents, and making careful plans for long-range care of the child.

As payment for his work, the foster parent receives from $25 to about $300 per month, average compensation being about $55 to $75 per month. Foster parents are thus expected to contribute their time and effort for a very low rate of financial return; the rewards are derived primarily from the satisfaction of helping children in need. Most foster families are not financially dependent on the social welfare agencies and can leave programs with relative ease; the turnover rate is about 30 percent per annum.

Agencies have operated on the general assumption that foster family care will be short term because the conditions of the child and/or his family will improve. The assumption has proven unfortunately to be overly optimistic in most cases. Two national studies have shown that only about 12–13 percent of children in foster homes return to their parents and that perhaps an equal proportion are adopted (Maas and Engler, 1959; Jeter, 1963).

A second assumption, which is perhaps less applicable to the very young child, has been that the period of foster family care will entail treatment of the child and of his natural parents. The available evidence indicates, however, that very few children in foster care are given any meaningful psychotherapy (Jeter, 1963). The notion that the families of these children receive treatment seems also to be a fallacy. In one study, for example, "more than 70 percent of the fathers and mothers . . . either had no relationship with the agencies responsible for the care of their children or their relationship was erratic or untrusting" (Maas and Engler, 1959).

A third assumption has been that the child will be placed in a stable situation until he can return to his own family, but this, too, is seldom the case. Most children who enter foster care will have more than one case worker and will be placed in more than one foster home.

Many, indeed, have four or more placements. Young children tend to be relocated less often than older children, but the long-term prospects for a stable family situation for any child in foster care are not good.

A fourth assumption has been that there will be an ample supply of foster homes. A recent study of nearly all child welfare agencies in the United States indicated, however, that there are far too few. Agency personnel indicated in the same survey that many foster families have an unrewarding and difficult role of which the community has little understanding or appreciation (Stone, 1969). The shortage of foster homes is related, in part, to recruiting new ones. Social welfare agency experience has been that only four to ten percent of the families applying as foster parents are eventually approved. Since personnel are scarce and home-study cost is high, this very low rate of approval is discouraging.

The foster home system, in spite of the difficulties, has obvious advantages. It is flexible as to numbers, permitting relatively easy and inexpensive expansion and contraction as contrasted with institutional care. It is flexible as to individualization, allowing for the matching of those things which specific families have to give with needs of specific children. It is relatively low in cost compared with institutional care. Finally, and perhaps most important, it leads to the dispersion of problem children throughout the community, avoiding their concentration in particular social settings.

In order to reduce turnover, assure greater agency control, and permit far better education of the parents involved, child welfare agencies have turned increasingly to agency-operated or controlled foster home arrangements. The several types of such arrangements have been described above. Generally, they are more expensive than the regular family homes, but allow considerably greater use of professional personnel and have greater capability to deal with unusual or disturbed children. They do not preclude the possibility of geographic dispersion of problem children nor the relative ease of adding or subtracting from the pool if necessary. They constitute a relatively new and attractive approach which has been receiving increasing attention and support.

Another increasingly common phenomenon has been pseudo-adoption. An agency assesses the probability of a child remaining in foster care for a long period of time and comes to an agreement with the foster family that it may keep the child to maturity. This arrangement tends to reduce agency and natural parent intrusion, but continues financial support. (Selected references: Maas and Engler, 1959; Stone, 1969; Taylor and Starr, 1967; Wolins, 1963.)

b) *Adoption* Given the various objections to the care of young children in institutions and the serious practical problems of caring for them in foster homes, it is not surprising that there has been a great deal of pressure toward placing young children with substitute families on a permanent basis through adoption.

About 175,000 children were adopted in the U.S. in 1970. Nearly half of these were adopted by step-parents (43 percent) or other relatives (6 percent); the others by persons unrelated to them (51 percent) (National Center for Social Statistics, 1972 b). Step-parent adoption ordinarily takes place when a couple marries and one of the partners already has children. This is a relatively simple legal procedure and does not involve agency intervention.

Non-relative adoptions are of two types in the U.S.—those carried out totally within the discretion of a social welfare agency (known generally as agency adoptions) and those independently transacted by the responsible parties and supervised by the court (referred to as independent adoptions). While independent adoptions have remained relatively constant at about 20–25,000 per annum, the number of agency adoptions has risen continuously (National Center for Social Statistics, 1968). Most children adopted by non-relatives are very young; 36 percent of the total are under one month of age, 64 percent under three months, 77 percent under six months, and 85 percent under one year. Only about 2 percent of the children adopted are six years of age or older.

About 63 percent of children adopted in 1969 and about 88 percent of children adopted by non-relatives were born out of wedlock (National Center for Social Statistics, 1970). The out-of-wedlock status of most adopted children may imply some profound changes in the statistical picture over the next several years. As abortions become easy to obtain, available services to single parents increase, and the stigma of illegitimacy declines, the supply of adoptive children may also be reduced.

Independent adoption is generally frowned upon in the United States because of the danger that the child may be placed in a home which is not conducive to his well-being and continued growth. While in every instance the final adoption requires a court review, usually carried out by a professional worker, these reviews are not always thorough nor can they reasonably lead to the withdrawal of children from questionable parental arrangements. The proportion of non-completed adoptions among independent placements, though relatively low, is nearly ten times as high as in agency placements, however. In 1962, for example, 4470 children from the state of California were placed through adoption agencies with only 85 uncompleted adoptions, while 4040 were placed independently with 792 non-completions (California Citizens' Adoption Committee, 1965). Once consummated, however, most independent adoptions seem to be reasonably successful (Witmer *et al.*, 1963).

Agency adoption is a three-step process, entailing a home study which constitutes review and approval of the family; placement of the child; and supervision of the family until the adoption becomes final. In reviewing the family's capability, the social worker takes into account the age of the adoptive parents relative to the age of the child whom they wish to adopt, their general health, the stability of their marriage, their ability to provide for the financial and social security of the child, their general capacity for parenthood, and their motives for adoption. Considerations of race and religion have varied over time. Until the 1950's both factors were of prime importance in "matching" the child and his adoptive parents. There was then a marked relaxation, first with respect to religion and then race. Recently cross-racial adoption has again come into disfavor, this time because many nonwhites are opposed to such adoptions.

Once a family is selected and a child is placed with them, there begins a trial period ranging in the various states from six to twelve months. If both the agency and the adoptive parents are satisfied, they jointly petition the court to transfer legal guardianship of the child from the agency to the adoptive parents.

Adoption has been a successful program in the United States. Findings on the adjustment of adoptive children differ from study to study, partly as a result of sampling procedures, but comparisons of adoptive children with school classmates and other normal populations reveal few, if any, meaningful differences (Kadushin, 1967). Adoptive parents tend perhaps to be more sensitive to childhood problems than are natural parents. Since they are more likely to be middle class, they are also more likely to seek treatment for their children. The somewhat higher incidence of the adopted in psychotherapeutic treatment facilities is, therefore, not easily interpreted.

There are a number of difficulties confronting adoption agencies today, the most serious being a persistent and increasing shortage of adoptive homes for some minority group children, handicapped children, and older children. Between 1958 and 1967, the annual number of adoption applications nearly doubled and the number of placements increased by 140 percent. But in the same period the ratio of approved applications per 100 available children declined from 158 to 104 (Riday, 1969). While in recent years the adoption chances of a nonwhite child may have risen somewhat, they are still consistently lower than for the white child. Between 1969 and 1972, for every 100 nonwhite children available, there were 61 approved homes; for every 100 white children there were 123 homes. In one study, approximately three-fourths of the available white children were placed in adoptive homes, while fewer than one-third of the available nonwhite children were placed (Riday, 1969). This discrepancy is not due to a lower adoption rate among minority families. Actually, the contrary is true. There were in 1967 approximately 9.2 adoptions per 1000 possible white families and 15.3 adoptions for every 1000 possible nonwhite families. Whatever the reasons, one thing is abundantly clear : the chances for adoption of nonwhite children in the United States are not good enough.

The shortage of homes has led to some rather innovative approaches, such as easing the financial consequences of adoption and attempting to be more flexible about matters such as religion, race, income of adoptive parents, etc. (c.f. Goldberg and Linde, 1969; Watson, 1972).

Exchange of information and services has also expanded the adoption potential. In addition to existing exchange arrangements within states and within the nation, the Child Welfare League of America has recently developed an Adoption Resource Exchange of North America. This projects intends to aid in finding adoptive families for children of minority groups, children with physical or emotional handicaps, older children, and groups of siblings, as well as families for the normal white infant.

Adoption is common, well accepted, openly discussed, and little if any stigma is attached to it in the United States. Clearly, we have move substantially from the time when it was a clandestine operation, deliberately concealed from family, friends, neighbors, and even the adopted child himself. More than any other American program, it embodies the preservation (or recreation) of a family for every young child—at minimal expense to the taxpayers. (Selected references: Andrews, 1968; Child Welfare League of America, 1958; Franklin and Massarik, 1969; Kadushin, 1967; Riday, 1969; Witmer et al., 1963.)

D. DAY CARE PROGRAMS

1. Background

Group day care for preschool children has, until very recently, been considered at best a necessary evil. It was undertaken during the 19th century for the protection of children, usually from poor families, whose mothers could not care for them because of employment or illness. Most programs were financed by urban churches and other charitable organizations, and had stringent restrictions upon family income level and sometimes upon the religion of the family as well.

As a consequence of this orientation and needs which were over-whelmingly disproportionate to available funds, programs tended to be under-equipped, under-staffed, and often housed in unsuitable quarters. Day care in a sense reinforced the worst aspects of child rearing in poverty homes, where overworked mothers had little energy, skill, or inclination to foster healthy growth in their children.

During the Great Depression of the 1930's, some members of the social work profession began to think of day care centers as resources to help families, rather than merely as facilities of last resort. Under the Federal Economic Recovery Act, and later the Work Projects Administration of the 1930's, funds were made available to departments of education in the states. By 1937, these programs were serving about 40,000 children in day care centers and nursery schools. Although the primary purpose was to provide employment for jobless adults, a relatively wholesome situation was created for the children. Support of some WPA nurseries continued until 1943. Meanwhile, in 1941, the Lanham Act (Community Facilities Act) was passed in response to a need for women workers in war-related industries. States were given federal funds to cover 50 percent of the costs of day care centers and nursery schools in areas where such industries were concentrated. By 1945, over 1.5 million children were involved in this program, about one out of every five children ages two to five. With the end of the war effort, however, federal support for the facilities were withdrawn. A mere five years later, there remained places for only 185,000 children in licensed day care, either in group settings or in families.

The sudden demise of day care facilities was in large measure the result of the distinct disapproval with which many professionals, religious leaders, and laymen regarded working mothers. The negative attitudes about women's working and group care of young children were translated into a welfare program designed to ensure that mothers in poverty families would remain at home with their children. The fact that women of all socioeconomic and educational levels were seeking and obtaining employment was deplored and largely ignored. Day care as a matter of public concern fell into limbo for nearly 20 years.

Not until the 1960's when the problems of the poor became a popular concern was there any real change. In 1962, amendments to the Social Security Act began to provide limited funds to state public welfare agencies as an incentive to improve day care standards and plans. With the declaration of the War on Poverty in 1965, a number of programs were organized to help poor people become competent and independent, and day care began to be seen as a means of fulfilling the basic needs of children while simultaneously permitting their mothers to accept training for employment.

By 1965, then, professional opinion about day care was changing rapidly. The earlier studies of "maternal deprivation" (see Section II, c) were re-interpreted and many professionals concluded that deprivation of stimulation and of (generalized) mothering were the real issues (Casler, 1961; Yarrow, 1961). Separation from the mother for a portion of the day would not, they suggested, lead to the dire results formerly predicted. Moreover, plentiful documentation had been accumulated demonstrating that many poverty homes were poorly suited to meet the needs of young children and that the relationships of these children with their own mothers did little to enhance cognitive or social development (c.f., Hess and Shipman, 1965). The opinions presented at a major conference in 1965 attested to the swing of professional and lay opinion toward the support of expanded day care services not only for the poor (Richmond, 1965), but for the nonpoor as well (Oettinger, 1965). An important policy paper by two leaders in the social welfare field called for expanded day care as "a social instrument to offer compensatory educational and child development experiences for the very young" (Mayer and Kahn, 1965). By summer of that year, the ambitious Project Head Start was under way (See Section VI, F).

Further amendments to the Social Security Act in 1967 required most recipients of federally funded state welfare programs to accept training for employment under the Work Incentive Program (WIN). Mothers of preschool children were exempt from this requirement, although training was made available to them. States were required to furnish facilities needed by the preschool and school-age children of WIN trainees, and the federal government agreed to meet up to 75 percent of the costs. State programs developed very slowly and uncertainly under these arrangements; further amendments in 1969 increased the federal contribution to 90 percent and made eligible a broader range of children—all previous or current recipients of welfare assistance, as well as children of those currently enrolled in training. By 1970, at least 127,000 children were receiving day care in centers or family homes under this program (U.S. Senate Committee on Finance, 1971).

In addition, numerous other special-purpose programs at the state, local, and federal levels began to involve day care. The provision of day care by private entrepreneurs began to expand also. A broad variety of public and private resources, thus, suddenly became available—but in so uncoordinated and fragmented a fashion that it was practically impossible to discern any pattern of development. In 1969, the U.S. Department of Labor identified 42 separate programs, in 15 subdivisions of 6 federal government departments, through which federal day care funds could be obtained.

Important legislation in 1969 permitted industrial employers and labor unions to engage in bargaining about day care services. Previously, employers willing to establish day care services had to take full responsibility, outside of any union contract, and it had been illegal for employees to exert collective pressure through their unions for such facilities. Hospitals, in need of nurses and other health-related personnel (80 percent of whom are women), have been among the leaders in this area (U.S. Department of Labor, 1970a), but no more than a handful of industries have as yet established day care centers.

Although day care facilities today serve only a small fraction of the young children of working mothers, they enjoy a new status in the eyes of many professionals, parents, and public-spirited citizens. Quality day care has, in addition, become one of the foremost demands and symbols of the new women's movement. Although the focus is still on poor children, day care programs are coming to be viewed as offering positive services needed as much by the children of families which are not poor (Ruderman, 1968). It is probably fair to say that children's needs are for the first time being considered equally important as the need for mothers to work.

In the midst of the movement to establish more and more day care facilities, some professionals are beginning to sound the warning that poor day care can indeed be dangerous for children, that impersonalized, regimented, and poorly conceived programs can negatively affect the minds of children as surely as adept, personal, stimulating programs can positively affect them. It is being stressed, too, that high quality programs will require extremely generous funding. Problems related to finance may indeed become a major public issue, since high-quality day care cannot be provided at a cost most parents can afford. How parents, employers, and local, state, and federal governments are to share costs is yet to be settled.

2. Forms of day care

A wide variety of child care arrangements presently exist in the United States, some involving the public sector, many involving the private (market economy) sector, and many more involving only the child's own relatives. Actual child care arrangements vary according to the situation of the family and the community and, to a minor extent, the characteristics of the child. Most out-of-family arrangements are paid for by the parents, and most facilities used for these arrangements (especially private homes) are privately run and not inspected by the states.

Ithaca Journa

FIGURE 8 Family day care mother and her charges

The *family day care home* is simply care in someone else's home. It may be used for children of any age, but is felt to be "especially suitable for infants, toddlers, and sibling groups and for neighborhood-based day care programs, including those for . . . after-school care," (Office of Child Development, 1968). Both the numbers and ages of children are strictly limited.

The *day care center* makes no attempt to simulate family living. Centers are found in homes, settlement houses, schools, churches, social centers, public housing units, or specially constructed facilities. Such centers are, for the most part, an isolated "child's world," with very few opportunities for outside contacts. The children are usually grouped by age and some centers have organized programs for cognitive, social and personal development. The sponsoring agency may be any interested institution : public or private, profit or non-profit. Most centers serve children of a specific group of mothers, and there tends to be little mixture of socioeconomic or ethnic groups. Although some centers accept two-year-olds, the *crèche* for infants and toddlers is almost unknown in the United States except for a few experimental programs. While many parents of infants are eager to place their children in day care centers because they are dissatisfied with the quality of care in home settings (Ruderman, 1968), many states prohibit group care centers for children under the ages of two or three.

The importance of the group care solution to day care needs in the United States today should not be exaggerated. Despite the increased discussion of group day care programs and the rapid appearance of new centers, the overwhelming majority of children whose mothers work are cared for in home settings of one kind or another (See Table 4).

TABLE 4
Available day care places for infants and preschool children
(licensed *and* unlicensed)

	1964	1970
Family day care homes	615,000	710,000
Day care centers	197,000	575,000
Total out-of-family day care	812,000	1,285,000
Estimated total young children of working mothers	4,500,000	4,500,000

Sources:

1964 – Low and Spindler, 1968
1970 – Westinghouse Learning Corporation, 1971

3. Working mothers — young children and child care arrangements.†

In March, 1969, approximately 4.2 million or about 30 percent of mothers of children under six years were working or looking for work. They had approximately two million children under the age of three, and 2.5 million who were three to five years old. Mothers of children under six without husbands present were more likely to work (44 percent) than those with husbands present (29 percent). Mothers of young children were less likely to work, however, than those whose youngest children were in school (See Table 5).

TABLE 5
Working mothers by age of child, 1969

Age of Youngest child	In labor force	Full-time	Part-time
Under 3	26%	16%	10%
3–5	37%	31%	6%
6–17	51%	39%	12%

Source: U.S. Dept. of Labor, 1970b

Developmental Psychology Laboratory, University of Washington
FIGURE 9   Center day care

† Most information in this section is quoted from U. S. Department of Labor (1970b, 1970c) and Low & Spindler (1968).

Opportunities for part-time employment are increasing and more mothers of very young children avail themselves of this possibility. There is concern that social welfare legislation not require mothers to make an all-or-none decision about work, and that day care be made flexible enough to preserve the mothers' opportunities for meaningful interaction with their children (Bronfenbrenner, 1969). Many women feel they function more effectively as mothers and as individuals when they are away from home for part of the day; they feel also that their children profit from this brief time

Developmental Psychology Laboratory, University of Washington
FIGURE 10   Center day care

in the company of others. Care must be taken to protect the possibility of individual and family decisions about this matter.

A national study conducted through the Bureau of the Census in 1965 sampled mothers who had worked at least 27 weeks the preceding year (Low and Spindler, 1968). Their arrangements for the care of their children are shown in Table 6. Combining the figures for children cared for in the home of someone else who was not a relative (615,000) and in group care centers (197,000), a total of 812,000 children under 6 were in placements subject to licensing procedures. Yet in 1965, fewer than half that number of licensed child care placements were available. Many young children remain

TABLE 6

Child-care arrangements: percent distribution of children
below six years of working mothers

Arrangement	Full-time Child age under 3	Full-time Child age 3 to 5	Part-time Child age Under 3	Part-time Child age 3 to 5	Mother's education Less than 4 years Hi school	Mother's education Completed Hi school	Mother's education One year or more College
Care in own home by:							
Father	9.5	10.8	20.2	24.5	14.1	14.6	14.9
Other relative							
under 16	0.6	1.3	3.7	5.0	4.6	0.8	1.9
16 or older	18.0	17.1	12.5	10.1	22.2	14.2	8.3
Non-relative							
child care only	8.7	9.7	5.7	6.8	5.4	10.0	9.9
additional chores	9.1	9.3	3.1	1.8	3.6	6.8	11.8
Care in other home by:							
Relative	22.0	14.8	9.4	8.9	17.0	13.6	11.3
Non-relative	19.8	19.5	10.3	6.5	13.4	18.3	12.8
Other arrangements:							
Group Care Center	4.8	9.7	0.9	1.5	3.4	6.4	7.3
Child looked after							
self	0.2	0.3	0.9	1.0	0.5	0.4	0.3
Mother (at work)	6.4	6.9	33.3	31.6	16.0	13.8	19.3
Work only in							
school hours	—	0.8	—	2.4	—	0.9	2.3
Other	1.0	—	—	—	—	0.2	—
	100.0	100.0	100.0	100.0	100.0	100.0	100.0

Source: Low and Spindler (1968). Tables A-3, A-5, A-21.

in inadequate circumstances and many mothers are prevented from working because they can not find or afford child care of a quality they will accept.

4. Costs of day care

Operational costs of day care vary by type of care, quality, and the region in which it is offered. An estimate by the U.S. Office of Education (1969) suggested a minimum for custodial group day care of three to five year olds at $1,245 per child per year; an acceptable general developmental program, including parent education, at $2,320. For a program of family day care for children under three, levels ranging from minimal supervision to a comprehensive, enriched developmental program were suggested at $1,423, $2,032, and $2,372 per child per year. One recent study has estimated a core day care program for children three to five at $2,349 per child per year for a center of 25 children, with a reduction of $2,189 for a center with 75 children (ABT Associates, 1971). It is estimated that building a day care facility for 100 children in 1972 would have cost about $135,000, more or less depending upon the locale (Fishman, 1970).

Many professionals are thus appalled by the very low levels of funding presently being suggested by federal, state, and local governments—as little at $400 per year (Todd, 1972). It has been proposed that parents in need might be issued vouchers by which they could pay for day care under any arrangements they chose to make, the vouchers funded by the government on a sliding scale according to income, and worth from $400 to $1,300 (Parker and Knitzer, 1971; Todd, 1972).

The actual annual costs of day care purchased by state welfare agencies for child care under the AFDC program averaged $1,140 in 1970 (Long, 1971). The average annual cost per child in 20 better-than-average centers recently surveyed was $1,632 (ABT Associates, 1971). These centers tended to pay low salaries to personnel at all levels. They offered fairly good programs that were, however, far from ideal. Even so, mothers who arrange for child care themselves typically pay far less. The average costs per year under the programs of the Social Security Act in which the mothers were reimbursed for their child care costs ranged from $315 to $428 per child (Long, 1971). Estimates of average annual costs to families in general are not much higher than $500 to $1,000 per child, depending on the region of the country, type of care, etc. How can there be such diversity? The answer seems to be that most mothers who use out-of-family care make arrangements with neighbors or friends and pay minimal amounts for what is likely to be very low quality care.

A great many mothers find it possible only to "park" their young children with a woman who assumes responsibility for too many children, and who is often available only because she is unemployable due to low ability, poor health, advanced age, or too large a family of her own. These conditions account, in part, for the fact that family day care mothers, even in licensed homes, often have less than a high school education, lack any formal training in child care, and have no contact with professional child care organizations (Ruderman, 1968). The situation is improving to some extent under pressures for professionalization and higher quality care, but costs must consequently be expected to rise.

It is significant that, in the period 1969–1971, a number of commercial enterprises seriously contemplated establishing chains of day care centers, and a few even opened their doors. This movement came to a rather abrupt halt, however, because it soon became obvious that day care of acceptable quality is simply not a money-making proposition. Care for the very young child cannot be justified solely on grounds that it allows mothers to work and therefore to be economically productive. Many mothers cannot earn enough to meet the costs of day care and other work-related expenses, especially if they have several young children. If day care actually leads, however, to enhanced development for the child and/or ultimately greater independence and fulfillment for the mother and family, then costs must somehow be judged accordingly.

5. Standards for day care

The quality of care varies dramatically from one setting to another. There are, for example, a few very high quality experimental centers with comprehensive programs which include intensive educational, health, and family components and a high ratio of staff to children (e.g., Robinson and Robinson, 1971). In addition, there are some reasonably good public and private centers with good staffs which are of acceptable quality. The standards of the public centers are, incidentally, generally higher than those of the private centers (Ruderman, 1968). The great majority of centers are of questionable quality, offering little more than custodial care. The quality of family day care homes is similarly diverse. It is probably safe to say, however, that the standards for the homes are, in general, even lower than for centers.

Each state sets its own licensing standards. Of necessity, these deal primarily with objective characteristics and leave open to question and erratic enforcement the less easily defined aspects of a healthy environment for young children (Wolins, 1968). Until the advent of federal funding, most state bureaus operated with token staff and usually without any provisions for mandatory licensing. Arrangements for care were considered private matters between the family and the individual or center providing the service. Few states systematically closed centers or homes which did not meet minimal standards. Recommended standards for day care have now been published by several national professional organizations such as the American Public Health Association (Dittman, 1967), the Child Welfare League of America (1969; Provence, 1967), and the American Academy of Pediatrics (1971).

The federal government has also established a set of minimal requirements, which must be met by facilities receiving its funds (Office of Child Development, 1968, 1972). These include strict limitations on the number of children in a family day care home and specifications of minimal staffing ratios according to the age of the child; safety standards; space requirements; provision for rest and nutrition; competency standards for caregivers; admission procedures; parent involvement, etc. No more than six children per caregiver may be present (12 in all) in any family day care setting, including the day care mother's own children. When infants or toddlers are present, the ratio is reduced to one to four or five, or even fewer. In a day care center, the ratio of caregivers must equal or exceed one for three infants, four toddlers, or seven preschool children. These ratios are defined in actual hours of care available for child contact and ratios may vary from one time of day to another. Noncontact personnel (secretaries, cleaning personnel) are not included. "Each child must be provided with experience, activities, equipment, guidance and support that contribute to physical and emotional development and health; develop mental abilities in such areas as language, numbers, spatial relations, abstraction and memory; foster individual and group interactions which contribute to general social competence."

In addition, the sponsoring agency must arrange for periodic monitoring of the program; must see to it that each child receives regular health evaluations and assistance in obtaining treatment; must provide psychological and social services; must see to it that caregivers and operators have the opportunity for continued training, etc. These requirements are, of course, relevant only to programs receiving federal funds (mainly operating under agency sponsorship for the poor), but they tend to set standards for other programs, especially those of a nonprofit nature, and may also affect state licensing procedures.

The United States is thus establishing a pattern of adult:child ratios which is among the highest in the world. It is also setting standards for child development which clearly reject the suitability of custodial care—though the nature of educational and developmental services are at the option of the contracting agencies and the caregivers.

It is current practice to keep children out of group care if they are suffering even minor illness. Moreover, the increased work necessary to maintain hygienic conditions for very young children has been one of the reasons that group care has not often been considered suitable for infants and toddlers. The American Academy of Pediatrics, considered the most authoritative group on health matters for young children, in 1971 issued a new and provocative set of standards for day care centers for infants and children under three years of age. To quote from this publication:

Current research indicates that children who are ill generally have harbored the infectious agent for several days prior to the appearance of symptoms and that the agent may have been present in the day care center population for a considerable period of time prior to its first appearance as symptomatic illness. Since day care is one method of assisting mothers and supplementing family care, children who are ill could be cared for in the day care center at the mother's discretion. . . .

The committee considered the value of cleaning of toys and other items the children come in contact with. Although such cleaning may be desirable from the aesthetic standpoint, the scrubbing of toys daily does not constitute a significant safeguard against the spread of infection. The staff should be attractively clothed; but frequent changes of clothing and the wearing of special scrub gowns or similar attire designed to prevent the spread of infection is thought to be unnecessary and should not be required (pp. 1–2).

6. Size of programs and staff-child relationships

A recent study of 50 public and private day care centers revealed some interesting differences among programs. The smaller programs, serving 30–60 children, tended to be of higher quality than those serving over 60 children. In the latter, there was much more emphasis on rules and restrictions; teachers appeared less sensitive, more often neutral or distant. "Conversely, in smaller centers . . . provision of opportunities for pleasure, wonder, and delight was significantly higher." In the larger centers, play areas were less well organized, and children tended to remain with their own age groups almost exclusively. While the larger centers had better trained teachers and an absence of crowding, the children seldom appeared to be highly involved or interested—the air was much more that of an "institutionalized" establishment, impersonal and devoid of intense or personal interactions (Prescott, 1970).

7. Parent participation and parent-staff relationships

Until recently there had been little systematic effort to involve parents in day care activities. Professional staffs and advisory boards of public-spirited citizens were thought to know what was best for the families and children. Communication with parents was often very restricted and channeled into formal contacts. One survey found, for example, that three out of four center directors severely limited teachers' and caretakers' discussions with parents (Prescott, 1965).

Even with closer contacts between parents and day care workers the two worlds of the child will probably continue to be more-or-less conflicting and uncoordinated. Prescott (1965) found systematic differences between attitudes expressed by mothers and day care personnel in methods of discipline and in their standards for the children. Parents were more often punishing, expected more immediate obedience, and were less attuned to the developmental levels of the children; they also had higher standards in areas which to them had moral connotations (e.g., bad words, aggression against adults, appropriate sex roles). Teachers were more often demanding with respect to behaviors concerned with the maintenance of order and routine. There were, of course, substantial differences among mothers which were somewhat related to their socioeconomic status.

Counseling services in public welfare agencies have tended to discourage mothers from what might have been healthy interchanges with center staffs. Organized day care centers have been, to some extent, reserved for children of poor, sick, or inadequate mothers who have had to justify their eligibility and abide by social welfare agency decisions. The mother who has wished to work or study, or who has found the full-time care of young children onerous, has often been made to feel guilty and uncomfortable. The mother whose child has been granted entry has been subtly expected to be grateful and uncritical. Changes from custodial to developmental goals of day care are changing this situation. Also, social workers now more often recognize that working mothers and their children are for the most part capable and well adjusted (Child Welfare League of America, 1969).

Mothers' degree of satisfaction with the arrangements they have made for child care reflects a great many factors, including how well the caretaker likes young children, how well the mother agrees with the caretaker on various aspects of child care, what the mother expects the caretaker to accomplish, the number of children being cared for, the age and sex of the child, the convenience, expense, and so on. Mothers who are less likely to be satisfied with their arrangements have children younger than 3, have more than one child, have boys, are from the middle-income brackets, and have a personal sense of being overburdened (Ruderman, 1968). Mothers tend to prefer care in their own homes by relatives, sitters, and to a lesser extent, fathers, but not by siblings. Out of their own homes, mothers tend to prefer relatives' homes to family day care homes or similar arrangements. Most satisfied of all, however, are mothers whose children are in day care centers, despite the fact that they expect more of the centers' personnel than is the case in any other caretaking situation.

8. The federal government and day care

There was, during the short period from 1965 to 1970, a proliferation of government sponsored day care programs, most of which were developed to combat, in one way or another, the problems of the poor. Several key programs, including AFDC and WIN (see Section VI, C), were organized under the provisions of the Social Security Act as amended in 1967 and 1970. Another series of programs, including Head Start and Parent and Child Centers (see Section VI, E), were organized as major components of the War on Poverty under the Office of Economic Opportunity.

Under a 1967 amendment to the Economic Opportunity Act, Congress directed that efforts be made to coordinate day care programs at the federal, state, and local levels. Two major expressions of this mandate have occurred. First, an interagency Federal Panel on Early Childhood was established to coordinate some of the multiple federal programs relating to early childhood. It has published the Federal Interagency Day Care Requirements (Office of Child Development, 1968), compiled comprehensive information bearing on federal programs for young children, and made recommendations for future action. Second, as the outgrowth of a recommendation made by the Federal Panel, the "4-C Program" (Community Coordinated Child Care) has tried to coordinate all the various child-care programs within single communities, regions, and states. This very low-budget program receives no new money for day care itself, however, and only a very limited grant to cover a tiny administrative staff. Furthermore, it does not even exist in many communities.

Since 1954, some deduction from taxable income for child care has been permitted for single parents and for low income married parents, both of whom worked. In 1972, the annual income below which deductions are allowed was raised from $6,000 to $25,000, thus drastically increasing the number of eligible families.

9. Results of day care

Research into the effects of ordinary, custodial day care is practically nonexistent in the United States. In view of the controversy which has surrounded this area, this fact is indeed surprising. The data which do exist are more properly labelled "educational" than "day care" in the sense that the services studied have really been compensatory education programs which have used day care only as a convenient vehicle (see Section VI, E).

Prior to the 1960's, few researchers were interested in the problems of day care, and the professionals involved in day care were not research-oriented. Now that educators, psychologists, pediatricians, and others with research training have become involved, they have been stymied in a number of instances because the difficulties in finding really equivalent groups of children in different settings, by the mobility of families, by the unwillingness of day care operators to have their work evaluated, and so on.

One concern which has troubled many people about day care has, however, been at least partially answered. Despite fears that day care would interfere with the early, strong relationship between mother and infant or toddler, observations of children who have received day care from infancy (usually around one year of age) to age $2\frac{1}{2}$ or 3 have found no diminution in the child's attachment to his mother, as compared with children without day care (c.f. Caldwell *et al.,* 1970).

E. CONVENTIONAL EDUCATIONAL PROGRAMS

If Americans do not believe that "all men are *created* equal," they do tend to believe that all men can be *made* equal through education. At the same time that schools are blamed for many social ills—the alienation of youth, racial inequalities, poor physical fitness, etc.— effective "cures" are vigorously pursued through educational programming (e.g., sex education, driver education, compensatory education, etc.).

In particular, the importance of the early years has been stressed by developmental psychologists, psychiatrists, educators, sociologists, and others. It is now the popular view that the first four to six years are the most important in determining the basic nature of cognitive, emotional, and social behavior patterns. This view has been taken rather seriously by better educated, more affluent families, as shown by the widespread development of private nursery schools and kindergartens. Until very recently, in fact, it was overwhelmingly the case that nursery schools were for the affluent and day care centers were for the poor. This distinction is much less true today; public nursery schools have been opened in great numbers for the poor and day care centers have become more popular with all families. Even so, there are sufficient substantive differences between educational programs for the majority and compensatory education for the disadvantaged to warrant discussing them as separate systems.

Educational programs for the years prior to the first grade of elementary school can be divided into three distinct phases: home, nursery school, and kindergarten.

1. Ages 0–3: Home and mother

The earliest years have been almost exclusively the province of the family. Fundamental emotional and social development has been thought to progress most favorably within the context of the home, building upon a close relationship with the mother and, to a lesser extent, other family members. Only recently have many investigators also begun to be interested in the function of early cognitive experiences in shaping the child's later growth (see Section II). This new concern has been popularized for parents through articles such as "How to Raise Your Child's IQ," "How to Teach Your Baby to Read," etc. Educational toys for infants and toddlers have multiplied in the marketplace with astonishing rapidity, and it seems clear that most middle class mothers are more aware now than previously of the possibilities of constructive play with their babies, the importance of language and other kinds of stimulation, and the potential for affecting the course of intellectual development. In fact, this aspect of motherhood has probably been exaggerated and is now perhaps out of balance with other aspects of growth.

2. Ages 3 and 4 : Nursery schools

Nursery schools were first popularized in the United States by university departments of psychology and teachers' colleges which started them as experimental centers. Others were soon established for children of the well-to-do.

a) *Background and philosophy* Out of concern for the well-being of children living under conditions of economic depression, and to provide constructive employment for adults, the federal government began in 1933 under the Federal Economic Recovery Act and later under the Work Projects Administration, to support nursery schools and day care centers. By the time America entered World War II, 1,500 federally supported nursery schools and 1,000 private nursery schools were in existence. Funds were diverted to day care at that point, and federal support of the part-day educational programs was withdrawn. The crucial decision to keep nursery schools separate from public school systems apparently occurred in 1933, when an independent National Advisory Committee, representing concerned professional and parent organizations, undertook the guidance of the Federal projects. This separation made a difference in their clientele and thus in their very nature.

It is not surprising that the predominant philosophy of nursery schools has reflected the ease with which children from favorable home environments benefit from a generally supportive, relatively non-structured and stimulating environment. With the trend toward urbanization and small, nuclear families, the preschool has been seen by many as a place for the child to "flower" naturally, to have access to space, freedom, and experiences with other children which formerly constituted the way of life in rural settings (Stone and Church, 1968). A typical manual states that, "The job of a thoughtful teacher of young children is to establish a situation full of interesting opportunities and then let the children respond as they will to a world that is constantly revealing itself to them in a variety of ways," (Alschuler, 1942).

Goals of nursery school education have generally focused on social-emotional growth, motor skills, and, to a lesser extent, intellectual growth, with emphasis on such factors as creativity, imagination, expressiveness, verbal skills, and knowledge of the world of nature. Specialists have tended to emphasize the "whole child" and to reject specific curricula in favor of spontaneous growth through play. Although there exist no explicit sets of directives or values in most nursery schools, the teacher has been expected to offer affection, to encourage independence, and to create the possibility of meaningful play and learning situations. Her role has thus been seen as supportive rather than actively educative. The conviction that biologically regulated timetables guide the maturation of skills underlay the original establishment of this approach, but it was supported by the observation that most children from stimulating homes do develop rather well with the kinds of opportunities provided.

This orientation, often termed "developmental" by its advocates, but "traditional" by its opponents, is still found today in most nursery schools, although many others are based on more contemporary theories of cognitive development. A number of the new curriculum approaches are described in a later section. They have been developed, for the most part, under experimental programs initiated since 1965, and are generally characterized by more specifically defined goals and more structured programming of content. Many professionals have charged that these new programs "force feed knowledge," and that they will turn children into "intellectual automatons," devoid of spontaneity. Nursery school education, then, continues to be the subject of spirited debate.

b) *Administration and staffing* Nursery schools exist in a variety of contexts. Some are commercial ventures; some are sponsored by churches and other charitable groups; some are run by the parents themselves, as cooperatives; and some are within universities and colleges to serve primarily as training centers and as sources of research subjects. There are no official national standards for nursery school programs, nor do nursery school administrators or parents take seriously the guidelines published by any respected authority or professional association. An apparently agreed-upon goal is a class of up to 15 three-year-olds or 20 four-year-olds, with a trained teacher and an assistant. Actual situations vary, however, from training programs so "enriched" that there are occasionally more adults than children, to "backyard schools" which offer little more than custodial care. Because many states require no license or certification for programs lasting only a few hours each day, many nursery schools are run by untrained persons who lack adequate resources and are completely out of touch with new developments.

Most programs operate for two or three hours, two to five mornings a week. Some nursery schools have afternoon sessions for a second group of children. Meals are seldom served except for a light snack. Because even high quality programs may differ greatly in the type of space, parent involvement, ratio of children to teachers, etc., cost estimates are very hazardous. It is likely that effective nursery programs are being run for perhaps $500 per child per year or for even less, when attendance is limited to two half-days per week for three-year-olds and three half-days per week for four-year-olds, as is often the case. Such programs seldom provide health or other supportive services except for occasional parent discussion groups. There have been no studies relating effectiveness of nursery school programs to cost, and it is far from clear that, above a certain minimum, program benefits are directly related to expenses.

c) *Users of programs* Almost 40 percent of young children three to five years old in 1971 were enrolled in part-time nursery schools or kindergartens or full-time day care centers offering an educational program. This figure, which includes both compensatory and conventional programs, represented an all-time high for the United States; the proportion was about 25 percent as recently as 1964. This substantial increase is, in part, a function of the large number of programs which have been recently established for the children of poor families. Public kindergartens and private nursery schools have also expanded, and at the same time there has been some reduction in the number of children in this age range. It is still the case, however, that enrollment is related to a number of economic, social and regional factors, so that children from higher income families in urban or sub-urban areas outside the Southeast are more likely to be enrolled (see Tables 7 and 8). At ages three and four, the enrollment of nonwhite children is greater at each socioeconomic level than is the enrollment of white children. At low income levels, this is probably a function of the greater number of nonwhites who have children in full-day

TABLE 7

Percentage of children three to five years old enrolled in preprimary programs by place of residence: October, 1971[a]

Age and race	Total U.S.	North East	North Central	South	West	Central City	Suburbs	Non-Urban
3 years	12.4	9.2	8.4	15.6	16.9	15.8	15.7	6.7
white	12.0	9.0	9.0	15.1	17.1	14.9	15.9	6.3
nonwhite	14.1	10.3	10.6	16.9	15.0	17.6	14.4	9.0
4 years	29.8	33.5	27.2	28.1	31.7	35.6	36.7	18.7
white	29.6	32.6	25.4	29.2	32.7	35.4	36.7	18.6
nonwhite	30.8	39.5	40.2	24.8	24.7	35.9	36.6	19.5
5 years	73.7	75.8	88.2	55.6	78.9	77.0	79.1	65.8
white	75.2	77.2	88.9	55.2	79.1	78.3	79.9	68.5
nonwhite	66.4	67.0	82.8	56.8	77.2	74.4	71.1	48.8

[a] From Barker (1972), Tables 3 and 4. An additional 9.6 percent white and 15.7 percent nonwhite five-year-olds are in elementary school programs.

TABLE 8

Percentage of children three to five years old enrolled in preprimary programs by family income: October, 1971[a]

Age and race	Total U.S.	Under $3000	$3000–$4999	$5000–$7499	$7500–$999	$10,000 and over
3 years	12.4	11.9	6.1	5.9	9.5	20.5
white	12.0	7.9	5.5	4.9	8.6	20.0
nonwhite	14.1	16.7	6.9	10.9	18.6	28.4
4 years	29.8	27.0	25.3	21.7	23.5	41.3
white	29.6	25.6	22.4	20.3	21.6	41.0
nonwhite	30.8	29.1	32.7	27.9	37.5	44.5
5 years	73.7	60.0	66.2	68.1	76.7	80.9
white	75.2	59.2	66.0	68.6	77.2	81.8
nonwhite	66.4	60.7	66.5	66.0	72.8	68.6

[a] From Barker (1972), Table 5. An additional 9.6 percent white and 15.8 percent nonwhite five-year-olds are in elementary school programs.

TABLE 9
Percentage of children three to five years old enrolled in
preprimary programs by full-day vs. part-day: October 1971[a]

Age and race	Total U.S.	Poverty Areas		Non-Poverty Areas	
		Full-day	Part-day	Full-day	Part-day
3 years	100.0	60.0	40.0	28.1	71.9
white	100.0	58.3	41.7	23.2	76.8
nonwhite	100.0	61.5	38.5	56.1	43.9
4 years	100.0	19.7	80.3	16.2	83.8
white	100.0	3.3	96.7	13.7	86.3
nonwhite	100.0	30.4	69.6	33.7	67.5
5 years	100.0	24.3	75.7	9.2	90.9
white	100.0	24.2	75.8	7.4	92.6
nonwhite	100.0	24.2	75.8	20.8	79.8

[a] From Barker (1972), Table 10.

TABLE 10
Percentage of enrolled children three to five years old in
public and nonpublic programs: October, 1971[a]

	Public	Non-public
Prekindergarten		
white	25.2	74.8
nonwhite	59.3	40.7
Kindergarten		
white	80.3	19.7
nonwhite	90.5	9.5

[a] From Barker (1972), Figure 2.

compensatory programs; at upper levels, it may reflect the large
number of working mothers and the emphasis these families place
on education.

d) *Parent Participation*   Parent roles vary from complete lack of
contact to responsible participation in cooperative nurseries staffed
partially or entirely by parents. The relationship of staff to parents
tends to be that of professional to lay person. Nursery schools are seen
as offering enrichment opportunities which are sought out and paid
for by parents. It is natural that parents consult the teacher for
advice, for they have selected the particular school and sometimes

the particular teacher for their child. Many nursery schools make an effort to involve parents in visiting the school while it is in session, in periodic parents' meetings and in teacher conferences. The parent remains essentially an outsider, however, because there is no role to be played except as onlooker. Fathers and other family members tend to be even less involved than mothers in both private and public nursery schools.

e) *Content* Most nursery schools present a variety of toys and equipment for free play, arranged in a kind of lavish "buffet" from which the child may pick and choose. Mainstays are large blocks and trucks, housekeeping and doll equipment, "dress up" clothes, puzzles, toys which encourage fine motor skills, picture books, and outdoor equipment for climbing, sand play, swinging, wheel play, and water play. Role-playing is facilitated by the setting, and the preferred toys are simple and functional, lending themselves to a variety of uses in the child's imaginative play. Most programs include opportunities for abundant creative expression activities with clay, paint, papier maché, paste, crayons and other media; nature study with class-room pets and plants; and music through records, simple instruments, and songs. Although help is also given with a few self-care activities needed during the program (e.g., putting on boots and coats), most training of this sort is expected to occur at home.

Much of the morning in the usual nursery school is devoted to free play. A child may spend his entire time in a single activity or flit from one to another as he pleases. The teacher may try to guide his choices, encouraging some variety and a reasonably sustained attention span, but in general the only essential rules communicated to the child are that he must "play fair" by sharing toys with others, taking turns, etc. In nursery schools with larger staffs, each principal play area tends to be staffed by an adult who serves as a resource for the children who come to her.

Interspersed with free play periods are times when the children are expected to act in concert. Snacks (e.g., juice and crackers) are served at mid-morning, for example, and children wash their hands before snacks, then eat together. There may be group activities such as singing, dancing, stories, or a field trip, but the disinterested child is seldom required to participate. Some nursery schools, of course, emphasize structured activities much more than do others, and the choices open to a child will differ according to the resources available and the cleverness of the teacher.

Although "socialization" is usually presented as a major goal of the nursery school, in fact explicit socialization training rarely takes place. There is reliance, instead, on the informal, natural give-and-take of children, the emulation of admired models, and the child's maturing control over impulsive acts as he discovers their consequences. Many teachers do not, for example, intervene in a fight between two children unless one seems physically endangered; it is tacitly assumed that some sort of "pecking order" will be established among the children, and that the oppressed will learn to "stick up for their own rights." Where helpfulness is specifically encouraged, it is more likely to be helping the teacher (e.g., to bring out snacks, to mix paints, to clean a table) than helpfulness toward other children. Neither teacher nor children have a concept of the "children's group."

The role of the teacher consists of setting the stage and being alert to the "teachable moment" when a child's spontaneous play has led him to the point at which a crucial bit of information would be

Ithaca Journal

FIGURE 11   Nursery school

Developmental Psychology Laboratory, University of Washington.

FIGURE 12   Nursery school

especially helpful, or a novel idea would enrich his exploration. Operating without an explicit curriculum, the good teacher is alert to a wide variety of developmental needs. On the play ground, for example, she is likely to be busy with one child after another, giving this one a swing, that one some help on a balancing board; standing at the bottom of a slide to reassure a timid child; setting up a group of packing boxes which soon become a ship, store, house, or fire station to some of the boys and girls; explaining to two boys that throwing sand is not allowed because sand hurts eyes; asking a little girl who seems frustrated by her toppling sand castle whether some water could help; kissing a bruised knee "to make it well"; and keeping an eye on things in general to be certain that no dangerous situation develops. Occasionally, the teacher or assistant teacher may introduce a circle game or clapping rhyme with a small group of children; or they may take advantage of a natural occurrence such as a fallen leaf on the playground to point out the veins and coloration to the few children who are nearby. If there are sufficient adults the children may go as a group on a neighborhood walk. When the children are indoors, a considerable amount of teacher time is likely to be occupied with facilitating creative endeavors by the children— e.g., preparing clay or papier-maché, mixing paints, putting on aprons, changing paper on the easels, hanging completed paintings to dry, and admiring the children's productions. Teachers seldom "teach" more than the simple mechanics of how to keep paint from running or how to blend two colors.

The most important exceptions to the role described above are to be found in two groups of nursery schools: the first follwing the work of Maria Montessori, and the second, the work of B. F. Skinner and his students. Although there are disagreements among various groups in the Montessori movement, all emphasize nonverbal manipulation of objects designed to be self-teaching, with the teacher in a background role. Most Montessori schools are privately run and are members of one of the Montessori associations. For the Skinnerians, socialization and cognition are both specific goals for the teacher, who carefully reinforces behaviors she wants to encourage, and for the most part ignores behaviors which she considers inappropriate. Most nursery schools of this type are in academic and/or clinical settings, where teacher: child ratios are particularly favorable.

The nursery school's place in the community reveals the isolation in which it exists, completely separated from the public schools. Aside from the regular staff and mothers who occasionally visit, other adults are rarely in evidence. It is clear that the children can claim this place as their own world, and that the adults' world is "somewhere else."

f) *Results* Nursery education for middle-class children is considered by most specialists and parents to be positive but not indispensable for the young child growing up in a stimulating home with plentiful neighborhood companions and good play space. Despite the existence of a large number of studies seeking to evaluate the effects of nursery school (Swift, 1964), the evidence remains inconclusive. Almost all of the nursery schools which have been evaluated have been exceptionally high quality according to the standards of the day. Even with these programs, although short range gains in social behavior (e.g., Hattwick, 1936; Jersild and Fite, 1939) and IQ (Robinson and

[133]

Robinson, 1971) have been apparent, enduring long-range gains have seldom been found (Bronfenbrenner, 1973; Brown and Hunt, 1961). Research in this area is hampered by many factors: equivalent non-nursery school control groups are difficult to locate; children attending school have been sent there by parents for reasons which cannot be easily ascertained; middle-class children tend to show gains in IQ without special intervention; early-beginners may be held back in school by other children who have not had nursery school experience; and finally, run-of-the-mill nursery programs have not been easily accessible to investigators.

3. Age 5: Kindergarten

Kindergarten is now an accepted part of the public school system in most states and communities, but in many ways, this year constitutes a no-man's land in the educational configuration, only one of the gateways through which children first encounter school. Some three- and four-year-olds begin "readiness preparation" with nursery school, while as many as a quarter of six-year-olds in first grade have had no preschool experience at all. Kindergarten, though, is known as the "readiness" year, the year when a child prepares for "regular" school.

a) *Background and philosophy* The first kindergarten, a private class, was established in America in 1855 by a disciple of Froebel, and the first public kindergarten was established in 1873. It soon became clear that, unlike the nursery school, kindergarten would be in large part a public school function. Since World War I, private programs have accounted for only 10–15 percent of the total enroll-ment, mainly in the cities (Simon and Grant, 1969). Growth of kindergartens was fairly steady, though slow, until a spurt of expansion in the 1960's. By 1971, approximately 3,263,000 children were en-rolled in public and private kindergartens. (72 percent of all five-year-olds, plus 12 percent of four-year-olds and 5 percent of six-year-olds).

Philosophy Kindergarten education is based for the most part on the works of Froebel, Dewey, and Montessori, although the original writings of these leaders are not widely read anymore, and many trained teachers are unaware of this heritage. Many of the usual activities are basically those suggested by Froebel, modified over the years in the American milieu. Froebel's standards for fine motor skills have been lowered, for example, and his materials have also been enlarged to fit young hands. From Montessori came a number of self-teaching materials, the insistence upon the importance of self-help and housekeeping responsibility, and the notion that the teacher should remain in the background as an inspiration, guide, and resource. The influence of John Dewey is seen in the emphasis on the present as well as the future in children's lives, on their happiness, expressiveness, and creativity. More contemporary cognitive theorists, learning theorists, developmental psychologists, and educators have also made their mark on various kindergarten programs, but few conventional, non-compensatory kindergartens of the nation are in the forefront of innovation or adaptation to a changing world. Indeed, most are not very different today from kindergartens a quarter century ago.

b) *Administration and staffing* The public school system is responsible for all matters related to public kindergartens, but the relationship is almost impossible to describe. Such involved, complex and varied patterns of interaction exist among the parties involved that what holds for one school district may not be at all true for another.

Responsibility for the schools is mostly a state and local affair. The division of responsibilities between state and local groups differs from one state to another. The federal government funds some programs, but in almost all instances, state or local matching funds are required and control of the programs remains with state and/or local authorities. The states provide basic funding for schools and set certification requirements for teachers and other personnel. Some school districts add to the funds provided by the state. A variety of authority patterns exist in such matters as planning curricula, choosing textbooks, planning and funding school buildings, and determining staffing patterns.

The schools of each community are under the jurisdiction of a local Board of Education. There are some 20,000 or more independent school districts in the nation, each with its own elected or appointed

Board. The Board, made up for the most part of prominent local citizens, has responsibility for policy matters, overall fiscal decisions, personnel decisions, etc. It selects a superintendent of schools, who is the chief administrative officer for the school district. The number, complexity, and relationship of his staff to the individual school, its principal, and classroom teachers, will vary according to district size and local custom. In some, for example, the individual teacher may be completely free to determine her approach with the children; in others, she will have a fairly specific curriculum guide and a set of materials which she is expected to use.

Provision of kindergartens is, for the most part, a local affair, with most state governments having passed permissive legislation allowing but not requiring local school districts to establish classes. Sometimes there is limited state funding or none at all; in 1968–1969, for example, 17 states provided no state aid for public kindergartens. The growth of the kindergartens began in the big cities, which have usually been more willing to vote additional taxes for school support, but they are now found in most communities.

The nationwide average per-pupil cost of the public school systems, omitting expenditures for new buildings, was $783 in 1969–70, varying among the 50 states from $438 to $1,237. The usual school year is September–June. Separate accounting for kindergartens is not available, but in most school systems it is approximately half as expensive as the other elementary grades because the children attend only a half day ($2\frac{1}{2}$ to 3 hours). Although some schools provide a teacher's aide, most classes are taught by a single teacher who has both morning and afternoon sessions. Tuition for private kindergartens generally falls in the range of $225 to $450 per year for half-day programs.

Kindergarten teachers are typically required to have a professional teaching certificate (see Section VII), although in many states it need not be based on special preparation to teach kindergarten. There are about 43,000 kindergarten teachers in the United States, almost all of whom are women. In 1969, the average class consisted of approximately 28 children.

c) *Users of the program* Every child of appropriate age is eligible for the public school programs which exist in his locality, with the rare

Developmental Psychology Laboratory, University of Washington.

FIGURE 13   Outdoor play at kindergarten

exception of the child whose mental retardation or other gross handicap makes school placement inappropriate. (States are required to
provide special classes for such children by age seven.) Typically a
child must be age five by some date between October 1 and December
31 of the year he enters kindergarten. A few districts make provision
for early admission of unusually bright children.

In October, 1971, 71.8 percent of all children then five years old
were enrolled in kindergarten; another 10.7 percent of this age group
were in first grade; and 1.9 percent were in prekindergarten programs
—a total of 84.4 percent (Barker, 1972). Approximately one in six
of these children was in a private school. As seen in Tables 7–10, there
are socioeconomic and ethnic differences in attendances of five-year-
old children. Income and place of residence are the strongest factors;
race has a more variable relationship with school attendance.

A number of factors enter into the process by which kindergarten
facilities are made available and are used by families. Local willingness and ability to pay extra taxes is a major factor. Where there are

no public kindergartens, Project Head Start tends to provide for children of poor families, while children of relatively wealthy families attend private kindergartens. Not surprisingly, most districts make little effort to see that eligible children enroll in kindergarten. Initiative is left to the parents; it is the very children who need kindergarten the most, therefore, who are likely to be left out.

d) *Parent participation* Parents may actually have less contact with kindergarten teachers than with subsequent elementary school teachers because of the double shifts of kindergartens. Many public schools schedule one or two routine conferences during the year, but these are usually too brief to provide any opportunity for real communication. With "problem" children, there is, naturally, special interaction between the parents and the school staff, and special conferences are also available to parents requesting them. Newsletters are often used to facilitate communication with and among parents.

The Parent Teacher Association (PTA) is a strong force in some schools and exists in some form in nearly all schools. Through this association, parents (mainly mothers), can enter actively into the school program by volunteer work in classrooms, playgrounds, and libraries; by tutoring children with special needs; by supplying transportation, parties, and money for items not covered by the school budget, etc. The PTA is a potentially strong force in determining school policies and practices. Some are active and effective; some are apathetic; some engender hostility between parents and school staff. Parents typically understand, however, that they are expected to work for the good of the school, and not to interfere with the administration or seek special advantages for their own children.

e) *Content* The content of the kindergarten curriculum has not been standardized, and there are few special achievements expected of its "graduates." Guidelines issued by state departments of education tend to resemble each other in their assumption that the test of kindergarten is to develop the child's "readiness to learn" in a classroom setting. Among other goals, implied or explicit, are the ability and/or desire to :

function within a large group with a minimum of individual
    attention
listen thoughtfully
follow instructions
inhibit most "spontaneous" behaviors except at recess
respect the teacher, other children, and oneself
notice visual likenesses and differences
recognize the printed alphabet and numerals to 10
want to read and to perhaps read some signs and names
manipulate drawing and writing materials
count and understand simple concepts of measurement
understand about the school and neighborhood
recognize the cycles of the year, including holidays
observe familiar scientific phenomena
use a variety of art materials
learn health and safety habits, etc.

The kindergarten year is expected to be an important and busy time
for the students. What actually occurs within a class is usually the
teacher's own responsibility—for better or for worse. Talented and
experienced teachers presumably work effectively with little guidance;
mediocre and new teachers probably do not. The teacher is almost
always expected to plan her classes' activities and to prepare her own
teaching materials. Each day typically includes time for both free play
and structured group activities.

Kindergartens have reflected the prevailing winds of educational
practice and have thus changed considerably over the years, at times
being more "formal" and at times more "progressive" or "permissive." For the past few decades, the ideal kindergarten has been
pictured as rather like a senior nursery school, where children work
and play spontaneously, and the teacher is free to interact with individuals or small groups, seizing upon the "teachable moments." Most
kindergarten programs, however, have in practice been more formal
than this. Classrooms are frequently too small for much free action
(typically about 80–85 square meters) and are located in buildings
where noise disturbs the upper grades. The large number of children
creates pressure for formal interaction between the teacher and the

class as a whole. In addition, many teachers have had no specialized preparation for work with this age group. Children coming from nursery schools where they have experienced abundant adult attention, space and freedom to explore, and encouragement of spontaneous play, are sometimes disappointed and become something of a problem to their teachers.

Until recently, it has been maintained by educational leaders that formal academic work has no place in the kindergarten; that workbooks, reading, printing, formal number concepts, are not good for five-year-olds. There are an increasing number, however, who feel that such activities are appropriate and desirable for children mature enough to handle them. Professionals are particularly divided about the inclusion of reading instruction, although they tend to agree that reading readiness activities are essential (Fuller, 1961). With the new compensatory programs and the dawning recognition of the untapped learning potentials in the young, there seems little doubt that modifications in regular kindergarten programs will follow.

f) *Results* The value of kindergarten experience for the normal child has been proclaimed by teachers, parents, and almost everyone else—but there is surprisingly little evaluative research. Results of compensatory programs for disadvantaged children cannot be generalized to standard kindergartens. One major research barrier has been the considerable difficulty in securing an equivalent comparison group, without kindergarten experience. Because attendance is voluntary, subtle differences exist between users and non-users. Even in states which have only recently or have not yet developed kindergarten programs, the situation is complicated by the presence of private classes and Project Head Start for two large segments of the socioeconomic continuum.

The studies which do exist tend to report favorable effects of kindergarten attendance on later achievement, self assurance, and social skills; none reports unfavorable results (Mindless and Keliher, 1967). Furthermore, kindergarten affords an opportunity to identify children with potential learning and personality disorders and to introduce early remediation efforts (de Hirsch, Jansky and Langford, 1966).

F. COMPENSATORY PRESCHOOL PROGRAMS FOR DISADVANTAGED CHILDREN

Preschool compensatory programs represent the convergence of several tides of concern and action discussed earlier : a new recognition of the critical nature of the earliest years of life, the civil rights movement, the War on Poverty, and the concern with mental retardation.

It has always been apparent that children from low-income homes are usually poorly prepared for school. They typically enter with undeveloped skills, a lack of self-confidence, a mistrust of adults, and a deep fear of the whole school operation. Disadvantaged children often seem to "tune out" environments which would be stimulating to middle-class children. Unpracticed in fine motor play, they shun puzzles, beads, scissors, or crayons which would develop fine motor coordination. Unable to utilize standard English patterns and often handicapped even in dialectical English, they avoid stories, conversations, and the other verbal mainstays of early education. Programs designed for middle-class children are probably inappropriate, then, for children who by the age of two or three already exhibit impairment of function in crucial areas of development.

While the need for action has long been obvious, meaningful programs to help the nearly one million poor children who enter schools each year were not established until 1965. It is not yet clear, however, how enduring will be this commitment to help the poor. President Nixon proposed to Congress early in 1973 that many federal programs stemming from the War on Poverty be eliminated and that federal funds be given to the states in block grants to do with as they see fit in areas of health, education, and welfare. It is doubtful that this proposal will be accepted by the Congress; there is no doubt, however, that a long and bitter debate will ensue and that some disruption of existing programs is inevitable.

1. Project head start

The concept of this compensatory program was first presented by a task force of President Kennedy's Panel on Mental Retardation, a special advisory group. In 1963, it suggested a national program of

intervention to prevent mild retardation traceable to cultural deprivation. In 1964, the new Office of Economic Opportunity (OEO)
established under President Johnson undertook a broad program of
community action activities for financially impoverished adults and
children.

a) *Philosophy*   A panel of experts was convened by the Director
of OEO to draw up a blueprint for a child development program.
Their report, delivered in February 1965, became the springboard for
Project Head Start. It stressed these points :

1) The overriding goal of each program should be to create an
environment in which each child has the maximum opportunity and
support in developing his full potential.

2) Programs must be comprehensive . . . to achieve maximum
effectiveness. This requires extensive activities in the fields of health,
social services, and education.

3) Careful attention must be given both to the evaluation of the
child's abilities and deficiencies and to the correction of deficiencies
and strengthening of abilities.

4) Programs should focus on the parent as well as the child.

5) There should be support for a variety of programs tailored to
fit local community conditions. OEO should specifically encourage
innovative and experimental ideas. There should, of course, be adequate evaluation and research to accompany these programs.

6) These programs can and should be initiated very quickly. There
already exists adequate understanding of the problems and processes
involved to permit an immediate and massive intervention in the
poverty cycle (Cooke *et al.,* 1965).

Project Head Start was originally intended as a pilot summer
program with funds of $17,000,000, but response to the announcement
of the project was so overwhelming that within a very brief time 2,600
commuities developed programs serving 561,000 children and the
total first-year appropriation was $96,400,000. At that point, Head
Start consisted of an intensive eight-week summer program reaching as
many poor children as possible just prior to their entry into public

school. Most programs have now been converted to year-round, half-day or full-day preschools, with some children attending for two or more years.

b) *Administration and Program operation*   The responsibility for operating Project Head Start was shifted in 1969 to the newly created Office of Child Development in the Department of Health, Education and Welfare. Between the federal and local levels are regional and state offices which are responsible for working with the local programs. Individual programs are initiated by a variety of agencies such as school systems, nonprofit agencies, churches, and community action agencies.

Eighty percent of the operational costs of local programs are borne by the federal government; the local share may include contributions of space, volunteer time, and other services. For full-year programs, the national average 1971 cost per child was $1,109, part-day programs averaged $1,050 and all-day programs, $1,400. For summer-only programs, the average cost was $234 per child. Actual costs ranged widely, however, from location to location. There is no charge to poverty families but the few participating non-poverty families must pay for the service. The total federal budget for Project Head Start in 1972 was about $360 million.

c) *Personnel*   The ideal Head Start classroom of 15–20 children is staffed by three adults : a teacher and two assistant teachers. One of the latter is a career development person from the poverty population served by the center, and one is an unpaid volunteer. The actual median ratio of teachers and aides to children is, however, one adult per seven or eight children. In addition, there are staff members for administration, health, social services, psychological services, nutrition, etc. In 1971 there were a total of 55,000 paid staff in full-year programs serving 275,586 children. Of special interest are the para-professional workers, most of them from the poverty population, whose task it is to bring together center, parents, and community. Volunteer workers, some 165,000 persons in 1971 (including some men and, in the summer, older siblings of Head Start children), are used throughout the program.

Pre-employment qualifications for jobs with Head Start, except for specialized professional staff, do not involve much formal education, training, or paid experience. Appropriately trained personnel simply do not exist anywhere in the United States in the numbers demanded by the program. Summer staffs tend to be better educated because they draw upon elementary school personnel on vacation. To create a coordinated and skilled staff team, continuing in-service training is required. In addition, brief specialized courses are offered in colleges and universities, and a special effort is made to further the formal education of adults from disadvantaged backgrounds through the Graded Career Development program. This system of "career ladders" has a double pay-off : workers profit from the chance to develop new skills and job possibilities, while the society acquires a badly needed corps of personnel trained in child development. In 1971, for example, 7,500 low-income employees of full-year programs were enrolled in college level training.

d) *Users of the program*   For full-year programs, children must be at least three years old and may not yet have entered public school (44 percent are age four; 31 percent, age five); for summer-only programs, they must be about to enter public kindergarten or first grade (three-quarters are five or six). Another major criterion is annual family income, judged according to an index based on the prevailing cost of living, the size of the family, and whether its residence is on a farm. Enrollment in 1971 of 275,600 children in the full-year programs provided coverage for about only one-seventh of all four- and five-year-old eligible children. The summer-only programs reached another 118,000, or about one out of seven of the eligible children ready to enter school. It is important to note that the summer-only programs initially reached up to half the eligible children, while all-year programs at that time reached only a very small minority. Many professionals have deplored the segregation of the poor in these programs, thus generating a move to include some children (up to 10 percent) from non-poverty families—a provision present from the inception of the program but seldom put into practice.

Head Start programs are generally less available in rural and southern communities, where personnel and financial resources are scarce and where white community leaders tend to resist local programs which are primarily for minority group children. Although most children living in poverty are, in fact, Caucasian, Head Start has enrolled high proportions of children from minority groups. In full year programs in 1970, for example, about three-quarters of the children were Negro, Mexican-American, American Indian, and other minorities, while in the 1969 summer program, approximately 57 percent were from minority groups. The summer and full-year

Ithaca Journal

FIGURE 14   Compensatory programs

[145]

programs tend to enroll younger children and a greater proportion from "hard core" poor families with lower incomes, more broken homes, etc.

e) *Parent participation* Paid and volunteer work provides important opportunities for parents to participate in Head Start programs. The proportion of Head Start parents on the paid staff has been about one-third of the full-year and summer programs (Bates, 1972). Family involvement is sought in a number of additional ways. For example, parents are involved in policy advisory committees at every level from the local center to the national office. There are also various kinds of parent committees which plan adult-oriented activities including lectures, demonstrations, workshops, social and recreational events, literacy training, job counseling, etc. Most important, perhaps, the parents are active participants in the classroom, not only as volunteer aides but also as observers, producers of materials and equipment, chaperones on field trips, etc. Finally, home visits by staff members also serve to link the centers and the families. Even so, practical problems, such as both parents working, interfere with full participation of some families and others are shy or simply uninterested. The degree of family involvement is more vigorous and enthusiastic in some centers than others, but on the whole it is an impressive index of the importance which these parents attribute to the program.

f) *Scope of the program* In addition to the education component, each child is supposed to be given a comprehensive medical and dental examination, routine screening tests, immunizations, dental fluoride treatment, and health education. His parents may also receive health education and introductions to community personnel who can assume responsibility for the family's future health care. Every Head Start program must have a social services program to link the center, the family, the related community services and resources. Nutritional services must include meals for the children as well as nutritional education for the parents. Other kinds of educational experiences for the parents are designed to improve their functioning as individuals, parents, and citizens. Head Start is thus a comprehensive child development program unlike almost any other in its broad-range approach to improving the environment of the young child and his ability to cope with it.

g) *Content of the educational component* There is a great deal of local autonomy in planning the educational program, from the guiding philosophy to the details of daily schedules. The national and regional offices of Head Start influence programs rather indirectly by furnishing optional guidelines, providing materials for training programs, and visiting local programs with guidance and the offer of resources. Some of the guidelines available are in line with the more traditional nursery school and kindergarten programs, while others are much more structured for concentrated learning experiences.

It is not surprising, then, that Head Start programs are enormously diverse. One observational study of 136 classes, for example, found that in some classes there was practically no dramatic role playing, while in others it occupied as much as 35–40 percent of the activities. Formal language training varied from less than 5 percent of the activities to 35 percent; informal language development ranged even more widely (5–75 percent), with some teachers ignoring this aspect and others seizing practically every opportunity to elicit language. Some classes were substantially teacher-controlled, but others were definitely child-directed; some paid little or no attention to "good behavior" while it was the focus of nearly a third of the incidents in other classrooms (Datta, 1969).

Across the country, there seems to be some movement now toward more coherent, planned and somewhat structured educational curricula. Common areas of emphasis are sensorimotor development, self esteem, language, social skills, cognitive concepts, and enhancement of the desire to learn. Development in academic skills generally receives little emphasis.

An important experimental component of Head Start was the "planned variations" program, which involved 12 models, each of which had been developed and pretested in a laboratory school, and each of which constituted a rather complete strategy for preschool education. The models were also implemented in Follow Through. These programs have had a "ripple effect" in their communities, influencing public school programs, other Head Start centers, and nursery schools. They range from a semitraditional approach to highly structured academic training, and are still available to local Head Starts as alternative approaches which they may choose. Eight of them are briefly described below.

The goal of the *behavior analysis approach* (developed by Bushell, University of Kansas) is to teach the child needed skills by means of a token exchange system and other systematic reinforcement techniques. Parents are hired and trained to use these techniques in the classroom, and also to teach them to other parents. Individual instruction is emphasized by careful diagnostic charting and the use of programmed materials.

In the *structured academic approach* (Becker and Englemann, University of Oregon), programmed materials are used to teach essential concepts and operations in reading, arithmetic, and language. Teaching is characterized by a high degree of child involvement, intensive pattern drills in small groups, and frequent, systematic social reinforcement of desirable behaviors, by teachers and parents who are trained as aides.

The ultimate goal of the *development approach* (Gilkeson, Bank Street College of Education) is to enable each child to become deeply involved in self-directed learning. The child is free to investigate objects and to explore media. A number of special instructional materials have been developed. The teacher is regarded as highly important—a consistent adult whom the child learns to trust, and who sensitizes him to his experiences, sensations, feelings, and ideas.

The *behavioral skills and attitudes approach* (Henderson, University of Arizona) emphasizes language competence, the heuristics of learning, motivation, skill acquisition (reading, writing, numbers) and socialization (e.g., cooperation, planning). The curriculum is carefully structured but flexible; a variety of options are available to each child, providing opportunities to develop individual skills at individual rates. One-to-one interaction with adults is stressed, but small, heterogeneous groups are also encouraged so that children learn from each other. Imitation is a formal part of the approach, particularly in language learning.

In the *cognitive orientation* approach (Weikart, High/Scope Educational Research Foundation), based in large measure on Piaget's work, there are three major foci : a cognitively oriented curriculum featuring a carefully sequenced progression (e.g., simple to complex, concrete to abstract); home visits by teachers or specially hired staff, to help mothers learn to promote cognitive growth; and continuous assessment for the purpose of individualizing instruction. Language training and the development of a positive self concept are also considered vital.

The *parent educator* approach (Gordon, University of Florida) utilizes community paraprofessionals (often mothers of project children) who work half-time assisting the teacher in the classroom. The rest of their time is spent making home visits, demonstrating and teaching mothers to present tasks chosen especially for their children. In this way, mothers (and often other family members) learn how to be successful teachers, directly promoting emotional and intellectual growth.

In the *responsive education* approach (Nimnicht, Far West Laboratory for Research and Development), the total environment is engineered to be responsive to the child's particular interests and learning style. Autotelic (self-rewarding) activities such as some of the Montessori materials and many electronic/mechanical devices are provided to encourage the child to try things out, risk, guess, ask questions, and make discoveries without risk to his self-esteem.

The *pragmatic, action-oriented* approach (Armington, Educational Development Center) draws heavily on ideas and practices from the British Infant schools. The goal is preparation for life in a modern world, and every effort is made to integrate learning with the life style outside the classroom. Parents are thus vital information resources. The teacher is viewed as a catalyst who takes her cue from the child's expressed interests, but provides guidance and structure.

h. *A "modal day" in Head Start*   The following two informal, fragmentary observations were made in Head Start programs in two neighboring communities. They illustrate the kinds of contrasts found from one program to another, which make it so difficult to describe or evaluate Head Start as a whole.

First, some similarities between the programs : Both were staffed by experienced Head Start teachers, each in her third year with the project. Each had some college education but no degree. Each program had a teacher's aide from the local poverty community, and on most mornings, one of several volunteer Head Start mothers as a helper. Both classes ran for the full academic year, half-day, and served a midmorning snack and lunch. Each enrolled 15 four-year-olds, who had been together about three months when observed.

Class 1. The first Head Start class illustrates traditional but rather passive teaching, an example which represents neither the best nor cleverest use of this approach. It is, however, unfortunately representative of many classes.

The physical setting is a one-story, modern building annexed to an elementary school. It houses some regular kindergartens as well as another Head Start class. The building is of concrete block construction, spacious, well-lighted, with an airy feeling. The classroom is approximately 84 sq. meters—a generous 5.6 sq. meters per child. Areas are set apart by the use of waist-high dividers and furniture grouped for special activities such as housekeeping play, reading and listening, painting and play with trucks and blocks. Next to the teacher's desk is a bulletin board on which are tacked photographs of each child taken during a recent trip to the zoo. On a low table nearby is a caged guinea pig. There is also a waist-high table for sand play and a water-play table, built by some of the fathers, which is covered today. Three low, colorful plastic-topped tables, each with six small chairs, are in the middle of the room. Each child has a "mailbox" cubicle for his special belongings and the things he has made to take home. Coats, hats, and boots remain outside the door in a cupboard. Some toys are on open shelves; some are put away in teacher-controlled space. It is a pleasant room, but it is also a sterile room, lacking a sense of intimacy.

On this day, 11 children are present, 7 boys and 4 girls, all of them Caucasian (as are the teacher and aide) including two of Mexican-American background. They are neatly and casually dressed. This center is located in a small town; most of the Head Start children live on scattered small farms and are transported by two school buses.

The teacher and her assistant have arrived at 9:00 a.m. to discuss the day's activities and to do chores such as preparing carrots for snack, cleaning the guinea pig's cage, preparing paper and paints. (These are all tasks with which the children might have helped.) The teacher selects the books to be read, including one about night sounds to reassure a child who has recently been unwilling to sleep in the dark.

9:45 First busload of children arrives. Teacher greets the five children and helps with coats. Charlie's mother, today's volunteer, arrives with him and with a young puppy in a box. "Watch out," she cautions, "he'll poop on you!" Teacher holds puppy gingerly while the children solemnly admire and tentatively pat him. The other children now arrive. Susie and Tony walk over to look at the pictures of themselves. "I'm right here," says Susie. "See me!" "Where is me?" asks Tony.

He gets no response and walks off, aimlessly. The children now scatter to various areas, the adults interacting minimally with necessary help (e.g. teacher helps Sam to put on headphones to listen to a record). Susie and Charlie bring his mother to the photographs; she admires their pictures and helps them name the zoo animals also shown. Mack is holding the puppy. Susie pats it; now Mack puts it on the floor to keep away from her. She slips in and pats it again, calling, "Teacher, I want to hold him." "O.K., after Mack's turn," is the response. Mack clutches the puppy.

Mother sits at a table, cutting paper plates in a prepared pattern for the children to paste green and red crepe paper circles (also pre-cut) as a Christmas wreath, and talks with the three on-lookers about the town's Christmas decorations. Then she plays the clown, putting a plate on her head as a hat, and the children giggle. Pedro and Tom are painting; the aide ties their aprons. As she removes their pictures from the easel, she comments with somewhat stereotyped approval on each.

Finally, Susie can stand it no longer and takes the puppy from Mack, who whispers fiercely, "Give him back!" She strides across the room and puts the puppy on a table. Mack makes a train of two chairs and "choo-choo's" toward her as she climbs on the table with the puppy. Mack begins to whimper. Teacher says, "Next is your turn." Charlie says, "You can only hold him one time!" Mother admonishes, "We'll be here all morning and everyone will have plenty of turns." Mack says gratefully, "You're the one who brought the cupcakes last time!"

10:05 Baskets of cheese-bread sticks and carrot sticks are made available near the aide, who calls the girls, and the teacher, who calls the boys, each for a story. The girls quickly assemble but the boys come more slowly. The puppy is crying; Mack and Charlie put the puppy's box on a curved board, rocking it. They quarrel; momentary tears; then Charlie returns to the group and Mack nuzzles the puppy. Finally, the story over, teacher says, "Mack, you were nice and quiet, but everyone must have a turn." Cindy is given the puppy.

10:20 Teacher and Mother arrange the prepared paper plates on two tables, each seating four children, who are given a paint brush, cup, and box of four water colors. They paint one side of the plates—all alike—which are then put away to dry. There is little talking. Some water spills; Mother cleans it up and offers more. Teacher is moving the chairs into a semi-circle with help from Betty. She puts a paper crown on Betty's head, saying, "It's Betty's birthday!" Betty, who seldom speaks, smiles but does not look at the teacher. She continues to wear the crown for the rest of the day. Play is now rather desultory and listless. Three girls have put on "dress up" clothes but now sit silently on a table, not interacting, aimlessly swinging their legs, apparently unable to carry through with dramatic play. Cindy is still hugging the puppy; Charlie and Tom are playing with blocks and trucks; the rest are finishing the wreaths. Teacher now starts a record and, taking two long sticks, keeps simple time. As the children come over to the chairs, she hands them shorter sticks and they follow her lead. (Meanwhile, Pedro is absorbed in the story on the tape, listening through the earphones.) Aide joins the group with an ecstatic Susie, whom she has helped to dress in a sequinned pink long dress, complete with cape, hat, and gloves. . . . The music over, free play resumes. Two children sit on a table, back to back, not communicating. Three girls play dispiritedly with dolls, mainly just holding them. Some children are

[151]

playing with large blocks, some with puzzles. Teacher and aide circulate, looking on, saying little. Quarrels over dolls and the puppy are arbitrated by the teacher.

11:00 Children put on their coats for outdoor play although it is gray and drizzling. There are swings and a slide under a roof. The aide begins a game of "A Tisket, A Tasket" and then, "Farmer in the Dell," traditional circle games. The teacher pushes others on the swings; they make no effort to "pump" themselves. After about ten minutes, the children are taken in a line to the first-grade classroom next door to admire a gingerbread Christmas house which the teacher has made.

11:20 In preparation for lunch, teacher and Mother set the table and arrange children's name cards. Children use the toilet, are helped by the aide to wash their hands, and sit down. The lights are turned out and they put their heads on the table (Mack and Charlie are making faces at one another). Lunch has been brought in from a truck. As they are waiting to be served, teacher recites a poem about snow, inviting the children to copy her as she motions with her hands. Then she calls the children one at a time to a serving table, where the kitchen helper gives each a portion of mixed vegetables, ground meat baked in biscuit dough, celery sticks, and a half-pint carton of milk with a straw. One adult is at each table. Each child puts his finished plate on the serving cart, and is given a bowl of vanilla pudding. Several have second helpings; Pedro has four! Teacher gives Betty a wrapped birthday gift, a book, which she hugs happily but will not open despite pleas from the children. Some food scraps are given to the puppy, who eats with an attentive audience.

11:45 Now begins a period of play when, for the first time, most of the children seem engaged in what they are doing. The aide sponges off the tables and modelling clay is placed on one, attracting four girls. Sam and Tony are assembling a plastic doll, Sam encouraging Tony to insert each feature. Pedro watches briefly, then begins to respond to a question-and-answer record teacher has placed on the phonograph. Sam, Tony, Charlie, and Mark then play for a long time at the sand table, each in his own corner, with his own truck and shovel. Susie, Cindy, Betty, and Debby are pounding clay into "cakes" with little sticks for candles. On another table, Mother has brought the circles to be pasted on the wreaths. She does one and encourages the children, as they come, to do theirs in their own way. When sand is spilled at the sand table, Sam uses broom and dustpan without being asked.

12:10 Except for the four boys who had been playing in the sand and are still finishing their wreaths, the children now select individual projects. They seem even more interested in these activities than the previous ones. One uses a buttoning game which was made by a parent; one has a box of magnets; one listens to a record; one is assembling wooden puzzles; one pets the puppy; one paints at the easel. Tony is making a lovely mess with crepe paper and paste as he finishes his wreath. Mother is critical of Charlie's effort ("Oh, you can do better than that!") but supportive of everyone else's. Sam and Tony are building an elaborate structure from giant dominos, with overtures from Susie which they ignore. This is a very quiet time, with everyone purposefully occupied in his pursuits.

12:30 Everyone puts on outdoor clothes, retrieves belongings, and has a note pinned on his coat about a parents' meeting that night. They sit in a semicircle in front of the teacher, who is reading a counting book. They count aloud with her from one to 22. One group leaves with the aide for the first bus; the others follow-the-leader after Debby around the room, encouraged by the teacher, until the second bus arrives.

Class 2. The second Head Start class illustrates an approach loosely built on the High Schope (Weikart, 1971) Piagetian model which more explicitly recognizes and capitalizes upon the challenge of teaching young children. Born of an active citizens' movement in the central area of a large city, this program involves 15 children: 4 Caucasian, 11 Negro. Thirteen come today, all dressed neatly in long pants. Both teacher and aide are Negro. The mother who was to assist does not appear, and the teacher, who has planned many activities for the day, wonders how she will manage without her.

The setting for this program is the basement of a rather old brick building, formerly an elementary school and now completely devoted to Project Head Start. The basement room is about 56 sq. meters—3.7 sq. meters per child—and despite the exposed pipes and "basement" feeling, it is colorfully decorated, well organized, and exudes a rather warm and intimate ambiance. In the hall, people come and go; water splashes in the bathroom. The classroom contains the same equipment as Class 1, and is similarly divided by low barriers and shelves. A gerbil cage is in one corner. There is a full-length mirror.

The morning is a busy, pleasant one and time seems to go quickly. The children are enthusiastic, purposeful, and lively; they are obviously fond of the adults, accustomed to cooperating well, and enjoying the challenging pace of the program.

9:00 The children arrive in three separate "minibuses." The teacher or aide meets the children at the curb. Meanwhile, the other sees to it that the children—who burst eagerly into the classroom—each find one of the games, puzzles, and books already laid out on the tables. ("This is a hard one, Robert. Do you think you can do it? Good!")

9:20 Teacher rings a bell, "Clean up time!" Mickey takes the bell, gleefully imitates. Teacher, amused, reminds him that the bell is for the grown-ups. "What can you help us with, Mickey? Can you take a chair? How do you carry a chair?" Children and teachers now arrange two tables, put away the puzzles and books. Two are absorbed in their books. Teacher asks them, "What was the bell for?" (With big grins,) "Reading time!" "You are teasing me! Would you put this book away when you put yours away?" Everyone is now sitting quietly, waiting. The children at the teacher's table are each given symbol-matching cards. She encourages each child to name the left symbol, and to turn the right wheel to match it. Each is matching a different symbol and checks his own by seeing if the colors on the card's back are matched. "I made a match!" "You did! Good! What color did you have? . . . Who has a shirt that color?" (The children at the other table are counting chips with the aide.) Now the teacher gives each child a card with six sections to be covered by a set of six smaller cards. Some cards have six dot pictures differing in position and number; some have pictures of children or

[153]

objects showing contrasting concepts (e.g. "fast and slow," "same and different"). Each child works diligently and cheerfully, conferring with the teacher. She circulates from child to child, getting each to verbalize his concept, praising efforts. (Now the aide is showing her group cards with the pictures of children, gay or sad. She asks, "How do the children feel? How do you know?" Then, two together, "Are these the same [feeling] or different?") As the children finish the cards, the teacher gives each a piece of paper torn from a butcher's roll and shows them how to fold the paper into a booklet. Passing a basket of crayons, she repeats for each child, "Please take a *green* crayon." They all watch each other. "Like this!" Darlene calls helpfully to Johnny. Mark grabs a crayon from his neighbor, having thrown his own on the floor. The teacher removes it gently. "If you want one, yours is there." He retrieves his own and breaks it. "Now I have two!" This is tactfuly ignored. Now, at a suggestion from Lizzie, the children trace their own hands. The teacher asks each to say what color he is using. They laugh, "Green, green!" After this, teacher asks them to turn to the inside and "Draw me a green triangle." She writes each child's name on his paper, after encouraging him to make as many of the letters as he can. Meanwhile, the aide's table has been cutting shapes of paper: squares, rectangles, and triangles. Then they draw curving lines on folded paper and cut along them. Aide says in praise, "It's a lot of work to do this! We work hard!" Then the children go to the bathroom and wash their hands by themselves. As they return, the aide asks Frances to help push the table. Two others quickly run to join her. "Oh, so many helpers! So strong, too! You are a help to me *every* day!" Other children are industriously putting crayons away, bringing snack food and napkins, setting table. Some stay in a corner, talking. Teacher says, "Darlene's sitting down. Arthur is sitting down now. Patsy is sitting down . . ." as the other children quickly join them. Table conversation between Arthur and Albert, who seem a little glum, but not angry: "I gonna push you down." "I gonna get that big box and chop *you* down." Teacher is passing out pre-sweetened dry cereal in cups and dried prunes to the children she worked with before, in turn to children "who are ready to be quiet." (Aide serves the other table.) She points out that the napkins are rectangles and the cups, circles. "What about the cookies?" ("Square!") "And when we break them in half?" ("Rectangles!") "Albert brought many crackers today. We're going to pass them around and you can take two." (To each she counts, "One two.") Plastic spoons are passed around and the children pour milk on the cereal from shared cartons. "Who brought the crackers today?" "Albert!" call the children. "He said he brought them for his friends. He has a lot of friends. Did he bring a lot of crackers?" Albert says, "May I please have another one?" Teacher: "You said that nicely. Take a *half* of one. No, that's a *whole* one." Joe asks, "Is that all we're having?" Teacher laughs, hugs him. During snack, each child chooses what he wants to do next. After cleaning up, they go immediately to their chosen places and the teacher and aide help them get started dressing up, painting at the easels, playing in the housekeeping corner, etc. Two girls wipe the table with sponges, making ready to fingerpaint. . . . Robert and Bobby are gaily racing trucks into the hallway and back. Aide says, "Not so fast!" When they fail to slow down, she teases, "It's against the law to go fast in the tunnel! I'll have to take your drivers' licenses away if you don't slow down." They giggle and comply, temporarily. Patsy, Frances, and Gloria are waiting patiently to fingerpaint, smocks on. Teacher says, "This takes a lot of clean-up. Will you help?" They nod happily. She puts down a large glob of liquid starch and sprinkles green tempera powder on it. The girls mix it with both hands and, smiling delightedly, smear with big, wide movements. Two more girls now want to join them. Teacher asks, "What do you need?" and they race off for aprons. There are now four activities: five children fingerpainting, four playing with trucks, two in the doll corner, and two making chains with precut paper and paste. The aide joins the truck play with blocks, building a complex structure which could be a garage. The boys quickly adopt this idea and build even more elaborate structures. Teacher now helps fingerpainters to make hand prints on construction paper. Arthur approaches doll corner. Patsy says, "You take the telephone and call me and we'll bake a cake, O.K.?" He does so as they are joined by Gloria, who brings him a tie from the dress-up supply . . .

10:30 Aide rings a bell for clean-up, but the children largely ignore her. She claps her hands and says, smiling, "All right. I want these blocks cleaned up right now!" Gradually, the children put things away. They have been having a very good time. Then they bring chairs to a story circle. As they settle down, Darlene begins to show the children pictures in a book by "Dr. Seuss," a popular children's author, and to tell the fantasy tale quite accurately. This is not what was planned, but the two adults are pleased, and put their own plans aside. The aide encourages Darlene by asking leading questions as she seems to need them. All the children are very attentive. Then the teacher gathers the children into a big circle on a rug. They follow her directions, faster and faster, giggling. ("Hands up. Open, shut them, open, shut them, give a great big clap. Put them on you head. Put them in your lap.") They all repeat a nursery rhyme, then sing, with hand motions, "Miss Polly had a Dolly." Mickey puts his arm around the teacher and she moves him to her lap.

11:10 Today, because of rain, the children play indoors for 20 minutes in the gymnasium. Here there is sturdy indoor play equipment—boards and ladders, balance beams, and a long wheeled toy on which several children ride, one pushing from behind. Teacher has stayed behind in the classroom to organize matters and to make ready for lunch. The aide plays "gas station" with children who ride up on tricycles. Everyone is happy and active.

11:30 The children return to the basement, wash hands, and again contented and industrious, they help to set the tables. Food is brought from a central, privately-run catering kitchen. Each adult sits at a table, helping the children to help themselves to rice, beef stew, green beans, and milk. Dessert is orange gelatin. There is table conversation about today's activities, tomorrow's plans, and the field trip planned for the day after to a downtown department store. The children return their dishes to the serving cart and make ready to board the buses at 12:15.

The atmosphere in Class 2 was purposeful and vigorous. In contrast, Class 1 was lacking in focus and energy. Class 2's teacher and aide utilized every available opportunity to teach, to encourage the children to use new words and grammatical constructions, to look at their environment through wiser eyes, to develop a sense of continuity and growth. They helped the children to see themselves as competent, strong, and dependable. Although these teachers took a more active role with the children than those in Class 1, the Class 2 children themselves assumed much more responsibility for their own care and for housekeeping duties, settled their own disputes, played together more frequently, cooperatively, helpfully, and creatively. There was ample time for self-selection and free play, but it seemed to be a very full morning in Class 2, perhaps even a bit too full. Class 1 seemed in contrast to move very slowly, to embody little challenge, and for a good part of the morning, to engage the children's interest rather minimally. Much of the teaching relied on stereotyped material—e.g., reading books, keeping simple time to a record, reciting a memorized poem. There was little capitalizing upon the "teachable moment." Indeed, the mother exhibited more vitality and sensitivity than did the paid staff.

Class 2 children come from somewhat poorer families than do the rural children in Class 1; more of their homes are lacking a father and more of the families are on welfare. At age 4, the Class 2 children may be behind average middle-class children in some ways (e.g., they still need to learn the names of some common colors), but Head Start has undoubtedly helped them to be receptive and eager to learn. One cannot be so optimistic about the contribution of Head Start to the Class 1 children.

2. Project follow through

Follow Through, which is literally an upward extension of Project Head Start, was undertaken in 1967 when studies revealed that children from low-income families tend to lose the gains made in preschool programs, when they enter the regular school system. The program begins in kindergarten or first grade and extends through grade three of the public schools. Follow Through projects for the most part implement the same educational models as those studied in the planned variation investigations of Head Start. In fact, the planned variation approach of Follow Through preceded that of

Head Start. Each program offers, in addition to its educational component, continued medical, dental, nutritional, psychological, and social services. It also provides educational services supplementary to and different from those ordinarily available in the schools: specially trained teachers, classroom aides, teaching materials, and, in some instances, additional sessions (e.g., extending half-day kindergartens to full-day). Forty-five percent of the children in the classes are Head Start "graduates," 20 percent have attended other preschools, and 30 percent have no previous preschool experience at all. In 1972–73, more than 90,000 children were enrolled in 4,000 Follow Through classrooms with a total of about 7,500 paraprofessional program workers employed in addition to the normal school staff. Most of these aides were parents of Follow Through children. Average expenditure was about $800 per child per year in addition to the regular school budget.

3. Elementary and secondary education act

In 1965, Congress passed the Elementary and Secondary Education Act (ESEA), another compensatory attack on the War on Poverty, to prod the nation's school systems into action on behalf of the poor. ESEA was a much-contested departure from the historic doctrine that each state must completely support—and control—its own schools. Most of the money was funneled, as a compromise, through the State Education Agencies. No state matching funds were required but the money had to be used to aid school districts with a high concentration of children from low-income families.

Title I of ESEA carried the lion's share of the money. Funds were granted for remedial reading, preschool, paraprofessional, and lunch programs. About seven percent of the 6,250,000 children and youth benefiting from this program in 1972 were in preprimary programs: 150,000 in compensatory preschools and 300,000 in kindergartens. Expenditures for special instructional programs and services for preschool participants were about $115 million that year, the total for all ages being $1.6 billion. The cost per preschool child was around $255, much lower than that for other programs because expenditures were primarily for enrichment of already existing programs.

Title I money has been under state and local control and there has been little systematic evaluation of its effects. Most local Title I programs have stressed reading, but they have not been spectacularly successful. The other programs have been so diverse that it is impossible to describe them. They have tended to be spread thinly over too many children and have not been very innovative.

Title III was at first bolder. Under its provisions, school districts were granted funds directly for demonstration programs, initiated at the local level, which were to be creative departures from established ways of educating poverty children. Funding of a project was not to exceed three years, on the assumption that if the new idea was good enough, other sources of funding could be found. Title III projects reached 430,000 preschool children in 1972, although the average cost per pupil was only $17.43.

By and large, the projects funded under Title III have been disappointing (Karp, 1970). Funds have too often been used to finance ill-conceived or hastily planned projects and so-called "innovative" programs which were already in existence. Little effort at evaluation has been made. In 1967, authority over these funds was put into the hands of the State Education Agencies—a move which severely curtailed the anti-bureaucratic thrust of the act.

Title IV authorizes the Office of Education to conduct research relating to early childhood education. A number of programs have been undertaken under these auspices. The yearly budget (1969) was $6.2 million. Emerging as the most important effort in this area is the National Laboratory on Early Childhood Education (see Section IX). The Laboratory operates the Clearinghouse on Early Childhood Education of the Educational Resources Information Center (ERIC), a national information network to assist in the dissemination of information on current research. Unfortunately, funds have been withdrawn from some of these activities for 1973.

4. Other compensatory preschool programs

A complex and very important but largely uncoordinated array of university-based, independent experimental education programs for young disadvantaged infants and children began about 1961. Funded by a variety of sources—federal agencies, private foundations, occasionally state or municipal funds—these programs, together with the National Laboratory on Early Childhood Education, have provided the innovative patterns on which Head Start and other service undertakings have been based.† A few programs for infants have operated in an enriched day care model with deliberate educational curricula; others have consisted of home tutoring for parents and/or babies (see reviews by Haith, 1971; Starr, 1971; Williams, 1972). Most of the models have used a nursery school or day care setting for three to five year olds, but some have covered the range from infancy through elementary school. They have differed strikingly along many dimensions, including theoretical underpinnings, degree of explicitness in the curricula, specificity of behavioral goals, emphasis (or avoidance) of school-related skills, teacher vs. child centeredness, reliance on self-teaching materials, teacher-to-child ratios, age of admission, attempt to match tasks to individual readiness, parent involvement, comprehensiveness of services, teacher-training emphasis, and so on. The programs range from "pressure cooker" tutoring in school-related skills; to child-centered nursery schools in which teacher and materials are "programmed" to respond to the child's spontaneous approach; to enrichment of a traditional program through individual tutoring in the abstract uses of language; and so on. Much of the most competent professional talent in the country has been involved in these programs.

Although funding for these programs has recently been much harder to obtain, they continue to offer independent beacons to large-scale projects such as Head Start. A number of these projects are actively cooperating with service programs to produce a meaningful base of research, development, and demonstration.

a) *Parent and child centers* On the recommendation of a White House Task Force on Early Childhood Development, a variety of experimental Parent and Child Centers (PCC's) were established in 1969. They were intended as demonstration facilities which would, for the first time, bring comprehensive services to poor families with

---

† For a description of leading programs, see Bronfenbrenner (1973), Hunt (1969), Parker *et al.* (1970), Stearns, 1971.

children under the age of four. Problems of coordination proved formidable, however, and the comprehensive nature of the PCC's has never been fully realized. They have tended instead to be downward extensions of Head Start, to which they are financially, administratively, and philosophically linked. The annual budget has been a scant $5,000,000 per year.

Planning has been carried on mainly by local committees, and the 33 PCC's are enormously diverse. They offer a great variety of stimulating activities for children at home or in group settings, opportunities for parents to enhance their effectiveness both as parents and as citizens, and health care and social services for the children and their families. Some provide group care for infants and toddlers; others have sponsored innovative patterns of family day care; still others are training parents and volunteers (including adolescents and elderly persons, some of them males) in effective child care; etc. Most render services in the center's building but at the same time reach out into homes. On the average, they each serve 70 families but they are targeted to work with 100 families. Seven of the centers have advocacy programs which are designed to ensure that poor families with young children use available community resources, and that the agencies are responsive to their needs. The impact of these extremely varied PCC's on young children and their families is only now being assessed, but initial results are encouraging. Evaluative research is somewhat handicapped by the small number and varied nature of the centers, which are nevertheless a testing ground for new approaches.

b) *Home start* An even newer experimental program, initiated in 1972 and based in large part upon the in-home parent-education studies reported below, is Home Start. This program is designed to reach families with children three to six years of age who do not utilize Head Start programs. All the comprehensive Head Start services (e.g., nutrition, health care, etc.) are furnished, but replacing the Head Start preschool classrooms are project workers who visit the homes to bring educational play materials and to develop and expand the parents' roles as educators of their own children. Many of the workers are low-income persons with limited special training. Each of the first 15 programs has been planned within overall guidelines by a local committee to meet the needs of its own population.

c) *Health start* Health Start was initiated in 29 locations in 1971 as an attempt to deliver health services (medical and dental examinations and treatment) to siblings of Head Start children and other disadvantaged children from 0 to 6 years of age. The health services component of Head Start had been both one of the cheapest (about 6 percent of the budget) and also one of the most clearly effective segments of the program. Nearly 10,000 non-Head Start children were reached the first year, with services which they almost certainly would not have received without this year-round program.

d) *Early education of the handicapped* The Bureau for the Education of the Handicapped, part of the U.S. Office of Education, administers programs for the education of handicapped children; states also provide a variety of special classes and services. The bulk of the funds at the federal and state levels is expended for children old enough to attend public school, but there are some funds establishing special preschool programs, for training personnel, and for conducting research.

The Early Education Assistance Act of 1968 made available funds to assist agencies and non-profit organizations to develop and operate model programs promoting comprehensive approaches to the education of preschool and early primary handicapped children. Under these auspices, the First Chance Network has been established, a demonstration involving some 70 projects. The wide diversity among them enhances the opportunity for communities to find a model which suits their needs. Numerous types and degrees of handicap, different age groups and educational approaches are encompassed in this attempt to stir the imagination and the will of communities to tackle the difficult job of very early, very specialized education and rehabilitation. Some 4,550 children were involved by 1972 in these model projects.

In 1968, about 100,000 preschool handicapped children in all were receiving some educational services; by 1973, perhaps double that number. Such program development is especially welcome because diagnostic and medical services, which are already relatively accessible for handicapped infants and children, are often rendered ineffective in the absence of specialized treatment services to meet other vital needs.

Parent organizations, particularly the National Association for Retarded Children, have also formed some cooperative programs largely run by the parents themselves, because they effectively support one another and because their children are so often excluded from the kinds of preschool experiences available to normal children. The children involved in these programs tend to come from middle-class homes, and to be so severely handicapped that they cannot fit in with a normal group of youngsters.

5. Effects of the programs

Professional personnel involved with compensatory projects and experimental programs have, from the beginning, taken very seriously the obligation to conduct both short-range and follow-up evaluations. A wealth of literature has been generated—some of it encompassing the broad scope of national programs, some of it limited to single projects; some with rigorous controls, others with less tight designs. In a sense, each of these independent studies has asked at least some of a small cluster of questions which educators and behavioral scientists have suddenly had to face :

• Can we design preschool programs that will make an immediate and/or a long-range difference in the lives of disadvantaged children? In their cognitive development? Their personal and social development? Their subsequent school achievement?

• Which kinds of programs work best? With which sorts of children?

• How long must intervention last? When should it begin?

• How can we best modify the environments of these children (e.g., through nursery schools, through programs reaching their parents, etc.) to enhance child development?

• What are the costs of various programs in relation to their estimated benefits?

Research has been hampered by the lack of assessment devices suitable for young, disadvantaged children, and particularly those which relate to variables other than cognitive development. There have been a large number of practical problems having to do with attrition of subjects, formation and location of control groups, uncertain funding, the lack of trained personnel, etc. There has also been a diffusion of program effects to younger siblings in the same family and indeed throughout the neighborhoods, which may have led to an underestimate of the outcomes of certain programs. The smaller projects seem to have a better chance of achieving control over slippery variables than do the large ones.

Despite these and other handicaps, the compensatory preschool programs, particularly Project Head Start, have made possible a great wealth of studies.† There have, for example, been surveys of random samples of Head Start programs to assess success in complying with Head Start guidelines; assessments of the performance of Head Start and non-Head Start children who were attending first, second, and third grades in 1968 (and therefore had experienced only the early and presumably poorer forms of the program); a long-range prospective longitudinal study of disadvantaged children and their first school experiences; a study of the effects of Head Start on community institutions; a Head Start/Follow Through longitudinal study of the planned variations program; and a very large number of single-site studies.

What are some of the major conclusions of these studies? Given the wealth of the available literature, space permits mention of only a few conclusions, though this is undoubtedly some of the most fascinating research on the effects of varied adult-child interaction ever conducted in this country.

One general conclusion to be drawn from the many compensatory programs which have centered their efforts on group intervention, is that while most programs make an immediate and positive impact on most children's development, the effects of a brief (e.g., summer only) intervention are negligible (Cicirelli et al., 1970; Smith and

---

† Project Head Start evaluations have been summarized by Datta (1969), Datta, McHale and Mitchell (1972), and Grotberg (1969).

Bissell, 1970; Westinghouse Learning Corporation, 1969). Compensatory activities need to begin rather early and to be continued or at least supported by special services through the third grade of school and possibly longer. Without these special and continued efforts, most of the gains achieved during the preschool program tend to wash out when Head Start "graduates" are compared with control children during the first three grades of school. The effects of home and school environments typical of poor neighborhoods cannot continue to be overcome by an "innoculation" of preschool experience.

Beginning school is a stimulating experience for the control children, and at that point their scores on intelligence tests tend to rise, at least for a time. The children who were in special preschool programs generally do no better than to maintain their status. The differences between the groups are, therefore, usually erased to statistical insignificance. Follow Through efforts have, however, tended to sustain (and sometimes enhance) progress made by Head Start children.

It is, unfortunately, difficult to be sure which programs have indeed been successful because apparently positive findings have so often unwittingly been confounded with other variables. One plaguing problem has been the selection of suitably matched controls. Too often, the control groups have been composed of children whose parents did not enroll them in the experimental programs even when they had the opportunity, or in some other way systematically differed in the degree of their concern about their children's development, the degree of their economic deprivation, of their social alienation, etc. When rigorous analyses of the research data from group programs for young children have been carried out, they have, in fact, uniformly failed to demonstrate positive long-term results (Bronfenbrenner, 1973).

Only small experimental programs run by the researchers themselves have thus far yielded scores for disadvantaged children which have been, on the average, in the superior level, i.e., mean IQ scores of 120 or higher, sometimes with an advantage of 30–40 points over controls (e.g., Robinson and Robinson, 1971; Sprigle, 1972). Head Start projects have had more modest results. Group gains during the year were 7–22 points on the Stanford-Binet for 35.1 percent of a sample of 111 Head Start projects in 1968–69; gains of 1–7 points for 44.2 percent; no change for 12.6 percent, and losses of 1–13 points for 8.1 percent of the projects (Datta, 1972). Head Start has apparently been associated also with changes toward increased child interest in new things, improved adult-child and child-child interaction patterns, increased task orientation, improved self-concept, increased trust in others, etc. (Datta, 1969).

A wide range of studies have suggested that structured preschool and primary grade programs designed to meet carefully specified behavioral goals are more effective in enhancing the cognitive development of disadvantaged children than are programs which are more generally defined and run in a more traditional manner. This is especially true of children with low pretest IQs, older, and nonurban children (Datta *et al*, 1972), who are aided by the orderly environment of a well-run center, low pupil: teacher ratios, an academic orientation, and an emphasis on language. It is possible, however, that the demonstrated effectiveness of structured, explicit, and carefully sequenced programs is confounded with successful program implementation which is easier to achieve with structured programs (Huron Institute, 1972). There is some mild indication (c.f. Bronfenbrenner, 1973) that structured programs, while effective in some respects, may lead to greater passivity on the part of children and to less positive attitudes toward school and learning than children taught a "discovery" method. It is perhaps worthy of note that in Project Head Start in 1967, non-Southern children showed the larger gains in intelligence test scores; in 1968, after many Southern centers had converted to a structured academic program, Southern children showed the greater gains.

There are suggestions that some important effects of preschool programs are delayed in their emergence, particularly those related to attitudes, interest, and social behavior. School achievement and motivational measures may be more sensitive indices once the child enters school than his scores on tests of general intelligence (Gray, 1969). Observational scales (e.g., Emmerich, 1971; Soar, 1972) may also provide an important key to measurement in this area.

One line of investigation deserves special mention because it is a distinct departure from the usual group approaches to education of the young, and because it has shown signs of being effective, economical, and long-lasting. This group of studies, reviewed in detail by Bronfenbrenner (1973), consists of frequent home visits by personnel, often poverty group mothers with only a moderate amount of training, whose purpose it is to enhance the effectiveness of the dyadic relationship between parent (usually mother) and infant or young child. The visitor is usually introduced as a demonstrator of toys for the children; in fact, it is the mother's way of using these materials, her view of herself as the most important educator, and her recognition of her child's potential learning capacity, which are the foci of attention. The most successful of these programs have had at least as potent effect on the children's cognitive growth as have nursery school programs (and much more than ineffective classroom-type approaches to parents), and furthermore, the effects have been maintained for some time after termination of the program. This approach has the added advantage of helping siblings of the target child and some neighborhood children as well. Interestingly enough, when these home visits are combined with other experiences for the children in such a way that the role of the professional child care worker seems more important to the parents than their own roles, the effectiveness of the intervention dissipates.

The research data have consistently indicated, as expected, that children from the most deprived backgrounds show the greatest developmental deficits. Bronfenbrenner (1973) points out, though, that children from the most deprived backgrounds profit least from intervention programs. He questions whether this may, in part at least, be attributable to their parents being so overburdened with the tasks and frustrations of sheer survival that they have neither the energy nor the psychological resources necessary to participate in the intervention program designed to benefit their children.

He also argues persuasively that the parents must be the key persons in any intervention effort. This means, of course, that professionals must have greater respect for the importance of the parents' roles and that more effective approaches must be developed for enlisting the participation of parents from the lowest socioeconomic levels. He suggests a phased approach to compensatory educational efforts, beginning in infancy with home visits supplemented later with group experiences—with the focus remaining throughout on the parent-child interactions.

A former director of Project Head Start's evaluation division has best summarized the effectiveness of various compensatory preschool programs :

By the criteria of uniformly high immediate and long-term benefits and economic feasibility, the existing programs are deficient; by the criteria of successes which show what is possible and contributions to creating apparently better approaches, the programs are valuable (Datta, 1972).

G. PROGRAMS FOR ENVIRONMENTAL PROTECTION/ ENHANCEMENT

A wave of concern for environmental quality is currently sweeping America, where the ugly byproducts of industrialization and affluence are all-too-visible. Air and water are polluted. Natural wildlife is fleeing as forests are diminished. The American automobile, which continues to grow in size and power, devours precious natural resources, kills thousands each year, pollutes the air, and assaults ears with harsh noises. Many of those who are reaping the fruits of industrialization are, at the same time, beginning to wonder whether the price is perhaps too high. Two interrelated movements continue to gain momentum : one to protect against environmental damage and the other to enhance the beauty of the surroundings.

Considerable progress has in fact been made with the former, although much work remains to be done. Many private groups have effectively directed public attention to important environmental dangers. Federal and state regulations concerning the labelling and sale of substances potentially harmful to children have become increasingly strict. Toys or other articles dangerous to children are banned under the 1966 Federal Child Protection Act. Product safety regulations pertinent to children are also to be found in most manufacturing codes. All states, for example, prohibit the use of lead-based paints inside dwellings, and the threat of lead poisoning to young children who ingest paint flakes has been almost eradicated in many areas (Lin-fu, 1970). Under the legal doctrine of the "attractive

[167]

nuisance," adults are held responsible for removing or rendering safe all naturally occurring situations on their own property which may be hazardous to children, including, for example, uncovered wells and swimming pools, unlocked automobiles, firearms, poisonous substances, etc.

Sanitation programs are, in large part, the responsibility of local communities. One matter completely under local control, for example, is fluoridation of the water supply to prevent dental caries in young children. Opposition based on religious grounds or simply resistance to mass "involuntary medication" has often been very strong, despite the unanimous support of dental and other health organizations. Only about 43 percent of the population now uses artifically or naturally fluoridated water (U.S. Public Health Service, 1970). In short, federal regulations and standards are enforced in a fairly uniform manner, but there is much more variance in state and local efforts.

In spite of many positive accomplishments, the United States still has a long way to go in promoting safety for children. The number

Ithaca Journal

FIGURE 15　Campground

one killer of children under five is accidents, claiming 7,263 lives in 1968 (National Safety Council, 1968). Almost 30 percent of these deaths were caused by traffic mishaps, while fires and ingestion of toxic substances accounted for another 30 percent. This record is a national disgrace and calls for determined, concerted action.

The need for environmental protection programs has perhaps overshadowed efforts to enhance environments, and much less progress has been made in this area. There are too few parks, zoos, small playgrounds, etc., for growing, active children. Furthermore, most existing facilities tend to be concentrated in middle-class neighborhoods. Commercial recreational facilities and children's cinemas likewise discriminate against the poor because they can ill afford the admission prices. Federal and state recreation areas, while reasonably plentiful, also tend to be inaccessible to low-income families who lack the means of transportation.

The overall picture, then, is one of slow but steady progress. It is worthwhile to note that programs of environmental protection and enhancement are presently attractive to citizens of almost every socioeconomic level and persuasion, a situation which bodes well for their continuation.

H. TOYS, BOOKS, AND MASS MEDIA FOR CHILDREN

1. Play materials

The production and design of toys, books, records, and other play materials are entirely functions of the free-enterprise system in the United States, and are, indeed, a thriving part of the economy. The public spends about $3 billion a year on toys alone, with 40 percent of the purchases going to children under the age of five (Swartz, 1971). In 1967, for example, nearly 65 million dolls and over 3 million tricycles were manufactured. It is not surprising then that this industry is extremely responsive to public opinion, not only to the opinions of child care experts and middle-class parents, but increasingly as well to those of lower-class parents.

Capitalizing on the new enthusiasm for early education, commercial firms are now producing great quantities of play materials billed as "educational." Although many of these are of good quality, others are mere gadgets, of little worth and poor durability. These playthings are seldom tested to see whether in fact they have any educational value, but some of the major producers do seek the aid of early childhood educators in designing and informally testing new toys.

2. Books

Records and toys must usually be purchased by a family if they are to be used at home, but books and sometimes records may be borrowed from free, neighborhood public libraries which in most states have well-stocked children's sections. Many excellent and appropriate books are commercially available for children, including a growing supply of inexpensive, illustrated books in paper bindings.

Lately a wave of criticism has been directed at the homogeneous, middle-class nature of children's books. There is, as a result, an increasing variety of contemporary books which show alternative life styles and sex roles. The goal is two-pronged : to enhance reading appreciation and skills among poor children by providing materials with which they can identify, and to give non-poor children more realistic, broader conceptions of "other worlds." One particularly strong movement has deplored the consistent, stereotypic family portrait : white-collar working father, devoted mother, two children— "Dick" and "Jane"—and the ever-present family dog—"Spot." Critics contend that a steady diet of such materials tends to lock children into rigid sex roles (i.e., girls are passive, emotional, verbal "mini-mothers," while boys are adventurous, aggressive and brave, less articulate, but good at arithmetic).

3. Mass media

Radio programming and magazines for preschool children are practically nonexistent. Television (TV) is by far the most important mass medium for all age groups. Almost every American home has one television; many have two. There is mounting concern about the effects of programming especially on young children. Many people are worried about the harmful potential, especially the possible effects of the considerable overt aggression not only in children's programs but also in adult programs watched by children and adolescents. There is also interest in the potentially beneficial outcomes of educational programming.

American television is dominated by three national commercial networks and a fourth public network supported by private and some federal government funds. Broadcasting is continuous, beginning in the early morning and ending around midnight or later.

Regulation of television and other media has been thus far largely voluntary. Explicit agreements exist among the members of the National Association of Broadcasters about general standards of programs shown on television or aired on radio during hours likely to include young audiences. There is no rating system, however, to warn parents of programs with content likely to be disturbing to young children, as there is with respect to films shown at cinema theaters. Television and radio advertisements of liquor and cigarettes are prohibited by the Federal Communications Commission, though, and there are other regulations on "truth" in all advertising.

Many attempts have been made to ascertain how much television young American children actually watch. One recent estimate indicates a whopping 27 hours a week (Nilsen TV Index, 1970). More than one-quarter of all school children report watching television for more than five hours during each school day (Television and Growing Up, 1972). In one survey of first graders, 43 percent of the boys and 29 percent of the girls reported viewing four or more hours on a randomly selected week day (Lyle and Hoffman, 1970). Another survey revealed that children between the ages of three and six watch an average of 56 hours per week (*Newsweek,* June 1, 1970). Some dispute these high figures, pointing out that in many homes the TV set is turned on for much of the day but that young children actively watch only a small fraction of the time. Regardless of the precise figure, it seems clear enough that preschoolers are exposed to television a great deal, especially during periods when the mother is likely to be occupied with housework, preparing meals, etc.

In fact, TV is often labelled "The Great American Babysitter," the ever-ready amusement for restless children. Certainly not more than 20-25 hours a week can be classified as children's programming. Although these hours are concentrated during times when children are most likely to watch, one wonders about the remaining hours of viewing.

Even a cursory examination of commercial children's programs reveals that there is little effort to benefit the audience. Productions are dependent on advertising revenues and the major aim is, therefore, to capture the largest audience possible. This is inexpensively accomplished by offering a steady diet of cartoons, clowns, and situation comedies. One of the few exceptions is the longstanding leader in commercial programs for preschoolers, "Captain Kangaroo," starring a gentle old sea captain who brings a daily morning hour of comedy, stories, music, and stimulating activities. Children also seem to watch great numbers of commercial advertisements and are, in fact, perfect targets for their repetitive "oversell." Prominent sponsors of children's programs are food (especially breakfast cereal) producers, and manufacturers of toys, toothpaste, and children's shoes. Finally, it seems clear that young children also watch a variety of programs not specifically devised for them, including news broadcasts, sports, police dramas, westerns, adult movies, situation comedies, variety shows, etc.

In contrast to commercial television, the public network is committed to enhancing the development of its viewers, young or old. It carries several excellent programs, including, for example, "Misterogers' Neighborhood," in which soft-spoken Mr. Rogers leads an exploration of the child's world, his feelings, problems and joys; "The Friendly Giant," whose speciality is reading children's stories; "Sesame Street;" and a program to aid in teaching reading to young school-age children, "The Electric Company."

"Sesame Street" is unquestionably the most important television program for 3-5 year old children. Launched in 1969 by a coalition of federal agencies and private foundations, the program's main target is the culturally disadvantaged, urban, at-home preschool child. It has been designed by child development specialists primarily to enhance cognitive development and capitalizes on principles long familiar to advertising experts as effective attention-getters: repetition, fast action, contemporary slang, music, etc. The daily, hour-long format is a swift change-of-pace composite which employs adults and children of several races, a variety of puppets, "commercials" to teach numbers and letters, problem-solving episodes, visual discrimination games, etc. Immensely popular among children of all social groups, it is estimated to reach perhaps half of the preschool children in the United States (Ball and Bogatz, 1970). To win acceptance from low-income parents, the program has emphasized academic skills more than most child development experts would recommend. A new program, beginning in the fall of 1973, emphasizes the child's social and emotional development.

In spite of tremendous concern and controversy over the impact of television on children, research efforts have been scarce and sporadic. Concern over violence in programming led to the formation of a Scientific Advisory Committee on Television and Social Behavior under the auspices of the U.S. Surgeon General, to investigate the effects of television violence on human behavior. The group investigated previous research and commissioned additional studies. It was concluded that there is indeed a casual link between watching TV violence and subsequent aggression by the viewer. It was also emphasized, however, that TV violence is not the *principal* cause of violent behavior, but rather can best be described as an exacerbating factor which may trigger aggression in those children "who have been predisposed to be aggressive by other influences in their lives . . . the least capable of interpreting and resisting the anti-social influence of TV violence . . ." (Siegel, 1972). The group also maintained rather forcefully that self-regulation in the television industry has not worked. They made no plea for government censorship, but recommended consumer pressure on commercial networks through refusal to purchase the products of or stock in those companies who sponsor programs with too much violence.

Regarding the impact of TV advertising on young children, there is much debate but very little research. Areas warranting investigation include the extent to which children's preferences are influenced by advertising and the extent to which they influence their parents' purchases; the nature of conflicts engendered within families when parents cannot or will not satisfy the desires of children which have

[173]

been created by advertising; and the degree to which children develop skepticism and critical consumer judgment after being disappointed in products highly touted in commercials.

A few scattered studies have looked at family viewing habits. It has been shown, for example, that television receivers are turned on for a larger proportion of the day in low-income families than in middle-income families, often with no one watching (Tulkin and Kagan, 1970). Another study has indicated that young children who are frequent watchers tend to be physically active but interpersonally passive (Murray, 1972). The preponderance of available empirical data regarding children's programming are in the domain of cognitive development, most of it stemming from evaluations of "Sesame Street." There is some evidence that this program has been relatively effective in achieving direct teaching goals, e.g., recognizing letters, counting, classifying, recognizing body parts, etc. Of particular interest is the fact that during the series' first six months, three-year-old viewers made more progress in those skills directly taught than did older children. Five-year-olds, on the other hand, showed greater indirect effects (e.g., reading words, which was not a direct goal of the early programs). It is not surprising that the more frequently children watched, the greater their learning, and that those whose mothers also watched and discussed the program with them made the greatest gains. With certain subcultures, such as the Spanish-speaking, the program has proved remarkably effective. Observations have also revealed that girls tend to give greater visual attention to the programs, while boys are more physically responsive; both, however, make significant gains.

It appears, then, that potential benefits of television are only beginning to be tapped. "Sesame Street" provides a clear example of a children's program which is both entertaining and beneficial to cognitive growth. Such programming requires extensive planning, careful and continuous evaluation, and generous funding. Many have recommended that temporary government support be given to public television for such endeavors in the hope that commercial networks can be made to understand that cartoons and violence are not the only genres to which young children can be attracted.

VII

Training of personnel

A. GENERAL EDUCATION

"Regular" school in America begins at age 6 and continues for 12 years. Organization of the 12 grades varies in different school districts, but a typical pattern includes a 6-year elementary school, 3-year junior high school, and 3-year senior high school. The school a child attends is determined by area of residence. The average size of elementary schools is 400 pupils and the average size of secondary schools is 750; in the large cities, elementary schools average 650 pupils and secondary schools 1,400 (Kahn and Hughes, 1967).

School attendance is compulsory until age 16 in most stages, yet through failure or disinterest some children leave school before the 10th grade. A U.S. Census Bureau tabulation of young adults (ages 22–24) in 1970 indicated that 95 percent had completed at least the eighth grade, 83 percent had finished at least high school, 37 percent had completed at least one year of college, and 15 percent had completed four years of college or more.

Following high school, a number of alternatives are open. Some students obtain informal on-the-job training, enter a trade school, a union-controlled apprenticeship program, or a two-year "junior" college, all of these more or less job-oriented. Others select a more academic program at a four-year under-graduate college or a university which has both undergraduate components and a number of postgraduate schools. Transfer from a two-year junior college to a four-year college or university is usually possible.

Undergraduates working for the Bachelor of Arts degree (B.A.) concentrate a portion of their studies in one "major" field, yet the B.A. degree in many of the arts and sciences is of little vocational value. Training for most professions begins after the completion of four years of general academic study; major exceptions are teaching, nursing, and engineering.

The graduate degrees awarded by a number of departments in the arts and sciences are the Master of Arts (M.A) after one or two years of graduate study, and the Doctor of Philosophy (Ph.D.), which requires, at a minimum, three years of study after the B.A. degree. There are a number of specialized professional degrees, for example the Doctor of Medicine (M.D.), Bachelor of Laws (L.L.B.), Doctor of Dentistry (D.D.S.), Doctor of Education (D.Ed.), etc. Some of these, such as the M.D., can be followed by still further formal education and intra-professional certification.

As might be expected, the proportions of young people pursuing higher education (post-high-school) are much greater in more affluent families and in those from metropolitan areas. Colleges and universities are now actively recruiting a broader range of students, and in many instances are making special arrangements for tutoring and other help, especially for students from minority groups. Some scholarships are available, but most students must find the means to pay their college tuition and to support themselves, or to be supported by their families. Tuition—excluding living expenses—ranges from a few hundred dollars per year in state-supported colleges and universities to approximately $3,000 in some private colleges and universities.

The largest educational aid program ever undertaken in the United States has operated since the close of World War II for military veterans. It alone has made possible the continued education of very large numbers of men and a few women from all walks of life, has placed more mature students in under-graduate classes, and has broken down socioeconomic barriers to education.

The growth of the junior colleges and community colleges since World War II has also increased the opportunities for post-high-school education. These colleges usually have very low tuition and are often situated in metropolitan areas so that students can live at home while they attend school. This development has opened a number of possibilities for training workers in the area of early childhood : medical assistants, child-care workers, social work aides, and others.

The entire educational system in the United States is quite an open one. At neither the elementary nor the secondary level is there academic selection for a particular school or program. No special examination is required for completion of any degree prior to graduate school. Even college admission is coming to be considered a right for all high school graduates, and many states try to provide a place in college for each qualified applicant who is a high school graduate. Many colleges and universities are selective, of course, under the pressure of too many applications, and most graduate schools are as well.

B. TRAINING OF HEALTH PERSONNEL

1. Physicians

Between 1910 and 1950, medical education all over the country followed a standard pattern suggested by the now-classic 1910 Flexner Report, which had thoroughly reformed a chaotic and unprofessional state of affairs in medical education. Training in the medical colleges (about half of them state-supported, half private) began after three or, preferably four, undergraduate years of premedical preparation in a college or university. It consisted of two years of work in the basic sciences without much patient contact, followed by two years of clinical training in a variety of specialty areas such as medicine, surgery, pediatrics, and obstetrics and gynecology. The four years leading to the Doctor of Medicine (M.D.) degree were followed by a mandatory year of internship which might rotate through several areas or concentrate on one, according to the student's preference. Residency training to achieve specialization gradually developed until it consisted of programs lasting two to six years more. Residencies in Pediatrics typically last three years; in child psychiatry, five. Because of this elaborate training, most physicians upon entering practice are approximately 27 years old if they have terminated their training with the internship (usually becoming general practitioners), 29–33 if they have taken a residency. About 70 percent of today's physicians are specialists.

The 18 schools of public health in the United States are additional sources of training for physicians and nurses. Many graduates of these programs become health department officials and supervisors of some of the large-scale programs for mothers and children.

Conservative forces may have been very strong in the field of medicine, but a variety of changes in medical education have slowly evolved since the 1950's. The American Medical Association has relaxed its opposition to the founding of new schools of medicine; the 8,000 physicians who have typically graduated each year constitute barely replacement level in a national supply of 300,000 physicians, many of whom have been recruited from foreign countries. In 1972, there were 89 schools of medicine in operation and 19 new ones being established. Student bodies in existing schools have also been modestly expanded, and recruiting patterns have been diversified in terms of social background, ethnic group, and sex; no longer are medical students almost invariably young middle-class white males.

Among the many curricular changes, some of the more important trends have been early contact with patients; decreasing the duration of the M.D. program from four to three years, often by curtailing vacations; interdepartmental teaching (e.g., around organ systems rather than traditional specialties); allowing for more elective courses; increasing the role of the social sciences and attention to non-organic factors in illness; utilization of non-hospital urban clinical facilities (especially community health centers and clinics) and some rural facilities; and the commitment to eliminate the free-standing internship by 1975, incorporating it into the regular graduate program. Many of the changes have emanated from the preferences of the students themselves, such as a shift toward family medicine as a specialization, an increasingly popular residency program.

Various committees and councils of the American Medical Association are the primary bodies which approve or disapprove medical education programs, internships, and residencies. To be licensed in most states, a physician must be a graduate of an approved school of medicine and have passed an examination (usually the one administered by the National Board of Medical Examiners). Half the states now require the internship but will no longer do so after 1975. Certification in a medical specialty is not a state matter; standards are set by the appropriate professional group itself and typically include a residency, various examinations, and other experimental requirements.

Metamorphoses in health care in the United States—expansion of public services, increased use of auxiliary personnel, alternatives to solo private practice, cognizance of the special needs of particular groups, and greater awareness of social and psychological factors in all areas of health for rich and poor alike—all these changes will continue to demand changes in the training of physicians.

2. Nurses

Professional nurses are known as registered nurses (R.N.'s); at lower levels of authority and responsibility are licensed practical nurses (L.P.N.'s), nursing aides, orderlies, attendants and home health aides.

Registered nurses may be trained in one of three types of programs : associate degree programs, usually of two years duration, offered primarily by junior colleges; diploma programs, typically lasting three years, conducted by hospital schools of nursing (these are disappearing rapidly); and four-year baccalaureate programs located in colleges and universities. All of these programs presuppose high school graduation and most of the baccalaureate programs require one or two years of preprofessional college preparation. Several avenues for postgraduate training are open to the registered nurse. Many diploma nurses return to school to obtain baccalaureate degrees, for example, and baccalaureate nurses often enter master's or doctoral programs in university schools of medicine. There are also some specialized nursing fields which require technical training but do not necessarily yield an advanced degree.

Nursing, like medicine, is subject to state licensure and a graduate of any of the three types of schools is eligible to be licensed. However, baccalaureate graduates usually receive preferential treatment in postgraduate educational opportunities, type of employment, and salary. The associate or diploma nurse is much more likely to be used in direct patient care, the baccalaureate nurse in supervisory and training positions.

Almost 70 percent of the approximately 723,000 currently active registered nurses are employed by hospitals and other in-patient institutions; about 16 percent are employed in doctors' offices and private duty settings; another 10 percent are employed by public health agencies, schools, and industrial concerns; and approximately 4 percent are engaged in teaching.

Nursing education and nursing practice are in a state of flux. One major development has centered around the creation of positions with increased responsibility for patient care, sometimes primary care of a type previously confined to physicians. One such position is in the field of pediatrics, where nurse practitioners provide a considerable amount of well-child and even sick-child care with minimal supervision. Highly specialized training in pediatric nursing is available in such areas as care of young burn victims and pediatric pulmonary disease. There has also been increased utilization of nurses in broad spectrum settings such as family practice clinics and community health centers. There is every likelihood that these trends toward increasingly sophisticated roles will continue, particularly as concerns the health care of mothers and young children.

3. Dentists

In the United States there are approximately 103,000 dentists, of whom approximately 91 percent are currently active in private practice. About 10 percent of these are recognized as specialists, nearly half in the area of orthodontics. Relatively few dentists have specialized in pedodontics. As in the other areas of health care, there is an increasing trend toward the utilization of auxiliaries in routine aspects of patient care.

Almost all the 52 dental schools operate four-year programs, and most of these require graduation from an undergraduate university or college. Specialization generally takes two additional years of training. State licensing is required and is contingent upon graduation from an accredited program and passing a state examination.

4. Pharmacists

Pharmacists are trained in Schools of Pharmacy which are associated with schools of medicine, are affiliated with four-year colleges and universities, or are independent. A total of five years of post-high-school education is required, including a minimum of three years in

the College of Pharmacy. State licenses may be obtained after graduation from an accredited school, one year of internship, and a written
examination. There are approximately 129,000 pharmacists currently
active.

C. TRAINING OF SOCIAL WELFARE PERSONNEL

1. Social workers

Although their distribution is quite uneven both geographically and
over different population groups, there are some 65 social workers
for every 100,000 people in the United States (U.S. Department of
Health, Education, and Welfare, 1966). These workers are almost
always women. Many begin their career before or early in marriage,
interrupt it while their children are young, and then return. Some,
therefore, hold their jobs for relatively brief periods; for example, in
the late 1950's, 27 percent of the workers who held a child welfare
job at the beginning of one year were no longer with the agency
toward the end of the same year (Tollen, 1960).

Most public and private agencies require a Master of Social Work
degree (M.S.W.). Preparation for such a degree usually entails a
college education—most often with a major in a social or behavioral
science or the humanities—and two years of graduate work divided
about equally between academic and field instruction. The basic
academic program usually includes courses in human growth and development; psychopathology; social institutions; social welfare programs and policies; and theory and methods of social work practice.
Most schools emphasize specialized work in specific problem areas,
including problems of children and youth, poverty, delinquency, etc.
All students undergo a supervised work experience. From their inception, nearly all schools of social work have been part of established
colleges and universities. An accrediting organization—the Council of
Social Work Education—sets standards and regularly reviews the
programs of individual schools. Most social workers emphasize their
desire to "work with people rather than with things," (Rosenberg,
1954), and prefer direct clinical work with troubled individuals rather
than object-oriented intervention. This emphasis has resulted in

[181]

gradations of prestige among the employing social agencies, with those dispensing psychotherapy having the highest and the economic assistance agencies having the lowest prestige.

In the past several years the work oriented and, more gradually, the training demands in child welfare have undergone considerable change. Although the final results of this transition are by no means clear, some salient developments can be identified : a sharp increase in liberal, fairly militant social work students; renewed interest in organizational and institutional change; a move to reduce formal academic requirements; greater emphasis on applied field work preparation; and a trend toward multidisciplinary approaches to problems of the individual as well as society.

D. TRAINING OF PRESCHOOL AND DAY CARE PERSONNEL

1. Nursery school teachers

Nursery schools seldom require a teacher to hold any kind of certificate and many teachers in fact have no specialized training at all. This situation in the pre-kindergarten programs has opened the door for minority-group and lower socioeconomic status individuals (almost exclusively women) to become teachers, a healthy development which must, however, be balanced against the unknown costs of the minimal training they have had.

The status of a nursery school teacher varies markedly with the setting, but almost invariably her pay is extremely low. The low pay results from the lack of agreed upon standards and from the fact that the job tends to attract mothers who desire only part-time work and do not need to be self-supporting. Reliable statistics are not available, but the general impression is of a high turnover rate and a lack of professionalism. It is, of course, easy to find exceptions, particularly in university-based nursery schools where teachers are usually highly trained but seldom paid commensurately.

Nursery school training has been available for many years to interested students. The department in charge may be education, psychology, home economics, or a special department of child development. A few specialized colleges are also devoted to preparing pre-school teachers.

The advent of Head Start has given new impetus to this field and there has been a rapid expansion of training facilities. Many are in community colleges offering two- and four-year programs. One such two-year program requires courses in history, English composition, science, and general psychology; theory and methods of early childhood education; curriculum design; dynamics of family relationships; child psychology; art, music, and science for children; nutrition; and parent education. Additionally, the expansion of specialized university-level training for teachers of young children (kindergarten through grade three) has made it possible for future nursery school teachers to take appropriate courses and degrees in early childhood education (see below).

2. Kindergarten teachers

Most school systems require only a general elementary school certificate for kindergarten teachers, although there is now a trend toward special certification for teachers of the primary grades—kindergarten through grade three. Certificates usually require a very specific and comprehensive course of study covering child development, methods of teaching various elementary school subjects, a selection of liberal arts courses, etc. Practice teaching for at least one semester is invariably required. In some states, the final certificate is not given until after a year of probationary employment. Programs of study are offered by most colleges and universities. Continuing education is promoted in most states by requiring occasional evening or summer courses for certificate renewal. In-service workshops may also be provided by schools. There is diversity among the states in the specific requirements for the certificate, making transfer from one state to another occasionally difficult.

Approximately half of teachers now come from middle-class backgrounds; most of the rest, from blue-collar and farm families. Previously, the proportion of middle-class teachers was considerably higher. Kindergarten teachers on the job tend to be isolated from the rest of the faculty, and to suffer rather low status. They are the only classroom teachers with two separate shifts of pupils, and their classes seldom participate in school activities which bring them into contact with the other pupils or teachers.

There are practically no male kindergarten teachers, although men constitute about 15 percent of elementary school faculty members. The profession is regarded by many women as temporary and as "insurance" against a time when it may be necessary or desirable to seek employment. In fact, more than a quarter of the college graduates who are prepared to teach never do so, and 60 percent of those who enter the field leave within five years. Although there now exist a surplus of teachers in some areas, this is not true of qualified kindergarten teachers, who are still rare enough to be assured of ready employment. Thousands more will be needed if the trend toward offering kindergarten as a regular part of elementary schools continues. Teacher salaries have improved markedly in the past decade, now amounting on the average to over $10,000 per year.

3. Child development associates

Day care workers and aides to nursery school and kindergarten teachers have had little if any professional status or means of advancement. The Office of Child Development has recently sought to develop a category of trained workers which will carry the certificate of "child development associate." The requirements of this new certificate are not yet clear, but they are expected to involve some training in the area of child development, as well as demonstration of competence in dealing with children. The junior colleges and community colleges are likely sites for the development of such programs, in cooperation with day care and early education programs.

E. TRAINING OF OTHER SPECIALISTS

1. Developmental psychologists

Only a few decades ago, the field of developmental or child psychology was an observational and descriptive discipline concerned with children's development. It has grown and diversified so that it now tends to be simply general psychology applied to human children and the young of other species. There are substantial numbers of developmental psychologists concerned with matters directly dealt with in this monograph but many more whose interests range far from the practical problems of upbringing. Developmental psychology constitutes a sometimes volatile mixture of basic theoretical science and applied technology; of concern with underlying fundamental laws of behavior and concern with the common, real-life experiences of children and families. Cutting across these diverse areas of interest are equally diverse theoretical frameworks. Broad psychodynamic theories stand side by side with a variety of cognitive theories, theories concerned primarily with the effects of patterns of reinforcement upon behavior, theories viewing behavior as having a substantial genetic component, and those which ignore genetic factors.

Most graduate programs in developmental phychology are components of Departments of Psychology and are aimed at the Ph.D. degree. Graduate training involves a rather limited amount of practical work with children, usually focusing instead upon basic theory and research. Most programs allow a great deal of personal selection on the part of the student. Ordinarily, the work requires about four years, although this period is somewhat shorter for some students, and considerably longer for others. During the latter part of graduate study, students undertake a substantial, independent and original empirical investigation which is the *sine qua non* of the Ph.D. degree, clearly establishing its character as a research credential.

Most Ph.D. recipients in developmental psychology become teachers and researchers in colleges and universities. Some are involved with research and evaluation in non-university settings, and a few are employed in early childhood programs as administrators and consultants. Employment opportunities have been relatively plentiful.

2. Clinical child psychologists

Clinical psychology is concerned primarily with the diagnosis and treatment of personal problems faced by children and adults. This applied professional orientation does not easily fit into the academic and research orientation of departments of psychology. Training programs have therefore utilized settings such as psychiatric clinics and hospitals, residential institutions for the mentally retarded, schools, etc. This practicum training has been supplementary to academic training for Ph.D. within academic university programs. A few universities are experimenting with a specialized degree, not the Ph.D., which would appropriately reduce the emphasis on conducting research and enhance opportunity for clinical training.

Most states require the practicing clinical psychologist to obtain a license, which is contingent upon obtaining the Ph.D. or an equivalent degree from an accredited university program, a stipulated amount of supervised clinical practice, and passing a state examination. Few clinical psychologists are involved in programs for preschool children.

VIII

Sources of information for parents

To JUDGE BY the paucity of organized efforts in parent education, one might believe that American parents are so skilled and secure that little need exists, an assumption not matched by reality. With the trend toward small nuclear families, large numbers of young people, inexperienced at child care, feel unprepared for the arrival of the first baby and tend to question themselves at every normal crisis as the child grows up.

A. WRITTEN MATERIAL

A natural step of the anxious parent is to turn to manuals on baby care. In the United States, there is a plentiful supply of such "do-it-yourself" manuals; indeed, they constitute the richest and most available source of help outside of friendly (sometimes unsought) advice from family and neighbors. The major public information resource is the U.S. Children's Bureau, which has published 11 editions (over 50 million copies) of *Infant Care*. *Your Child From One to Six* is a similar all-purpose manual, and there are numerous other booklets and folders dealing with special topics, most of them available for ten to twenty-five cents.

As might be expected, many commercially published books are also available. By far the most popular has been *Baby and Child Care* written and periodically revised since 1945 by Dr. Benjamin Spock. More than 24,000,000 copies have been sold. This practical manual, while telling the parent to trust himself, discusses a wide gamut of child-management matters. The younger half of the nation's present population is sometimes called, with some justification, the "Spock Generation."

There are currently large numbers of other books dealing with infant and child care, both from the point of view of practical problems (e.g., Better Homes and Gardens Baby Book, 1969) and from the perspective of the child's feelings and fears (e.g., Fraiberg, 1959;

Ginott, 1967). A few authors have attempted to bring parents the message of the new revolution in early childhood education (e.g., Pines, 1966) and some manuals have been prepared in conjunction with compensatory education programs (e.g., Wittes and Radin, 1969). Parents can also obtain free pamphlets on childrearing, published by drug companies for advertising purposes and distributed in doctors' offices. Almost every women's magazine and the women's section of many daily newspapers publish regular features of advice to parents by recognized experts in pediatrics, child psychiatry, or developmental psychology.

B. RADIO AND TELEVISION

Radio broadcasts in the United States now consist almost entirely of music and news, but it might have been expected that television would capitalize upon the new focus of attention on the young and the photogenic nature of children. This has unfortunately not been the case : except for isolated programs, television has played a negligible role in parent education.

C. CLASSES

In most public schools, teenagers have been given little help in preparation for parenthood. Home economics courses for junior and senior high school girls are offered in most schools but they are seldom compulsory and they are rarely concerned with the problems of motherhood. Recently, however, a major program has been launched jointly by the U.S. Office of Education and the Office of Child Development to teach adolescents—both male and female—how to become good parents. During its first year, 1973, the "Education for Parenthood Program" calls for establishment of 500 local projects, serving about 500,000 students, in which classroom instruction is combined with practical, field-based experience. Students will work with children in Head Start classes, day care centers, and kindergartens. The program will entail development of a curriculum model covering child development, household management, health, nutrition, and aspects of interpersonal relationships in families with young children.

Since 1967, one of the most important developments in parent education has been the emergence of comprehensive service programs designed for pregnant, unwed school-age girls who will probably keep their babies. Some programs provide day care, primarily in order to enable the young mothers to continue their schooling after the birth of the child; classroom discussion and practical experience also focus upon improving mothering skills. These programs typically include counseling services, and arrangements are made to ensure the health care of mothers and infants.

At the college level, courses in child development in departments of psychology and home economics vary from some oriented toward the future parent or teacher to other oriented toward the science of human development.

Among the classes for the adult general public, the most important, with 83,000 students in 1969, have been those offered for pregnant women by the American Red Cross. The classes deal primarily with prenatal care, delivery, and health and nutrition during the infant's first year. A few other courses in family life education are offered through community colleges and various local groups.

A number of efforts to reach low-income families have been undertaken recently. Traditional classroom approaches have not worked with such parents (Amidon and Brim, 1972; Kraft and Chilman, 1966)† but when they have been required to become involved in activities with their children, parent education has apparently been more effective (Miller, 1969). So many different efforts have been made to find the "right" combination to reach parents that, in fact, no typical pattern in compensatory and community programs has yet emerged (Stearns and Peterson, 1973).

---

† Amidon and Brim, it should be pointed out, take the position that none of the programs involving parents has been effective in enhancing children's development.

IX

Research relating to the infant and preschool child

RESEARCH ACTIVITIES in the United States related to the early periods of human development have been numerous and varied. During the past few years, in particular, there has been a burgeoning of research efforts concerned with the beginning months and years of life. At the 1971 and 1973 biennial meetings of the interdisciplinary Society for Research in Child Development, for example, papers concerned with the very young, especially infants and toddlers, far outnumbered those concerned with older children. About two-thirds of the studies reported in this group's research journal, *Child Development,* in 1970–71 utilized infants or preschool children, at least in part, as did 43 percent of the studies reported in the American Psychological Association's journal, *Developmental Psychology.* Among studies sponsored in 1970–71 by the National Institute of Child Health and Human Development, biomedical and behavioral studies of prenatal and infant development outweighed those of any other age period. The National Institute of Mental Health and the Office of Education have also given a high priority to research with young children. Finally, the intervention programs for disadvantaged young children already described are each being carefully evaluated and modified by concurrent research.

1. Personnel and funding

Universities maintain by far the major concentrations of research talent and facilities in this country. More than 200 such institutions are scattered about the 50 states. Faculty members are usually expected to be involved in research endeavors on their own initiative, and in fact personnel decisions (e.g., promotion, salary) are often largely based upon the quality and quantity of research productivity. Graduate students, especially candidates for the Ph.D. degree, also constitute an important pool of sophisticated investigators.

Most of the research supported by public and private agencies actually takes place within the universities, sometimes in university-based centers set up to accomplish specified goals. The U.S. Office of Education, for example, has given funds to universities to establish seven major laboratories, dealing with problems in early childhood education, and eight important research and development centers, most of which also include some studies of the preschool child. Similarly, the National Institute for Child Health and Human Development has made sizable grants to establish and run twelve university centers devoted to multi-disciplinary approaches to the causes and treatment of a broad range of childhood handicaps with particular emphasis on the problems of mental retardation.

Some early childhood research also takes place within the laboratories of government agencies, notably the National Institute of Mental Health and the National Institute of Child Health and Human Development. Coordinated evaluation programs related to Head Start and similar programs are controlled by appropriate government agencies (e.g., Office of Child Development, Office of Education) but large-scale evaluation studies are often contracted out to private research corporations. The combined private and public agency research efforts, however, are dwarfed in comparison with research activity within the universities.

Among the professional fields most active in child-oriented research endeavors are developmental psychology and the pediatric health sciences. The field of education, previously oriented almost exclusively toward service, is becoming increasingly research-oriented, particularly as schools recognize and communicate their difficulties in meeting the needs of special groups of students. Social workers have been singularly uninvolved with research, although there are signs of change. Finally, researchers in home economics, nutrition, and in behavioral sciences such as sociology, anthropology, and political science, are turning their attention toward the environment of the young child.

During the past decade, the availability of research funds was sometimes greater than the ability and the number of appropriate researchers to use them. Particularly for studies concerned with problems of mental retardation, disadvantaged populations, and early education, this was a period of very rapid expansion during which numerous large-scale research centers were established. For a time is seemed that almost anyone who wanted to study almost any aspect of the development of infants and young children could obtain rather generous support. Most areas of research, however, had reached a funding plateau or even a slight reduction by 1970 (Searcy, 1970b), which in view of inflationary pressures actually resulted in a reduction of research activities. The field of early childhood research has probably not undergone the same degree of retraction that has characterized other sciences (Handler, 1971), but the days of seemingly unlimited funding are certainly over.

Most research funds have come from the federal government, particularly from branches of the Department of Health, Education, and Welfare, including the various National Institutes of Health, the Children's Bureau (now reorganized under two agencies), and the Office of Education, as well as from the Office of Economic Opportunity. Other important sources of research funding have been private foundations such as the Carnegie Corporation and the Ford Foundation, which have tended to use their resources to encourage socially significant but neglected fields. With their more limited funds, interest groups such as the National Association for Retarded Children (a parents' association) and the March of Dimes (which some years ago shifted its interest from prevention and treatment of poliomyelitis to the prevention of birth defects), and state and local governments have supported research related to young children.

Most research projects are undertaken at the initiative of the researcher himself, or in combination with other researchers who have coordinated interests. They submit grant proposals to one or more agencies which are potential funding sources. As a general policy of all federal agencies (and many state and private ones as well), the scientific merits of proposals are reviewed by panels of qualified independent researchers from outside the agency. Agencies may accept proposals suggested by researchers within a broad area of interest, or they may invite proposals which address a more specific research need. When money is made available for a specific purpose, there is almost always a shift to that topic by some qualified researchers. Sometimes this process works well and productively; sometimes, however, the research represents a more apparent than real attack on the problem. The pattern of making funds available for investigations of specific problems, although still not the dominant routine, is becoming more frequent.

Just as we have seen in the areas of programs and services, there is in the area of research considerable fragmentation of effort. Numerous governmental agencies with overlapping responsibilities are concerned with children's development, but few, indeed, are aware of the total picture. A report of a special federal Interagency Committee convened to develop a coherent picture of federal sponsorship of research in early learning, for example, found that the goals and objectives of research activities, as well as planning for future activities, were largely uncoordinated (Searcy, 1970a). Most professionals in the United States believe that there are inherent dangers in centralizing financial control over research, particularly because of the temptation to neglect basic research, unpopular theories, and even applied problems not directly related to ongoing programs. The present situation, on the other hand, is probably more disorderly than is desirable.

2. Current research interests

The far-flung child development research community is, in fact, studying many aspects of development, and a broad range of factors in the environment which influence that development from the moment of conception on. Just as in other affairs of human concern, there tend to be fads in content and styles of research. New and interesting areas and methods will for a time catch the fancy of large numbers of researchers who later move on to other topics to approach old problems with new techniques.

Within the past few years, the following have been some of the more important areas which have attracted the interest of researchers in many parts of the country:

Prenatal and perinatal factors and their effects on later behavior
    Anesthesia at delivery
    Chromosomal and genetic abnormalities
    Complications of pregnancy and delivery
    Detection of genetic disorders *in utero*
    Malnutrition

Infancy and toddlerhood

    Assessment of developmental patterns
    Attachment behavior (child to mother)
    Attention to novel and familiar stimuli
    "Critical periods" hypotheses (e.g., studies of imprinting)
    Early experience, effects on later behavior (predominantly animal studies)
    Enhancement of learning (infant stimulation)
    Instrumental learning
    Mother-infant interaction
    Sensorimotor development
    Sensory processes

Preschool age

    Assessment of development (especially cognitive and language)
    Curriculum development for preschool programs
    Discrimination learning
    Intervention (group educational programs, home tutoring, parent education)
    Language acquisition
    Moral judgment
    Operant conditioning and behavior modification
    Piaget-inspired studies, especially conservation
    Sex-role acquisition
    Social learning, modeling and imitation
    Television's effects on behavior (especially aggression)

In almost every aspect of development, there has been interest in children and families of differing social status, particularly those of very low economic status compared to those of the middle class.

The decade of the 1960's brought an intense involvement in compensatory intervention programs, as we have seen in previous sections of this report. Considerably more than half the research funds in early learning were devoted to this area by 1970. This probably signals the profound transformation of the field of child development from that of rather passive on-looker, preoccupied with descriptive and theoretically-based laboratory research, so that of active participant, committed to social engineering and to enhancing the development of children, particularly those whose life circumstances are most handicapping.

Within the behavioral sciences, the greatest proportion of research activity has been devoted to cognitive development. Research in this area has been spurred on by a number of factors. Controversies over definitions of intelligence, the types and organizations of mental abilities observed in children and adults, and the role of genetic vs. environmental factors have been central issues in psychology ever since its establishment as a separate discipline. Assessment of intellectual abilities (general and specific) has long occupied the attention of investigators, and a number of reliable instruments are already at hand to be utilized in various settings. More recently, the wave of interest in Piaget's work, stimulated especially by publication of the translation of *The Origins of Intelligence in Children* (1952), has given a new impetus to investigations of cognitive development in the very young. Then, too, the desire to develop the optimal intellectual potential of all citizens who are to participate in an increasingly complex technological society has lent an urgency to investigations of early child care and education programs. The growing conviction that it is the earliest years of life which are most crucial to cognitive development (Bloom, 1964) has been of special importance.

Research efforts concerned with the social-emotional development of young children have been considerably less satisfactory than those efforts concerned with cognitive development. They have been hampered primarily by the lack of an accepted orientation—either theoretical or practical—which relates early social-emotional development to adult patterns. The works of Freud no longer seem as promising as they once did, but no substitute has taken their place. Furthermore, suitable measurement instruments to assess social and emotional development have been lacking; although there have been a number of recent efforts to develop such tools, none has proved very satisfactory with young children. Actually, some of the most successful American psychological research in this area has dealt with the extinction of discrete "problem" behaviors and the establishment of specific, socially-approved behaviors. These studies, based on the work of B. F. Skinner (1938) and his followers, have utilized operant conditioning procedures and developed a behavior modification technology capable of being applied in many settings.

Much of the research of a developmental nature has not dealt with human subjects. Indeed, most of the investigations dealing with the effects of early experience have been conducted with lower animals such as rats, dogs, and primates. Although there are inevitable problems in generalizing to the realm of human behavior, such studies are of considerable theoretical interest, and they, of course, permit numerous manipulations which would be both impractical and unethical with human infants and children. Observation of the behavior of different species in their naturally occurring habitats have also made significant contributions to knowledge about the complexities of development.

Within the health sciences there has been an expanding interest in research from the prenatal period through early childhood. Biomedical investigations into the identification, prevention, and treatment of diseases, and the development of a technology permitting treatment of many life-threatening disorders, have been vigorously pursued. As in the behavioral sciences, attention is now being devoted to the delivery of services to all children, not just the privileged few, so that demands upon the field of health sciences are intense indeed.

There has been the wholesome trend in the past few years toward inter-disciplinary cooperation in research. For example, studies of the long-range effects of biomedical complications of pregancy and delivery have been assessed both in physiological and in behavioral terms. Developmental psychologists have entered prominently into the educational scene. Studies of language development involve both psychologists and specialists in linguistics. The early discovery and attempted remediation of learning disabilities in nonretarded children (e.g., reading handicaps) have profited from the combined efforts of educators, neurologists, and psychologists. Studies of retarded and severely disturbed children have been carried out jointly by professionals from many disciplines. Finally, a number of professional groups have become involved in investigations related to day care. This healthy trend seems likely to continue, although it must be admitted that cooperation is sometimes more apparent than real, and that investigators have often settled for studying similar problems in their own way rather than in genuine interaction. Even so, the growing awareness within each profession of the tools and insights of other disciplines has already led to many favorable outcomes.

3. Relevance of research findings to problems of child care

During the period since World War II, the entire scientific community has enjoyed a sort of honeymoon with the public at large. New technological advances built on "pure science" discoveries have helped to encourage public acceptance of science for its own sake. Many Americans—even young children—have been aware that Newtonian physics was important to the spectacular achievements in outer space, and that the work of Einstein helped pave the way to the Atomic Age. The potential effects of the new knowledge about the biochemical nature of heriditary mechanisms have been sensed without the demand for immediate applications. There has been confidence, too, that support for the behavioral sciences would have beneficial consequences, even if they were somewhat slower in coming. There has been, then, a rather uncritical support of research for its own sake, with little concern about the wisdom of the investigator's choice of questions.

There has recently emerged, though, an increased concern about the relevance of publicly supported research activities. With the advent of the large scale social action programs of the 1960's, many behavioral scientists were invited to leave their laboratories and to enter the arenas of education, health care, infant and child care, and community dynamics as active participants. These scientists have been asked to demonstrate what they accomplished and this new emphasis on accountability has been increasingly applied to all scientific endeavors.

An analysis of early learning research in 1970 revealed that approximately 27 percent of funding went to basic research activities, 58 percent to research related to intervention programs, and 15 percent to evaluations of various projects (Searcy, 1970b). This represents a decided reduction in the proportion of basic research activities as compared with a decade ago, but a proportion likely to be maintained in the foreseeable future. The Interagency Committee under the auspices of the Office of Child Development has recommended a future

[197]

allocation of 25 percent for basic research, 37 percent for intervention research, and 37 percent for evaluation of projects.

4. Communication within and between disciplines

The rapid growth of research endeavors related to children has made it difficult for the professional to keep abreast of his own field. In spite of a plethora of professional journals relevant to the various aspects of children's development, there is simply not enough journal space to publish many of the sound studies being carried out. There is, moreover, sometimes as much as a two-year lag from the time an article is accepted until it is published.

Various means have been undertaken to simplify the process of scanning the literature. Collected abstracts of published articles in fields such as child psychology and mental retardation are published regularly. Clearing houses in fields relevant to education have been established under the Educational Resources Information Centers (ERIC) sponsored by the U.S. Office of Education. Investigators and practitioners can obtain bibliographies on special topics and can view microfilm documents in library centers.

Professional meetings continue to be an important source of information exchange, and there has been a proliferation of professional societies devoted to particular specialties and subspecialties. Some societies (such as the Society for Research in Child Development and the American Association for Mental Deficiency) have members from several disciplines, though, and their journals and meetings thus serve as vehicles for cross-disciplinary communication. Books and articles reviewing the literature and intended for broad audiences also help, as do symposia sponsored by universities, government agencies, and foundations.

Researchers, faculty members, students, and practitioners continue to decry the compartmentalization of both research and teaching into narrow specialties. The perennial problems remain, though, and as it becomes more difficult to keep up with advances in knowledge, there is ever more reason for the professional to restrict his interests. The situation, then, is somewhat paradoxical: current research and evaluation problems often require interdisciplinary teamwork, but at the same time, individual research workers are forced to become ever more specialized in order to maintain a high competence level.

5. The status of research

Child development research is a thriving activity in the United States today. It is free-ranging, vigorously debated, reasonably well supported, and generally of satisfactory quality. In these respects, the field has never been healthier. It cannot be stressed too strongly, however, that research efforts have failed to ask many questions relevant to the situations in which children and families actually live.

In some areas, considerable progress has clearly been made, and the future appears promising. In the field of cognitive development, for example, new insights about the way young children learn have had a significant effect on intervention programs, particularly at the pre-school level. Studies of the effects of a broad range of variables in the poverty backgrounds of young children have also shown encouraging progress.

Research into the social and emotional development of young children lags far behind. Surprisingly little research has been devoted to investigating the character development of the young child, his modes of developing internal control over his behavior, his moral development, the development of a responsible orientation toward others. Except for vague references to enhancing the positive self-concept of the young child or concern with the obviously deviant child whose behavior is annoying or symptomatic of profound emotional disturbance, researchers have attended rather sporadically to this complex area of development. Yet, paradoxically, several follow-up studies of early intervention programs show that the most significant long-range effects of these early experiences may lie in improvement in the child's environment and his concomitant attitudes rather than in his school achievement.

The area of day care has been subjected to little research as yet. Questions centering on the desirability of admitting infants, different staffing patterns, single-age versus multiple-age grouping, home-based care vs. center-based care, optimal size of group or center, and alternative plans for children with minor illnesses, have only begun to be asked.

The field of social welfare has likewise suffered from too little serious research attention. Little is known, for example, about the relative effectiveness of various modes of intervention in disordered families. Policy decisions about extensive work-training and financial-aid programs for families with young children have been and continue to be made in the absence of any data.

A large variety of aspects of the total social system in the United States obviously affect young children, yet few ask how. What would be the outcomes of a work week of four 10-hour days on the opportunities for fathers to be with children? What would be the effects on work output and child welfare? How would children be affected by changing the housing patterns to provide ethnic, socioeconomic mixes rather than homogeneous neighborhoods? Such questions are seldom asked of the research community and such policy decisions are seldom based on considerations of family and child.

There remain many other unasked and unanswered questions, both basic and applied. There is, however, an encouraging degree of inter-action between the research community and the nation—an interaction which has brought about fruitful questioning from all parties. It is hoped that there will be continued support for the broad scale research effort which has been established on behalf of children, and also that future research will be more concerned with the real life problems of children and families.

X

Future directions and recommendations

A. CHANGING LIFE STYLES

The present document is, more than anything else, a testament to change. Like the people of other industrialized countries, Americans have made a series of major accommodations to conditions created by a burgeoning technology. For some, the age of automation has invested their dreams with a positive, concrete reality : less work, more leisure, increasing material wealth, and better health—in short, "the good life." Others see it as "the full catastrophe"—a technocracy gone awry, unharnessed, unleashed, out of control. Regardless of the individual perspective, it is clear that change will continue to touch people's lives.

One of the most important results of technological advances has been the tremendously increased amount of leisure time, which in turn has led many to explore a variety of independent, idiosyncratic activities popularly known as "doing your own thing." A personalized apolitical anarchism has become increasingly in vogue, then, particularly among the young, and has been accompanied by increased recognition, tolerance and even appreciation of different lifestyles.

As conditions have changed and people have entered realms heretofore unexplored, substantial shifts in roles have occurred. It is no longer an automatic assumption, for example, that the father will be the sole breadwinner, disciplinarian, and final authority in family decisions. Women have entered the labor force in greater numbers, broadening their roles beyond tending to children, house and home. Children are no longer seen as miniature adults, but as persons having their own valid needs, rights, freedom and dignity. These role changes are viewed with sentiments ranging from appreciation to disgust—but seldom with indifference.

The changing roles within the family and society have rendered many parents confused and anxious. At one time in American history, there was a pretty fair consensus that the ideal citizen was bright, industrious, and achieving. These and many other previously cherished values have been called into question, however, so that parents are no longer confident of the goals they should have for their children, much less of the best methods to achieve whatever goals they do believe in. If there ever was a "right way" to bring up children, then, it has in large part disappeared, leaving in its void a host of unanswered questions.

The effects of accelerated urbanization, the growth of residential suburbs outside cities, and the concentrations of poor people in inner-city ghettoes have been strongly felt. Although housing has generally improved, the housing patterns *per se* have led to increasing segregation, isolation, anonymity. The stereotypic middle-class, lonely house-wife, for example, is all-too-familiar and real in America. Zoning restrictions against businesses in residential areas have created a situation in which children grow up without ever seeing the workers, craftsmen, designers, and others who produce the goods and services used by their families. Most neighborhoods tend to be very homogeneous, devoid of variety or color. This condition has increasingly led some people to explore communal living, neighborhood cooperatives, community preschools—anything to enhance their sense of participation and belonging.

The problems of housing patterns are paralleled in the work force of America : as jobs have become more specialized, the gap between an individual's endeavors and the final product has widened. Many are beginning to re-evaluate job satisfaction using new and different criteria : meaningfulness as opposed to salary level, enjoyment versus security. At the same time, however, corporate conglomerates have grown so huge and impersonal that there is little responsiveness to many of the more personal needs of the workers. It is common practice, for example, to relocate employees periodically without regard for the impact on them, their children, families, or friends.

Concomitant with an ambivalent, if not decreasing emphasis on material wealth has been the growing realisation that the world's natural resources are not unlimited. There is a great deal of talk, particularly among youth, of drastically lowering consumption of material goods. The extent to which rhetoric will be put into practice, though, is unclear.

Finally, the importance of developments in contraception and abortion should be reiterated. It is now relatively easy to control pregnancies and births, so that only those parents who really want children need have them. This situation will almost certainly accelerate the already-declining birthrate, and raises an important question : who will have children? Ideally, it should be those who desire children and are capable of raising them well. Historically, though, birthrates have been highest among the poor and uneducated, many of whom neither want large families nor do a particularly good job of raising them. Attempts to introduce birth control have met with great resistance by some groups who see such efforts as a subtle form of genocide. Certainly, this is a touchy area, lacking any easy answers.

It is almost impossible to predict the changes which may emerge in the next few years. As we have indicated, the United States tends to be an on-again, off-again nation, with alternating periods of dynamic change and stagnation. It seems clear, though, that the pendulum is swinging back toward more conservative points of view generated by desires for stability and less rapid change.

B. THE CHANGING COMPACT

There were vast changes during the decade of the 1960's in the nature of the compact between society and individuals in the form of tremendously increased governmental activity at all levels on behalf of citizens, especially poor ones. The Social Security program was broadened and its benefits increased. Health programs for the aged and the young were undertaken. Government entered the fields of early education and day care with a variety of compensatory programs. Environmental protection and safety became popular causes and began to be the subject of more stringent regulations. Consumer rights and civil rights had been expanded rather steadily for several decades, but with accelerated speed during the 1960's.

The expanding social welfare programs have led to a rather paradoxical situation. With increasing personal freedom and a social climate tending to favor increased individuality and "doing your own thing," the government has simultaneously entered a much wider arena of the problems of living, attempting to create a more uniform and just society. Indeed, there is some evidence that the government may have gone farther than the majority of citizens would like in furnishing public services and, consequently, increasing government participation in and regulation of people's lives. There is concern today about where to draw the line between the desire for individual responsibility and determination, unrestrained except to protect the rights of others, and the desire to live in a smoothly functioning society which is more responsive to the needs of all the people. In some areas, it is beginning to be understood, these two desires may be incompatible.

Most professionals in the medical field would, for example, like to establish a recording and monitoring system for individual health records, in order to maximize the continuity and effectiveness of health care. They fear, though, the dangers of uncontrolled access to computerized records as an abusive invasion of personal privacy. Most welfare recipients react negatively to the detailed scrutiny of their personal lives which has often been required in connection with assistance. Many other citizens, including most professional welfare workers, are also concerned about the routine invasions of privacy, and maintain that any reform of the welfare system will have to be arranged differently in this respect.

Given the current state of ambivalence about government sponsored social action programs, it is particularly difficult to predict future patterns of government activity with respect to domestic problems. President Nixon is committed to removing the federal government from a wide range of social welfare programs. He has strongly advocated that most programs in the areas of health, education, and welfare become, as they once were, the responsibility of state and local governments, bolstered in part by federal funding. If, as seems quite possible, this turn of events should occur, few new programs for children can be expected and present programs may even be reduced. It is likely, however, that there will be increased activity in day care and early education at both federal and state levels in the form of standard-setting, certification, and licensing procedures. The fulcrum of the compact of the society with the family may well shift from the present active participation of the federal government, to enhanced cooperation among the family, the local community, and the state.

[204]

Some matters will, however, probably continue to demand federal action. The byproducts of our industrial age in the form of pollution of sundry kinds must be brought under control, and the enormity of the technical and regulatory problems which transcend local and state boundaries and capabilities will require major responsibility on the part of the federal government. It seems likely, too, that the federal government will play a leading role in the devlopment of a better coordinated, more functional, fairer, and less expensive health system for all citizens, not just the elderly and the very poor.

C. SOME RECOMMENDATIONS ADDRESSED TO THE AMERICAN READER

We have examined the ways in which Americans provide for their children, and we have found diversity in almost every aspect of the upbringing process. Tendencies toward individuality and self-reliance, coupled with compassion for and commitment to children, have created a society in which most children fare relatively well but too many do not.

Americans are far from accomplishing a utopian society. Indeed, there exists in our nation a poignant awareness of the many ways in which we fall short of commonly held goals for a peaceful, safe, and just world, with opportunities for everyone to find self-fulfillment and happiness. A consensus is emerging, however, that the welfare of children is everybody's responsibility, and that new steps to create a better America must, first and foremost, consider the needs of children.

We cannot resist the chance, in the final pages of this monograph, to suggest to our American readers a few ways in which our country, by considering the needs of children, might enhance the quality of life for all. The recommendations we will make are surely not meant to be exhaustive. Much needs to be accomplished, and many meritorious proposals have been forcefully presented by other bodies of concerned Americans. Many of these have been touched upon in the preceding sections. We understand the urgent need for more effective measures to prevent accidents, to eliminate hunger and malnutrition, to improve housing, to rejuvenate the cities, to improve the training and status of

[205]

those who work with children, to make a full array of social, education, and health services available to all families, to integrate various
uncoordinated programs, etc. We want to focus now, though, on a few
proposals which seem to us to have special significance for the young
child and his family, but which have received relatively little attention.

1. The need for relevant research

We must face the fact that we only guess at the consequences of much
that we advocate for children and their families, and hope that we
help rather than hinder. Today there is a wave of support for day
care; a few years ago, day care was an anathema to the specialists in
early childhood. Minimal research on the effects of day care has been
accomplished in the intervening years and our positions now, and
then, are based much more on opinion and faith than on empirical
evidence.

It has become a cliché that man's understanding of the physical
world has far outstripped his understanding of his own human-social
world. We must counteract this state of affairs with strong support
for both basic and applied research in the social and behavioral
sciences in general and in the field of child development in particular.
We need to enhance the social relevance of much research we do, to
begin to investigate those matters which parents, professionals, and
planners need to understand in improving the lot of children and
families. We should especially examine the ecology of childhood and
its potential to help or hinder the development of children. There is
no dearth of questions, but until now there has indeed been a dearth
of researchers looking for the answers. We are at a point when many
of our federal social-action programs may be dismantled, and many
of those which survive will do so under the auspices of the states. It
is essential that there be no similar dismantling of the research community, which functions effectively as a cooperative national coalition,
surmounting state boundaries and institutional affiliations.

Many Americans feel that we have as a nation lost our way, that
we no longer know how to proceed in constructing the great society.
In our headlong rush toward that goal, we have clearly outstripped
the state of our practical knowledge. Certainly the problems are very

complex and solutions will not be easy, yet lasting solutions can only be firmly rooted in scientific theory and empirically demonstrable facts. We must do our utmost to encourage our best and most dedicated minds to work on human problems, and we must strongly support them in their efforts to light the way to a better, and better understood world. During what may be something of a pause in the growth of social support for families, we must take advantage of the lull to develop new solutions, to pave the way for wise decisions and realistic choices when we gather momentum again.

2. Part-time employment

Having said that we need more research on which to base our recommendations, we are nevertheless emboldened to make some specific suggestions. It seems abundantly clear to us that there exists today a number of imbalances in the life of American women. Freed by modern conveniences of much of the physical labor of their households, they have shown increasing eagerness to establish contacts outside the home, to participate in the social and economic world, and to reject, at least in part, the notion that their sole mission in life should be as wife and mother. Yet day care services are now difficult to arrange and often not of a quality which the mother can conscientiously accept. As longevity increases and the size of families decreases, child rearing requires a decreasing proportion of the average parent's life. It is clear, too, that there has been a growing acceptance of a variety of life styles for individuals and families, only some of which are oriented toward the accumulation of material wealth and the pursuit of security.

An obvious and relatively simple solution to many needs of many children and parents under such conditions is to increase the possibility of part-time employment. Employers have tended to reject the notion of part-time work because training costs and the present tax structure make such an arrangement more expensive than full-time employment. Solutions to these practical problems can be worked out with relative ease. They must not stand in the way of the possibility that parents be permitted the option to be responsible caretakers of their own children for part of the day (to their mutual enjoyment and benefit)

[207]

and yet remain in contact with the world of adults and with the continuity of their own careers. Some husbands and wives might arrange their working schedules to spend more time together and with their children; others would prefer an arrangement which obviated the necessity for an outsider to be called upon for child care. The beneficiaries of such a system would include both families and those employers who could use the special talents and enthusiasms of several individuals working part-time more fruitfully than those of fewer full-time employees. Existing high-quality day care facilities could also accommodate more children on a part-time basis than they can now serve full time.

And the children? Surely they would benefit most of all. Full day programs for them are often fatiguing, especially when they are very young, but children do profit, we believe, from shorter days in stimulating environments different from their own homes. Mothers and fathers still fresh and happy to see them when work is over are far to be preferred to weary parents at the end of a long day. Most important of all, we must affirm and support the crucial roles which parents play as the principal figures in the lives of their children, a very demanding task for which they need time, energy, and purpose.

3.   Revitalizing the role of parents

Whatever the services society can provide to improve the conditions under which children are brought up, the available evidence convinces us that attempts to substitute for the place of parents are makeshift and inferior at best. There seems to us danger in the United States that the roles of the parents are being usurped in subtle ways and that we need strongly to reaffirm that parents are in charge of what happens to their children. It is essential that parents understand that it is they who are the most important upbringers of their children—the chief teachers, the chief health workers, the chief socializers, etc. They must be able, of course, to rely upon help with all these functions but their primary responsibility must be abrogated. We have mentioned the subtle damage to preschool programs when the parents feel that the preschool is educating their children and that they themselves are simply ancillary to the program (Section VI, F).

If this is not to happen in every realm, it is essential that the parents retain decision-making powers, and that they have the time and the resources to remain personally and actively involved with their children.

Services to families in the United States have for the most part been based on small units, chosen by parents, and often directed by them. We have seen that most primary health care services are administered in private offices and small clinics; that private day care centers, family service agencies, and other small units have played a major role in welfare services, and so on. Parents have been free to select services and practitioners as they have seen fit.

The preschools still tend to fit this pattern. They are small units, most of which have substantial parent involvement, and together they offer a considerable variety of programs. Even the Public preschool programs have maintained considerable diversity and have been small enough and open enough to allow parents to play major policy roles.

The contrast with the situation in the public schools is striking. Although they, too, tended to begin as small units with intense parental involvement, many public schools have evolved, especially in large cities, into monolithic, impersonal, and bureaucratic structures with parents' roles tangential at best. The expectation in such schools is that services will be provided "by them" (the school personnel), rather than "by us" (parents, other citizens, and school personnel). It is easy to forget that, in America, government *is* the people, particularly easy once a gigantic bureaucratic structure has emerged.

We recommend that every effort be made to preserve the involvement of parents in the preschool in fundamental ways, and that the possibility of families' meaningful choice among services be enhanced wherever possible. It seems a good idea to us, in fact, to reexamine the system of public education—indeed, all our public institutions which are designed to strengthen families—with the aim of increasing parental determination.

We recommend that services be designed to strengthen the parents' effectiveness. Too often parents surmise that their children "get enough education" at preschool or regular school, that they "get enough play and exercise" with their friends—in short, that teachers, playground supervisors, Sunday school teachers, music teachers, and even other children are *the* important upbringers. We are not suggesting that all parents should devote themselves full-time to child care; we are suggesting, however, that they be fully aware of their own irreplaceable position in the lives of their children.

4. Including the needs of children in all economic and social planning

Almost everything which occurs in the United States has some impact on the lives of small children, and yet how few are the plans and decisions which actually take children into account! We are convinced that most people are sincerely motivated to promote the welfare of the young and that they need only to be made aware of ways in which they can help. Let us point to a few areas in which the "awareness quotient" is rather low at present.

In some instances, business decisions create serious disruptions of family life. Some of the worst offenders are large companies that routinely require some employees, particularly those in executive positions, to move from one site to another. The military services for many years have similarly required a periodic change of station of all their active forces, though to their credit the tours of service are now longer. Many religious denominations also move ministers routinely. Other less disruptive business practices which adversely affect family life are evening and weekend meetings and after-hours involvements required of many employees. It seems likely that if the benefits to children and families were weighted on a scale with potential advantages to the organization, a surprising number of decisions might be in favor of the former.

There are many more decisions in the world of work which represent simply missed opportunities to enrich the lives of children and families. Industries could, for example, adjust the work day to allow greater opportunities for parents to be with their children at favorable hours. This could take the form of more part-time work, earlier or later working days for some groups, or the possibility of working longer hours for fewer days. Arrangements might also be made to involve children in the work-life of their parents by periodic visits and even active participation on the job.

Many aspects of community planning and decision making should also, we feel, begin to take the needs of children and families more centrally into account. The increasing isolation and resulting alienation of individuals is one of the most serious problems facing America today. Many of us live in ever more homogeneous and increasingly sterile neighborhoods, lacking opportunities to interact meaningfully with people who differ in important ways. In most middle-class communities, for example, commercial enterprises are separated from residences. One must leave the neighborhood to purchase necessary goods and services. The automobile, the freezer, and other technological advances make it sensible to trade with large stores in shopping centers which collect in one area everything needed for daily living. This style of life is very efficient, but its robs us of relationships with others who contribute to our lives—the butcher, the baker, the dry cleaner, the shoe mender. Children have no chance to understand that someone has baked their bread, made their clothes, etc. The craftsman who takes pride in his work is unknown to them. We regard these as missed opportunities for the cognitive and the personal-social development of children, and for their parents as well.

There are many other ways in which communities might increase the occasions for meaningful interdependence of people. We must pay more attention to human needs in designing buildings, recreation areas, transportation systems, etc. In American neighborhoods, there is a large capacity for helpful, cooperative, "neighborly" interactions. Young children are able to visit friends without formal arrangements being made; one mother will "babysit" for the mother next door, and vice versa, with little thought about it; when the child enters preschool or school, his parents will often become involved with others in projects for the school; car pools (taking turns driving children to preschool, music lessons, etc.) are readily arranged; etc. There is, then, a great capacity for "togetherness" in American life but the opportunities for its expression are fewer and less meaningful than they should be.

How can we become cognizant of the needs of children and families, and include them in the planning and decision processes? At the grass roots level, parents and other interested citizens must be allowed to take a more active role, as they have in the new compensatory programs such as Project Head Start. To ensure that the recognition of needs is translated into action, we need a series of strong children's advocates. At the level of the Office of the President, a Presidential Council of Advisors on Children and Families (perhaps analogous to the Council of Economic Advisors) is called for. Continued support for the advocacy role of the Office of Child Development is also required. Similarly, child advocacy councils and/or offices of child development are to be recommended for all the 50 states (some of these are already in existence) and their local communities. Simply bringing to the attention of business and community leaders what they might do is likely to go a long way in introducing change . . . especially in a favorable climate of opinion.

References

ABT Associates. A study in child care 1970–71. *Child Care Bulletin*, No. 3. Washington, D.C.: Day Care and Child Development Council of America, 1971.

Alschuler, R. H. (Ed.) *Children's centers*. New York: William Morrow, 1942.

American Academy of Pediatrics. *Standards for day care centers for infants and children under three years of age*. Evanston, Ill.: Author, 1971.

Amidon, A. and Brim, O. G. What do children have to gain from parent education? Paper prepared for the Advisory Committee on Child Development, National Research Council, National Academy of Science, 1972.

Andrews, R. G. Permanent placement of Negro children through quasi-adoption. *Child Welfare*, 1968, **47** (10), 583–586, 613.

Ball, S. and Bogatz, G. A. *The first year of Sesame Street: An evaluation*. Princeton, N.J.: Educational Testing Service, 1970.

Ban, P. L. and Lewis, M. Mothers and fathers, girls and boys: Attachment behavior in the one-year-old. Paper presented at the meetings of the Eastern Psychological Association, New York City, 1971.

Bandura, A. and Walters, R. H. *Social learning and personality development*. New York: Holt, Rinehart and Winston, 1963.

Barker, L. A. *Preprimary enrollment, October, 1971*. Washington, D.C.: National Center for Educational Statistics. DHEW Publication No. (OE) 72–197, 1972.

Bates, B. D. *Project Head Start 1969–1970: A descriptive report of programs and participants*. Washington, D.C.: Office of Child Development, July, 1972.

Bauer, M. L. Health characteristics of low-income persons. DHEW Publication No. (HSM) 73–1500. Rockville, Md.: National Center for Health Statistics, July, 1972.

Beck, D. F. *Patterns in use of family agency service*. New York: Family Service Association of America, 1962.

Bee, H. L., Van Egeren, L. F., Streissguth, A. P., Nyman, B. A. and Leckie, M. S. Social class differences in maternal teaching strategies and speech patterns. *Developmental Psychology*, 1969, **1**, 726–734.

Bell, W. *Aid to dependent children*. New York: Columbia University Press, 1965.

Bernstein, R. *Helping unmarried mothers*. New York: Association Press, 1971.

Better Homes and Gardens Baby Book. Des Moines, Iowa: Meredith Press, 1969.

Birch, H. G. and Gussow, J. D. *Disadvantaged children: Health, nutrition and school failure*. New York: Grune and Stratton, 1970.

Bloom, B. S. *Stability and change in human characteristics*. New York: Wiley, 1964.

Bogatz, G. A. and Ball, S. *The second year of Sesame Street: A continuing evaluation*, 2 vols. Princeton, N.J.: Educational Testing Service, 1971.

Bowlby, J. *Maternal care and mental health*. Geneva: World Health Organization, 1952.

Briar, S. Why children's allowances? *Social Work*, 1969, **14**, 5–12.

Bronfenbrenner, U. Socialization and social class through time and space. In. E. E. Maccoby, T. M. Newcomb and E. L. Hartley (Eds.), *Readings in social psychology*. New York: Holt Rinehart, 1958.

Bronfenbrenner, U. The impact on families and children of the President's proposals for welfare reform. Statement to the Committee on Ways and Means, U.S. House of Representatives, November 6, 1969.

Bronfenbrenner, U. *Is early intervention effective?* Washington, D.C.: Office of Child Development, 1973.

Brown, P. and Hunt, R. G. Relations between nursery school attendance and teachers' ratings of some aspects of children's adjustment in kindergarten. *Child Development*, 1961, **32**, 585–596.

Bureau of the Census, U.S. Department of Commerce. *Women by number of own children under 5 years old, March, 1969.* Series P–20, No. 205. Washington, D.C.: Government Printing Office, July 22, 1970.

Burgess, E. M. and Price, D. O. *An American dependency challenge.* Chicago: American Public Welfare Association, 1963.

Burns, E. M. *The American social security system.* Boston: Houghton-Mifflin, 1949.

Burns, E. M. *Children's allowances and the economic welfare of children.* New York: Citizen's Committee for Children, 1968.

Caldwell, B. M., Wright, C. M., Honig, A. and Tannenbaum, J. Infant day care and attachment. *American Journal of Orthopsychiatry*, 1970, **40**, 397–412.

California Citizens' Adoption Committee. *Serving children in need of adoption.* San Francisco: Author, 1965.

Casler, L. Maternal deprivation: a critical review of the literature. *Monographs of the Society for Research in Child Development*, 1961, **26**, No. 80.

Child Welfare League of America. *Standards for adoption service.* New York: Author, 1958.

Child Welfare League of America. *Standards for foster family care service.* New York: Author, 1959.

Child Welfare League of America. *Standards for day care service.* (2nd ed.) New York: Author, 1969.

Children's Aid Society of New York. Nine- to 24-hour homemaker service project. *Child Welfare*, **41**, March-April, 1962.

Chilman, C. S. *Growing up poor.* Washington, D.C.: U.S. Department of Health, Education, and Welfare, Welfare Administration, 1966.

Cicirelli, V. G., Evans, J. W. and Schiller, J. A reply to the report analysis. *Harvard Educational Review*, 1970, **40**, 105–129.

Citizens' Board of Inquiry into Hunger and Malnutrition in the United States. *Hunger, U.S.A.* Washington, D.C.: New Community Press, 1968.

Coleman, J. *et al.* A comparative study of a psychiatric clinic and a family agency. *Social Casework*, January–February, 1957.

Condry, J. C. and Siman, M. A. Characteristics of peer and adult oriented children. Unpublished manuscript, Cornell University, 1968. (a)

Condry, J. C. and Siman, M. A. An experimental study of adult versus peer orientation. Unpublished manuscript, Cornell University, 1968. (b)

Cooke, R. *et al.* Memorandum to Director, Office of Economic Opportunity, February, 1965.

Datta, L. E. A report on evaluation studies of Project Head Start. Paper presented at the 1969 American Psychological Association Convention, Washington, D.C., September, 1969.

Datta, L. E. New directions for early child development programs. Invited address: Child Development and Child Psychiatry Conference, University of Missouri, October, 1972.

Datta, L. E., Mitchell, S. and McHale, C. The effects of Head Start programs on some aspects of child development: A summary. Washington, D.C.: Office of Child Development, October, 1972.

DeFrancis, V. *The fundamentals of child protection.* Denver: American Humane Association, 1955.

de Hirsch, K., Jansky, J. J. and Langford, W. S. *Predicting reading failure.* New York: Harper and Row, 1966.

Devereux, E. C., Bronfenbrenner, U. and Rodgers, R. R. Child rearing in England and the United States: A cross-national comparison. *Journal of Marriage and the Family*, 1969, **31**, 257–270.

Dittmann, L. *Children in day care with focus on health.* Washington, D.C.: Children's Bureau Publication No. 444–1967.

Dollard, J. and Miller, N. E. *Personality and psychotherapy.* New York: McGraw-Hill, 1950.

Education Commission of the States. *Early Childhood Project Newsletter*, No. 5. February, 1973.

Emmerich, W. *Structure and development of personal-social behaviors in preschool settings.* Princeton, N.J.: Educational Testing Service, PR–71–20, 1971.

Erikson, E. *Childhood and society.* New York: Norton, 1950.

Eysenck, H. J. The effects of psychotherapy. *International Journal of Psychiatry*, 1965, **1**, 97–178.

Fishman, L. *Constructing FAP child care facilities.* Washington, D.C.: Office of Child Development, August, 1970. (Quoted by Parker and Knitzer, 1971.)

Flavell, J. H. *The developmental psychology of Jean Piaget.* Princeton, N.J.: Van Nostrand, 1963.

Fraiberg, S. *The magic years.* New York: Charles Scribner's Sons, 1959.

Franklin, D. S. and Massarik, F. The adoption of children with medical conditions. *Child Welfare*, 1969, **48**, 459–467, 533–539, 595–601.

Fuller, E. M. About the kindergarten. In *What research says to the teacher.* Washington, D.C.: American Educational Research Association, National Education Association, 1961.

Galbraith, J. K. *The affluent society.* Boston: Houghton Mifflin, 1958.

Garbarino, J. A note on the effects of television viewing. In U. Bronfenbrenner (Ed.), *Influences on human development.* Hinsdale, Ill.: Dryden Press, 1972, 499–502.

Gardner, D. B., Hawkes, G. R. and Burchinal, L. G. Non-continuous mothering in infancy and development in later childhood. *Child Development*, 1961, **32**, 225–235.

Gavrin, J. B. and Sacks, L. S. Growth potential of preschool aged children in institutional care: A positive approach to a negative condition. *American Journal of Orthopsychiatry*, 1963, **33**, 399–408.

Gesell, A. and Ilg, F. L. *Infant and child in the culture of today.* New York: Harper & Bros., 1943.

Gil, D. C. Nationwide survey of legally reported physical abuse of children. *Brandeis University Papers in Social Welfare*, No. 15, 1967.

Gil, D. C. *Violence against children.* Cambridge, Mass.: Harvard University Press, 1970.

Gil, D. C. and Noble, J. H. *Public knowledge, attitudes, and opinions about physical child abuse in the United States.* Waltham, Mass.: Brandeis University, September, 1967.

Goldberg, H. L. and Linde, L. H. The case for subsidized adoptions. *Child Welfare*, 1969, **48**, 2.

Goldfarb, W. Psychological privation in infancy and subsequent adjustment. *American Journal of Orthopsychiatry*, 1945, **15**, 247–255.

Gray, S. *Selected longitudinal studies of compensatory education—a look from the inside.* Nashville, Tenn.: George Peabody College for Teachers, 1969.

Grotberg, E. H. *Review of research 1965–1969.* Washington, D.C.: Office of Economic Opportunity, Research and Evaluation Office, Project Head Start, June, 1969.

Gula, M. *Agency operated group homes: A special resource for serving children and youth.* Washington, D.C.: Children's Bureau, 1964.

Haggerty, R. J. Do we really need more pediatricians? *Pediatrics*, 1972, **50**, 681–683.

Haith, M. M. Day care and intervention programs for infants under two years of age. Paper prepared for Day Care Workshop Conference, Warrenton, Va., July, 1970.

Handler, P. The federal government and the scientific community. *Science*, 1971, **171**, 144–151.

Harper, A., Queen, S. and Harper, E. *American charities and social work.* (4th ed.) New York: Crowell, 1940.

Hattwick, B. W. The influence of nursery school attendance upon the behavior and personality of the preschool child. *Journal of Experimental Education*, 1936, **5**, 180–190.

Heinstein, M. *Child rearing in California.* Berkeley: California Bureau of Maternal and Child Health, Department of Public Health, 1965.

Hess, R. D. Maternal teaching styles and the socialization of educability. Paper presented at the meeting of the American Psychological Association, Los Angeles, California, September, 1964.

Hess, R. D. Class and ethnic influences upon socialization. In P. H. Mussen (Ed.), *Carmichael's Manual of child psychology.* (3rd ed.), Vol. 2. New York: Wiley, 1970.

Hess, R. D. and Shipman, V. C. Early experience and the socialization of cognitive modes in children. *Child Development*, 1965, **36**, 869–898.

Hunt, J. McV. *The challenge of incompetence and poverty.* Urbana: University of Illinois Press, 1969.

Huron Institute. *Midyear data on four models: Implementation in Head Start planned variations.* Cambridge, Mass.: Author, November, 1972.

Hylton, L. F. *The residential treatment center.* New York: Child Welfare League of America, 1964.

Jenkins, S. and Sauber, M. *Paths to child placement.* New York: New York City Department of Welfare and the Community Council of Greater New York, 1966.

Jersild, A. T. and Fite, M. D. The influence of nursery school experience on children's social adjustments. *Child Development Monographs*, 1939, No. 25.

REFERENCES

Jeter, H. R. *Children, problems, and services in child welfare programs.* Washington, D.C.: U.S. Government Printing Office, 1963.

Joint Commission on Mental Health of Children, Inc. *Crisis in child mental health: Challenge for the 1970's.* New York: Harper and Row, 1970.

Kadushin, A. *Child Welfare services.* New York: Macmillan, 1967.

Kahn, A. *Planning community services for children in trouble.* New York: Columbia University Press, 1963.

Kahn, G. and Hughes, W. A. *Statistics of local public school systems, 1967.* Washington, D.C.: National Center for Educational Statistics, 1967.

Karp, R. Education: A show of power over funds for innovation. *Science,* 1970, **167,** 1709–1711.

Kohn, M. Social class and parent-child relationships: An interpretation. *American Journal of Sociology,* 1963, **68,** 471–480.

Kraft, I. and Chilman, C. S. *Helping low-income families through parent education: A survey of research.* Washington, D.C.: Children's Bureau, 1966.

Kram, K. M. and Owen, G. M. Nutritional studies on United States preschool children. In S. J. Fomon & T. A. Anderson (Eds.), *Practices of low-income families in feeding infants and small children.* DHEW Publication No. (HSM) 72–5605. Washington, D.C.: Government Printing Office, 1972.

Lee, P. R. and Silver, G. A. Health planning—a view from the top with specific reference to the U.S.A. In J. Fry and W. A. J. Farndale (Eds.), *International medical care.* Wallingford, Pa.: Washington Square East, 1972, 284–315.

Levitt, E. E. Psychotherapy in children: a further evaluation. *Behavioral Research and Therapy,* 1963, **1,** 45–51.

Lin-Fu, J. S. Childhood lead poisoning—an eradicable disease. *Children,* 1970, **17** [1], 2–9.

Long, R. B. (Chm.) *Child care: Data and materials.* Washington: U.S. Senate Committee on Finance, 1971.

Low, S. *Foster care of children: Major national trends and prospects.* Washington, D.C.: Children's Bureau, 1966.

Low, S. and Spindler, P. G. *Child care arrangements of working mothers in the United States.* Washington, D.C.: Children's Bureau Pub. No. 461–1968.

Lowe, C. U. and Alexander, D. F. Child health and federal care programs, advance copy, 1972.

Lyle, J. and Hoffman, H. R. Television in the daily lives of children. Paper presented at the meeting of the American Psychological Association, Washington, D.C., September, 1971.

Maas, H. S. and Engler, R. E. *Children in need of parents.* New York: Columbia University Press, 1959.

Maas, H. S. and Kahn, A. Socio-cultural factors in psychiatric clinic services for children: A collaborative study in New York and San Francisco metropolitan areas. *Smith College Studies in Social Work,* 1955, **25.**

Maccoby, E. Television: Its impact on school children. *Public Opinion Quarterly,* 1951, **15,** 443–444.

Meyer, H. J., Borgatta, E. F. and Jones, W. C. *Girls at vocational high: an experiment in social work intervention.* New York: Russell Sage Foundation, 1965.

Miller, J. O. *Review of selected intervention research with young children.* Urbana, Ill.: ERIC Clearinghouse on Early Childhood Education, 1969.

Mindess, M. and Keliher, A. V. Review of research related to the advantages of kindergarten. *Childhood Education*, May, 1967.

National Center for Health Statistics. Changing trends in illegitimacy. *Vital Statistics*, Vol. 15, **13,** 1966. (a)

National Center for Health Statistics. *National Health Survey*, Series 10, No. 29, April, 1966. (b)

National Center for Health Statistics. *School achievement of children by demographic and socioeconomic factors: United States*. Vital and Health Statistics, Series 11, No. 109, November, 1971.

National Center for Health Statistics. *The health of children, 1970*. Washington, D.C.: Public Health Service Publication No. 2121, 1970.

National Center for Social Statistics. *Adoptions in 1968*. Washington, D.C.: Government Printing Office, 1968.

National Center for Social Statistics. *Child welfare statistics, 1969*. CW–1 (69). Washington, D.C.: Government Printing Office, 1969.

National Center for Social Statistics. *Social services for families and children*. NCSS Report E–6 (12/69). Washington, D.C.: Government Printing Office, 1970.

National Center for Social Statistics. *Children served by public welfare agencies and voluntary child welfare agencies and institutions, March, 1970*. Washington, D.C.: Government Printing Office, March 10, 1972. (a)

National Center for Social Statistics. *Adoptions in 1970*. Report E–10 (1970). Washington, D.C.: Government Printing Office, June 26, 1972. (b)

National Center for Social Statistics. *Public assistance statistics, May, 1972*. Washington, D.C.: Government Printing Office, August 31, 1972. (c)

New York State Commission on the Quality, Cost and Financing of Elementary and Secondary Education. Report. Advance Copy, Chapters 1, 2, and 3. (January) 1972.

Newsweek. TV's switched-on school. June 1, 1970.

Nielson TV Index, Winter 1970.

Oettinger, K. B. A spectrum of services for children. In *Proceedings of the national conference on day care services, May 13–15, 1965*. Washington, D.C.: Children's Bureau Publication No. 438–1966.

Office of Child Development. *Federal interagency day care requirements*. Washington, D.C.: Government Printing Office, 1968.

Office of Child Development. *Federal day care requirements*. Washington, D.C.: Government Printing Office, 1972.

Pappenfort, D. M. *et al*. Children in institutions, 1966: A research note. *The Social Service Review*, 1968, **42,** 252–260.

Parker, R. K., Ambron, S. *et al*. *Overview of cognitive and language programs for 3, 4, and 5 year old children*. New York: City University of New York, Center for Advanced Study in Education, 1970.

Parker, R. K. and Knitzer, J. Background paper on day care and preschool services: Trends in the 1960's and issues for the 1970's. In *Government research on the problems of children and youth*, Washington, D.C.: U.S. Senate Committee on Government Operations, September, 1971.

Philbrick, E. *Treating parental pathology—through child protective services*. Denver: American Humane Association, 1960.

REFERENCES

Piaget, J. *The origins of intelligence in children.* (2nd ed.) New York: International Universities Press, 1952.

Pines, M. *Revolution in learning: The years from birth to six.* New York: Harper & Row, 1966.

Pinneau, S. The infantile disorders of hospitalism and anaclitic depression. *Psychological Bulletin,* 1955, **52**, 429–452.

Prescott, E. *A pilot study of day care centers and their clientele.* Washington, D.C.: Children's Bureau Publication No. 428–1965.

Prescott, E. The large day care center as a child-rearing environment. *Voice for Children,* 1970, **3 [4]**, 3.

President's Commission on Income Maintenance Programs. *Background papers.* Washington, D.C.: Government Printing Office, 1970.

President's Panel on Mental Retardation. *A proposed program for national action to combat mental retardation.* Washington, D.C.: Government Printing Office, 1963.

Project Head Start, Booklet No. 4. *Daily program I.* Washington, D.C.: Government Printing Office, 1967.

Provence, S. *Guide for the care of infants in groups.* New York: Child Welfare League of America, 1967.

Rebelsky, F. and Hanks, C. Fathers' verbal interaction with infants in the first three months of life. *Child Development,* 1971, **42**, 63–68.

Rein, M. Child protective services in Massachusetts. *Brandeis University Papers in Social Welfare,* No. 6, 1963.

Report of Forum 15. Washington, D.C.: White House Conference on Children, 1970.

Report to the President. Washington, D.C.: White House Conference on Children, 1971.

Richmond, J. B. Twenty percent of the nation. *Proceedings of the national conference on day care services, May 13–15, 1965.* Washington, D.C.: Children's Bureau Publication No. 438–1966.

Richmond, J. B. and Weinberger, H. L. Program implications of new knowledge regarding the physical, intellectual, and emotional growth and development and the unmet needs of children and youth. *American Journal of Public Health,* 1970, **60**, 23–67.

Riday, E. Supply and demand in adoption. *Child Welfare,* 1969, **48**, 489–491.

Riessman, F. *The culturally deprived child.* New York: Harper & Row, 1962.

Robinson, H. B. and Robinson, N. M. Longitudinal development of very young children in a comprehensive day care program: The first two years. *Child Development,* 1971, **42**, 1673–1683.

Rodgers, R. R. Changes in parental behavior reported by childern in West Germany and the United States. *Human Development,* 1971, **14**, 208–224.

Rosenberg, M. Occupational values and occupational choice. Unpublished doctoral dissertation, Columbia University, 1954.

Ruderman, F. A. *Child care and working mothers: a study of arrangements made for daytime care of children.* New York: Child Welfare League of America, 1968.

Sauber, M. and Corrigan, E. M. *The six-year experience of unwed mothers as parents.* New York: Community Council of Greater New York, 1970.

Schorr, A. L. *Poor kids.* New York: Basic Books, 1966.

Schultze, C. L., Fried, E. R., Rivlin, A. M. and Tecters, N. H. *Setting national priorities: The 1973 budget.* Washington, D.C.: The Brookings Institution, 1972.

Searcy, E. O. *Interagency committee report on early childhood research.* Washington, D.C.: Office of Child Development, 1970. (a)

Searcy, E. O. *Interim report on federal early learning programs.* St. Ann, Mo.: National Coordination Center, National Program on Early Childhood Education, 1970. (b)

Senn, M. J. E. Early childhood education: For what goals? *Children*, 1969, **16**, 8–13.

Siegel, A. E. Children's television. Testimony before the Subcommittee on Communication of the U.S. Senate Committee on Commerce, March 2, 1972.

Siman, M. Peer group influence during adolescence: A study of 41 naturally-existing friendship groups. Unpublished doctoral dissertation, Cornell University, 1973.

Simms, M. Some highlights from the nutrition conference. *Children*, 1970, **17**, 69–71.

Simon, K. A. and Grant, W. V. *Digest of educational statistics*, 1969. Washington, D.C.: National Center for Educational Statistics, Pub. No. OE–10024–69, 1969.

Skinner, B. F. *The behavior of organisms.* New York: Appleton-Century-Crofts, 1938.

Smith, M. S. and Bissell, J. S. Report analysis: The impact of Head Start. *Harvard Educational Review*, 1970, **40**, 51–104.

Soar, R. S. *Follow-Through classroom process measurement and pupil growth (1970–71).* Gainesville: University of Florida, College of Education, 1972.

Spitz, R. A. Hospitalism: An inquiry into the genesis of psychiatric conditions in early childhood. *Psychoanalytic Studies of the Child*, Vol. 1. New York: International Universities Press, 1945, 53–74.

Spock, B. *Baby and child care.* New York: Pocket Books, 1957.

Sprigle, H. A. The learning to learn program. In S. Ryan (Ed.), *A report of longitudinal evaluations of preschool programs.* Washington, D.C.: Office of Child Development, 1972.

Starr, R. H., Jr. Cognitive development in infancy: assessment, acceleration, and actualization. *Merrill Palmer Quarterly*, 1971, **17**, 153–186.

Stearns, M. S. Report on preschool programs: The effects of preschool programs on disadvantaged children and their families. Final Report, Contract No. HEW–CS–71–16, 1971.

Stearns, M. W. and Peterson, S. Parent involvement in compensatory education programs: Definitions and findings. Report prepared for Elementary and Secondary Education Division, Office of Program Planning, Budgeting and Evaluation, U.S. Office of Education, March 16, 1973.

Stone, H. B. *Reflections on foster care.* New York: Child Welfare League of America, 1969.

Stone, L. J. and Chuch, J. *Childhood and adolescence.* (2nd ed.) New York: Random House, 1968.

Streissguth, A. and Bee, H. L. Mother-child interactions and cognitive development in children. *Young Children*, February, 1972, 154–173.

Swartz, E. *Toys that don't care.* New York: Gambit, 1971.

Taylor, D. A. and Starr, P. Foster parenting: An integrative review of the literature. *Child Welfare*, July, 1967, 371–385.

REFERENCES

Television and growing up: The impact of televised violence. Washington, D.C.: Government Printing Office, 1972.

Thomas, A., Chess, S. and Birch, H. G. *Temperament and behavior disorders in children.* New York: New York University Press, 1968.

Todd, S. P. Alternative federal day care strategies for the 1970's. *Child Care Bulletin,* No. 9. Washington, D.C.: Day Care and Child Development Council of America, 1972.

Tollen, W. B. *Study of staff losses in child welfare and family service agencies.* Washington, D.C.: Government Printing Office, 1960.

Tulkin, S. R. and Kagan, J. Mother-child interaction in the first year of life. *Child Development,* 1972, **43,** 31–41.

U.S. Children's Bureau. *Your child from one to six.* Publication No. 30–1962. Washington, D.C.: Government Printing Office, 1962.

U.S. Children's Bureau. *Infant care.* Publication No. 8–1963. Washington, D.C.: Government Printing Office, 1963.

U.S. Department of Agriculture. Background paper on food and nutrition. In *Government research on the problems of children and youth.* Washington, D.C.: U.S. Senate Committee on Government Operations, September, 1971.

U.S. Department of Health, Education, and Welfare. *Closing the gap in social work manpower.* Washington, D.C.: Government Printing Office, 1966.

U.S. Department of Health, Education, and Welfare. *The effectiveness of compensatory education: Summary and review of the evidence.* Washington, D.C.: Government Printing Office, April, 1972.

U.S. Department of Labor, Wage and Labor Standards Administration. *Federal funds for day care projects.* Washington, D.C.: Government Printing Office, February, 1969.

U.S. Department of Labor. *Child care services provided by hospitals.* Bulletin 295. Washington, D.C.: Government Printing Office, 1970. (a)

U.S. Department of Labor, Workplace Standards Administration, Women's Bureau. *Who are the working mothers?* Leaflet 37 (Rev.). Washington, D.C.: Government Printing Office, October, 1970. (b)

U.S. Office of Education. *Standards and costs for day care.* Urbana, Ill.: Educational Resources Information Center (ED 042 501), 1969.

U.S. Public Health Service. *National nutrition survey.* Washington, D.C.: Government Printing Office, 1968.

U.S. Public Health Service. *Fluoridation census,* 1969. Washington, D.C.: Government Printing Office, 1970.

Vadakin, J. C. A critique of the guaranteed annual income, *The Public Interest,* No. 1 (Spring, 1968), 53–66.

Watson, K. W. Subsidized adoption. *Child Welfare,* 1972, **51,** 220–229.

Wegman, M. E. Annual summary of vital statistics, 1971. *Pediatrics,* 1972, **50,** 956–959.

Weikart, D. P. *The Ypsilanti preschool: Curriculum development 1968–1971.* Ypsilanti, Michigan: High/Scope Educational Research Foundation, 1971.

Weinberger, P. E. *Perspectives on social welfare.* London: Macmillan, 1969.

Welfare Administration, U.S. Department of Health, Education and Welfare. *Social development: Key to the great society.* Washington, D.C.: Government Printing Office, 1966.

Westinghouse Learning Corporation. *Evaluation of the effect of Head Start on children's cognitive and affective development.* 2 vols. Springfield, Va.: U.S. Department of Commerce, Clearing House for Federal Scientific and Technical Information, 1969.

Westinghouse Learning Corporation. *Day care survey: 1970.* Report to the Office of Economic Opportunity, April, 1971.

White, B. L., LaCrosse, E. R., Litman, F. and Ogilvie, D. M. The Harvard preschool project: An etho-ecological study of the development of competence. Symposium presented at the meetings of the Society for Research in Child Development, Santa Monica, California, March, 1969.

White House Conference on Children. *Profiles of children.* Washington, D.C.: Government Printing Office, 1970.

Wilde, Oscar. *A woman of no importance.* Act I. 1893.

Wilensky, H. L. and Lebeaux, C. N. *Industrial society and social welfare.* New York: Russell Sage Foundation, 1958.

Williams, T. M. *Infant care: Abstracts of the literature.* Washington, D.C.: Consortium on Early Childbearing and Childrearing, 1972.

Wiltse, K. T. Aid to dependent children: The nation's basic family and child welfare program. *Social welfare forum, 1960, official proceedings of the 87th annual forum of the National Conference of Social Welfare.* New York: Columbia University Press, 1960, 208–231.

Witmer, H. (Ed.) On rearing infants and young children in institutions. *Children's Bureau Research Reports,* No. 1, 1967.

Witmer, H. L. *et al. Independent adoptions.* New York: Russell Sage Foundation, 1963.

Wittes, G. and Radin, N. Ypsilanti home and school handbooks. *Helping your child to learn.* San Rafael, Calif.: Dimensions Publishing Company, 1969.

Wolins, M. *Selecting foster parents.* New York: Columbia University Press, 1963.

Wolins, M. The societal function of social welfare. *New Perspectives,* Spring, 1967, 1–18.

Wolins, M. Licensing and recent developments in foster care. *Child Welfare,* 1968, **47,** 570–614.

Wortis, H., Bardach, J. S., Cutler, R., Freedman, A. and Rue, R. Child rearing practices in a low socioeconomic group. *Pediatrics,* 1963, **32,** 298–307.

Wright, R. S. *Report to the nation on children and youth.* Washington, D.C.: National Commission for Children and Youth, 1968.

Yarrow, L. J. Maternal deprivation: toward an empirical and conceptual re-evaluation. *Psychological Bulletin,* 1961, **58,** 459–490.

Yerby, A. S. The administration of public health. In E. D. Kilbourne and W. S. Smillie (Eds.) *Human ecology and public health.* (4th ed.) New York: Macmillan, 1969.

Young, L. *Wednesday's child.* New York: McGraw Hill, 1964.

Appendix

FAMILY INCOME AND EXPENDITURE ESTIMATES

TABLE A1

Average annual incomes for representative occupations, 1970

	Males	Females
Physicians	$24,727	—
Engineers	13,819	—
Nursing personnel	—	$10,049
Teachers (primary and secondary)	9,180	6,078
Secretaries	6,883	4,488
Retail salespersons	4,832	1,257
Foremen	10,033	4,595
Craftsmen	8,091	2,768
Private household workers	—	400

Source: Statistical Abstract of the United States, 1972. Washington, D.C.: U.S. Government Printing Office, 1973. Discrepancy between male and female incomes accentuated by inclusion of part-time and irregularly employed workers and by lower-ranking jobs typically held by women. Substantial pay discrepancies exist, however, even when identical jobs are held by men and women.

TABLE A2

Intermediate level 1970 budget for an urban family consisting of a 38-year-old employed husband, a house-wife, an 8-year-old girl and a 13-year-old boy

Food	23%
Housing (includes utilities, property tax)	23%
Clothing	10%
Transportation	9%
Medical care	5%
Other consumption (e.g. child care, recreation)	6%
Other costs (e.g. life insurance, savings)	5%
Social security/disability insurance	4%
Personal income tax	14%
Total budget	$10,664

Source: Statistical Abstract of the United States, 1972.

TABLE A3

Average costs of supplies, 1972

Bread (454 gm.)	$ .25
Milk (1 liter)	.30
Eggs (12)	.50
Jar baby food (128 gm.)	.11
Standard crib with mattress	63.90 (43.44–87.90)
Play pen	26.95 (24.95–28.29)
Carrier seat	6.24 (4.99– 7.49)
Stroller (usually substitutes for pram)	31.95 (19.95–39.95)
Diapers (12)	3.39 (1.95– 4.44)
Complete set of clothing for infant	5.03 (3.97– 6.36)
(Stretch suit, undershirt, diaper, plastic pants)	
Complete set of clothing for toddler	11.53 (9.50–12.16)
(Overalls, shirt, undershirt, pants, socks, canvas shoes)	

Source : Food costs, Statistical Abstract of the United States, 1972. Equipment and clothing costs not available. These represent median, highest, and lowest costs of items advertized by the most popular mail-order firm (Sears Roebuck Co.), Spring-Summer, 1972.